18/2/18

Teach Yourself®

Get started in Mandarin Chinese

Elizabeth Scurfield
and
Song Lianyi

For over 60 years, more than 50 million people have learnt over
750 subjects the **Teach Yourself** way, with impressive results.

Be where you want to be with **Teach Yourself**.

For UK order enquiries: please contact Bookpoint Ltd, 130 Milton Park,
Abingdon, Oxon, OX14 4SB. Telephone: +44 (0) 1235 827720.
Fax: +44 (0) 1235 400454. Lines are open 09.00–17.00, Monday to
Saturday, with a 24-hour message answering service. Details about
our titles and how to order are available at www.teachyourself.com

For USA order enquiries: please contact
McGraw-Hill Customer Services, PO Box 545, Blacklick, OH 43004-0545, USA.
Telephone: 1-800-722-4726. Fax: 1-614-755-5645.

For Canada order enquiries: please contact
McGraw-Hill Ryerson Ltd, 300 Water St, Whitby, Ontario, L1N 9B6, Canada.
Telephone: 905 430 5000. Fax: 905 430 5020.

Long renowned as the authoritative source for self-guided learning –
with more than 50 million copies sold worldwide – the **Teach Yourself**
series includes over 500 titles in the fields of languages, crafts, hobbies,
business, computing and education.

British Library Cataloguing in Publication Data:
a catalogue record for this title is available from the British Library.

Library of Congress Catalog Card Number: on file.

First published in UK 1996 by Hodder Education,
338 Euston Road, London, NW1 3BH.

First published in US 1996 by The McGraw-Hill Companies, Inc.

This edition published 2010. Previously published as
Beginner's Mandarin Chinese.

The **Teach Yourself** name is a registered trade mark of Hodder Headline.

Copyright © 1996, 2003, 2010 Elizabeth Scurfield and Song Lianyi

Typeset by MPS Limited, a Macmillan Company.

Printed in Great Britain for Hodder Education, a division of Hodder Headline, an
Hachette Livre UK Company, 338 Euston Road, London NW1 3BH.

The publisher has used its best endeavours to ensure that the URLs for external
websites referred to in this book are correct and active at the time of going to
press. However, the publisher and the author have no responsibility for the websites and can make no guarantee that a site will remain live or that the content will
remain relevant, decent or appropriate.

Hodder Headline's policy is to use papers that are natural, renewable and recycla-
ble products and made from wood grown in sustainable forests. The logging and
manufacturing processes are expected to conform to the environmental regulations
of the country of origin.

Impression number 10 9 8 7 6 5 4 3 2 1

Year 2014 2013 2012 2011 2010

Contents

Dedications

In memory of a much loved mother, Ella Jessie Scurfield, whose loving spirit and quiet courage will always be with me.

To Rong, my wife, whose support has been invaluable.

Acknowledgements

Our grateful thanks to all those who made this publication possible. In particular we wish to thank our editor, Virginia Catmur, for all her encouragement and support.

Credits

Meet the authors

Elizabeth Scurfield and Song Lianyi are both experienced and enthusiastic teachers of Chinese. Elizabeth Scurfield graduated with a first-class honours degree in Chinese from the School of Oriental and African Studies in London and has taught Chinese for nearly 40 years, 30 of them at university level. She was co-founder of the Chinese Department at the University of Westminster (1974) at the age of 23 and brought new ideas and enthusiasm to its creation. She has made numerous short and extended visits and study trips to China since her first visit in 1976 as the only woman participant on a delegation of younger sinologists.

Song Lianyi (Song being the surname) grew up in China. He obtained his BA in China and his MA and PhD in the UK. Currently he is Principal Teaching Fellow in Chinese at the School of Oriental and African Studies, University of London, where he has taught Chinese for over 15 years. He has been an active member of the British Chinese Language Teaching Society and is a life member of the International Society for Chinese Language Teaching.

Elizabeth Scurfield and Song Lianyi were colleagues in the same university nearly 20 years ago and their fruitful collaboration has continued ever since. In addition to *Get started in Mandarin*, their current titles in the **Teach Yourself** series include *Speak Mandarin Chinese with Confidence* and *Read and write Chinese Script*.

Elizabeth Scurfield and
Song Lianyi

Only got a minute?

Chinese, in one form or another, is spoken by more people around the globe than any other language and China is now starting to claim a major role for itself in the global economy. For these reasons alone, it is worthwhile trying to learn at least a little of the language. It is also the world's oldest language still in use and its cultural history can be traced back over 3500 years. Mandarin Chinese, which you will be learning in this course, is the Chinese language with the most speakers; and even those Chinese for whom Mandarin is not the mother tongue will be proficient in Mandarin, as it is the dominant language of the People's Republic of China. It is also the main language of Taiwan and one of the official languages in Singapore.

While you may have an idea that Mandarin will be a difficult language to learn, this is not necessarily true, at least as far as speaking it is concerned. Its grammar is remarkably simple and regular. For example, there is only ever one form of the verb, unlike in English, where we have to be, am, is, are, was, were, will be … In Mandarin one verb form covers all these functions. Some learners worry that they won't be able to learn the 'tones' of Mandarin: but if you learn the tone every time you learn a new word, you will soon find that you produce the correct tone automatically. Even if your tones are not brilliant, people can still understand you fairly easily when they are actually speaking with you.

We hope that, with the aid of this course, you should have a decent grounding in spoken Mandarin Chinese and that, by the end of the course, you will have the confidence to give it a go when you go to China, whether that be for business or for pleasure.

10

Only got ten minutes?

The Chinese language

Chinese can now be considered as very much an international language and is one of the six official languages of the United Nations, alongside Arabic, English, French, Russian and Spanish. With over 1.4 billion mother tongue speakers spread across the globe, Chinese is, quite possibly the fastest growing spoken language in the world, in terms of numbers. In addition to its being an official language of the UN (and, obviously, in China itself), Chinese is also the official language in Hong Kong (with the spoken language being Cantonese of course, rather than Mandarin, with English as the other official language), Taiwan and Macau (with Portuguese the other official language) and one of the four official languages spoken in Singapore (but it is not the main language in this country). It is recognized as a regional language in Malaysia and, interestingly enough, in the United States of America. The large immigrant population is obviously the reason for this and it can be seen that similar immigrant populations to other parts of the globe are having the same sort of effect.

Although written Chinese is a very different proposition, spoken Chinese has a high level of internal diversity and even though all spoken regional varieties have tonality in common, the number of tones may differ. There are generally considered to be around 13 main dialectic/languages (even this distinction is controversial) groups but the language that is spoken by the most people by far is the language we are going to be learning in this course: Mandarin Chinese, which is spoken as a mother tongue by approximately 900 million people. Other groupings include Wu and Cantonese, the latter being spoken by between 60–70 million people. Furthermore, it is usually thought that these main groupings are mutually unintelligible.

Chinese as it is spoken within China shows huge variations, as we have just seen, from north to south, west to east. It is, therefore, to be expected that there is no one form of Chinese when it is spoken as the main language in another country (see earlier for these other countries) – each of these countries has its own dialect and once more we find that even within these countries, there are marked differences from one region to another, whether this be accent, pronunciation or more marked and profound differences that might render a speaker of one dialect not understood by a speaker of another.

With China's expansion into the global market, the numbers of non-Chinese people, businesspeople and other people alike, who are turning to the learning of Chinese as an essential medium of communication for the future, are booming. With so much manufacturing taking place in China nowadays and outsourcing of other industries and with China's own push to leave the third world behind and try to forge entry for itself and its people into the first, it makes enormous sense for westerners to learn at least the basics of Chinese, because protocols are very different from those of the west and, if we wish to avoid antagonizing our friends, business colleagues and other people, these protocols must be learnt, too.

Of course, there are so many native speakers of Chinese because of the size of the Chinese population: some 1.4 billion worldwide. Until fairly recently, Chinese government policy included a 'one child' requirement for families, in order to try and keep population growth within bounds. This requirement has now been dropped and the expectation is, therefore, that China's population will swell even more rapidly. Another reason to learn some Chinese, because you will have many more people to practise your language skills with!

So, we can see that globalization, international trade and, now, tourism have all played a huge role in contributing to the continuing and wide spread of Chinese – and, of course, Beijing's staging the Olympic Games in 2008 has boosted China's image on the worldwide stage, in addition to its possessing some of the most famous tourist attractions in the world (the Great Wall being but one).

Written documentation on the development of Chinese goes back for nearly four centuries, making Chinese the oldest language on the planet. And, as the speakers of the language have developed and changed over this time, so, too, has the language itself. Probably the main change would be the apparent simplification of the form of the language, resulting in the 'alphabet' (i.e. character set) consisting of a mere 400 or so syllables. And yet, the language continues to be vibrant and evolving, due to the extensions possible through compounding and tonal additions.

Other languages spoken in China

We have mentioned that, in addition to regional variations and dialects, there are several other actual languages spoken in China – although Mandarin is spoken by the overwhelming majority of the population. The second language, in terms of numbers speaking it, is Wu, which is estimated to be spoken by anywhere between 90 and 100 million, e.g. in Shanghai and surrounding regions, Min, spoken by a further 60–70 million (estimated number, e.g. in Fujian Province and Taiwan) and, the other language you have undoubtedly heard of, Cantonese, which is also spoken by approximately 60–70 million people (e.g. in Hong Kong and Guangdong Province). Then there are two reasonably widespread languages that are spoken in China, namely, Xiang and Hakka, although, as we referred to briefly earlier, there is some controversy as to whether these constitute languages as such or whether they are really dialects. Xiang (known also as Hunanese, as it is spoken predominantly (but not exclusively) in Hunan Province) is a language that has been profoundly influenced by Mandarin and is spoken by about 35–40 million people in Hunan and also Sichuan Province. (It may be of interest to know that Mao Zedong was born in Hunan Province and belief has it that, although a native speaker of Xiang, he was not at all fluent in Mandarin!) Hakka is spoken mainly in the south of China and was originally confined to the Hakka people, but is now also predominant in Taiwan and in Chinese immigrant populations around the world (very approximate numbers of Hakka speakers 35–40 million).

Grammar: the essentials

The fundamental building block of the Chinese language is the **character**, a single-syllable morpheme whereby each individual character forms one idea. And there are in the region of 400 of these basic monosyllables in Chinese – when these individual 'cells' of the language are combined, they form homophones, in which Chinese abounds. Unfortunately, this is what adds to the complicated nature of the language. This difficulty (for us as learners of Chinese) is ameliorated somewhat by Chinese's being a **tonal** language. **Putonghua** has four tones, so our original paltry 400-odd monosyllables become over 1400 different sounds (as some sound plus tone combinations do not exist) in one fell swoop. But also the characters that in Chinese we find combined in this way have similar meanings when used to form the new 'word' – confusion here is avoided since, when used separately, individual characters may take on another meaning, in combination, they can usually only mean one thing.

Most syllables in Chinese consist of two elements: an **initial** and a **final**, the former being a consonant at the beginning of the syllable and the latter, the rest of the syllable.

Initials

There are some 21 initials in Modern Standard Chinese (MSC), which is what you will be learning on this course. The semi-vowels 'w' and 'y' are considered by some to be initials, too. In addition, there is 'ng', a sound that occurs at the end of a syllable, as the same sound does in English. This sound includes six aspirated initials and six unaspirated initials, all 12 of which are voiceless. When making an aspirated sound, a feather or a sheet of paper held in front of your mouth will move; when making an unaspirated one, it should not. Lack of vibration in your vocal chords renders the initial voiceless.

Finals

Chinese has 36 finals, which are composed of a simple or compound vowel or a vowel plus a nasal consonant. Some syllables may lack the initial consonant but none lack a vowel.

Tones

The four tones in Chinese (remember from our earlier discussion that their presence multiplies the number of possible sounds available to about 1400) are variations in pitch – rising, continuing and falling. Each syllable in the language has its own specific tone, so they are an important component in 'word' formation.

The first tone is high and level, the second is rising, the third tone is a short fall followed by a rising tone and the fourth tone is a falling tone. (Note, however, that you do not have to produce a particular sort of sound in your own speech – all the tones occur naturally within the voice range.)

There is also a **neutral** tone, i.e. the syllable is toneless: all particles are neutral, the second half of a repeated word may be in neutral tone, fill-in syllables are neutral and the second syllable in a compound may be neutral (but on other occasions, not, so this neutrality has to be indicated in the text). One example is **xièxie**, *thank you*.

In the spoken language, you will find that it is rare for tones to be given their full value, but this doesn't let you off the hook! You should still learn them as if they were and, also, be aware that learning the words with their tone takes time, practice and lots of listening and repetition on your part. So do persevere!

Some additional points

Here are a couple of little extras, to cheer you up as you are about to embark on this course – it's all in the mind, you know:

One way in which to ask questions in Chinese is to use both positive and negative forms of the verb together. And then the corresponding answer is neither **yes** nor **no** but either the positive or negative form of that verb.

As you know by now, Chinese does not have a phonetic alphabet and *pinyin* is the nearest we in the west get to a recognizable form of transcribing it. It will be very useful for you in this course, as it provides a relatively accurate guide to correct pronunciation.

Where names in the west appear in the form title, given name, surname, in Chinese, they appear totally the other way around, viz. surname, given name, title. Hence, Mao, to whom we referred earlier on in this section, is the Chinese leader's surname and Zedong is actually his given name.

Some adjectives function as verbs, a form known as *stative verbs*, meaning that, in a 'to be' verb, there is no need for the 'to be' bit of it.

Unlike in English, an adverb will always go in front of the verb it is qualifying.

One feature of the language that should please you immensely (especially if you have learnt other languages in the past or if English is not your first language and you have had to struggle with this aspect) is that all verbs are invariable – meaning that they remain exactly the same, no matter what else is going on! Another feature of verbs that you will like is that (with one exception – the verb *to have* yǒu), negation comes through the use of **bù**, which precedes the verb.

We hope that this short introduction has kindled that spark of interest that led you to pick up this book in the first place.

About the course

Get started in Mandarin Chinese is the right course for you if you are a complete beginner or feel that you need to start back at the beginning again to rebuild your confidence. It is a self-study course which will help you to understand and speak Chinese sufficiently well to function effectively in basic everyday situations, both business and social. The course will also offer you an insight into Chinese culture and there is even an opportunity for you to find out something about the Chinese writing system if you want to.

Which Chinese will you be learning?

In one form or another, Chinese is the language most spoken in the world. It has many different spoken forms, but they are all written in almost exactly the same way, the difference being that the simplified script is used in the People's Republic of China and in Singapore and that full-form characters are used in Taiwan and Hong Kong (this may change in the future in the case of Hong Kong). The characters used in this book are always in the simplified script. For more information on the Chinese script, you can refer to *Get Started in Chinese Script* and to *Complete Chinese*.

More than 70% of Chinese people speak the northern dialect so the national language is based on this. More Chinese speakers can understand this national language than any other form of Chinese so it is what you will be learning in this book. In China it is called **pǔtōnghuà** 'common speech', but it is sometimes referred to in the west as Modern Standard Chinese.

What is romanization?

Chinese cannot be written using a phonetic alphabet in the way that European languages can. It is written in characters. You will find out more about characters in Unit 11. Various ways have been devised for representing Chinese sounds alphabetically. The standard form in use today is known as **pīnyīn** (literally 'spell sound') and is what we have used in this book. In 1958 **pīnyīn** was adopted as the official system of romanization in the People's Republic of China. Please note that **pīnyīn** is not an accurate phonetic transliteration of Chinese sounds for English speakers.

How the course works

The book is divided into two main parts. Units 1 to 10 introduce you to the basic structures and grammatical points you'll need in everyday situations. These units should be taken in order as each builds on the previous ones.

Units 12 to 21 deal with everyday situations such as booking into a hotel, changing money, buying tickets, seeing a doctor, travelling and being entertained in a Chinese home. They give you the opportunity to put into practice and consolidate the language you have learnt in the first ten units. You can take these units in any order, although the vocabulary does build up from unit to unit.

A few words about the recording

This book can be successfully used on its own, but you are advised to obtain and use the accompanying recording if at all possible. This will help you to pronounce Chinese correctly and to acquire a more authentic accent. The recorded dialogues and exercises will also give you plenty of practice in understanding and responding to basic Chinese. The **Pronunciation guide** and the new words in the first few units plus items such as the days of the week, the months of the year and simple numbers are all recorded. This will help you to speak Chinese correctly in the important early stages of your study. Readers without the recording will find that there are some units which contain an exercise that cannot be done with the book alone, but a written alternative is always provided.

About Units 1–10

Each unit starts by telling you what you are going to learn in that unit. The **Before you start** section prepares you for the unit ahead. Then there is an easy exercise **Let's try** to get you speaking straight away.

Quick vocab sections contain the most important words and phrases from the unit. Try to learn them by heart. They will be used both in that unit and in later units. There are various tips throughout the book to help you learn new words.

Dialogue. Move on to the dialogues once you have read the new words a few times. The dialogues will show you how the new words are used and hopefully reinforce them. If you have the recording, listen to each dialogue once or twice without stopping or read through it without looking anything up. You don't have to understand every word to get the gist of it.

Now, using the pause button, break the dialogue into manageable chunks and try repeating each phrase out loud. This will help you gain a more authentic accent. If you don't have the recording, use a ruler or a bookmark to cover part of the dialogue so you can concentrate on a small bit at a time. The most important thing in either case is to **speak out loud** because this will help you gain confidence in speaking Chinese.

Learning tips give you advice on everything from how to master vocabulary to how to improve your listening and reading skills and develop confidence in speaking.

Language notes. This section provides you with the nuts and bolts of the language. It goes over all the main grammar and structures for the units along with plenty of examples. Once you are confident about a particular grammar point, try making up your own examples.

Practice/Exercises. Each exercise in this section helps you practise one or more of the points introduced in the **Language notes** section. For some exercises you will need to listen to the recording. It is not essential to have the recording to complete this course and most of these listening exercises can also be completed without them. However, listening to the recording will make your learning easier and provide more variety.

Quick review, at the end of each unit, gives you the opportunity to test yourself on what you have learnt in that unit. In Unit 10, you are given the chance to test yourself on Units 1–10 with a **Halfway review** and to go back over anything you're not sure about. At the end of Unit 21 there is a **Final review** – here, you will be surprised at how much you have learnt.

Insight. These boxes are short notes in English that give you an insight into different aspects of Chinese culture and society and are usually linked to the situations being covered in that particular unit.

In each unit you will find at least one useful sign written in Chinese characters (**Hànzì**) so you can familiarize yourself with what they look like even though you haven't actually learnt any characters.

About Units 12–21

These units give you the opportunity to practise what you have learnt in meaningful and useful situations. The first page of each unit tells you what you are going to learn and under **Revise before you start** there is a check list of the structures you have already learnt which will reappear in that unit. This gives you the opportunity to look at some, or all, of these again and to go over them so you feel fully confident before beginning the unit. You will find that some structures come up time and time again so that you will not find it necessary to revise them after a while. You will also find a short text in Chinese (except for Unit 13, which is in English) about the topics in each unit followed by a comprehension exercise.

Cartoons and **proverbs.** You will find cartoons in some of the units which will give you an insight into Chinese humour and hopefully make you laugh! We have also included some proverbs (written in Chinese characters and in **pīnyīn**) which have some relevance to the topic and add some cross-cultural interest. These are short phrases which have their origins in classical Chinese.

Quick review (As in Units 1–10)

Key to the exercises. The answers to the **Practice/Exercises, Let's try, Quick review, Halfway review** and **Final review** can all be found at the back of the book. Do remember that variations are possible in some of the answers but we couldn't include them all.

Unit 11 – Let's look at Chinese characters!

Contrary to what most people believe, Chinese is not a difficult language to speak – particularly at beginner's level. Pronunciation and grammar are generally straightforward even if they require you to do a few things you're not used to. Even tones are not intrinsically difficult and can be fun, though they do involve a lot of time and practice.

Nobody can say, however, that learning to read and write Chinese characters is easy – fascinating yes, but not easy. That is why we have written this book in **pīnyīn**, so that the learner can get straight down to speaking Chinese without the barrier of an unknown form of writing.

Unit 11 is a special unit designed to give you the chance to find out something about the origin of Chinese characters and to have a taste of what's involved in reading and writing them. This unit is designed as a 'one-off' so that those of you who would rather concentrate solely on listening and speaking can miss it out without it affecting your understanding of other units.

At the back of the book

At the back of the book is a reference section which contains:

Key to the exercises
A **Chinese–English vocabulary** list containing all the words in the course.

An **English–Chinese vocabulary** list with the most useful words you'll need when expressing yourself in Chinese.

An Appendix: character texts which give you all the dialogues and texts in Chinese characters.

How to be successful at learning Chinese

1 **Little and often** is far more effective than a long session every now and then. Try to do 20–30 minutes a day if you can. If you can't manage that, then set yourself a minimum of 2–3 times a week. Try to make it at roughly the same time each day – when you get up, or at lunchtime, or before you go to bed for instance. This will make it easier for you to get into the habit of studying regularly.

2 **Revise and test yourself regularly.** Find a balance between moving through the book and revising what you have already learnt. If you move forward too quickly, you will find later units difficult and you will get discouraged. Try to avoid this.

3 **Hear yourself speak!** If at all possible, find yourself a quiet place to study where you can speak out loud. You need to build up your speaking and listening skills and your confidence, so make it as easy and as comfortable for yourself as you can.

4 **Find opportunities to speak Chinese.** You don't have to go to China to do this. Join a Chinese class to practise your Chinese with other people, find a Chinese native speaker to help you (but make sure he or she speaks **pǔtōnghuà**) and find out about Chinese clubs, societies, and so on.

5 **Don't be too harsh on yourself!** Learning a language is a gradual process – you have to keep at it. Don't expect to remember every item of vocabulary and every new structure all at once. The important thing is to get your meaning across. Making mistakes in Chinese will not stop a Chinese person understanding you.

But most of all remember that learning and using a foreign language is fun, particularly when you find you can use what you have learnt in real situations.

Symbols and abbreviations

◀ﺔ   This indicates that the recording is needed for the following
        section. (But often there is an alternative way of completing
        the section if you don't have the recording.)

Insight   This indicates information about Chinese culture and
        society.

(sing)	singular	(*lit.*)	literally
(pl)	plural	(MW)	measure word

Punctuation

Chinese punctuation is very similar to that of English but a pause-
mark (、) is used in lists instead of a comma, even if the list only has
two items in it. A comma is used for longer pauses.

Use of apostrophe

An apostrophe (') is used to show where the break comes between
two syllables if there is any possible ambiguity in pronunciation, for
example, **shí'èr** (not **shíèr**), **nǚ'ér** (not **nǚér**).

Use of hyphens

We have used hyphens to show how words are built up in Chinese:

> **Zhōngguó** *China* + **rén** *person* → **Zhōngguó-rén** *a Chinese*
>   *person*
> **Déguó** *Germany* + **rén**   → **Déguó-rén** *a German person*

A hyphen is also used to link a verbal suffix or verbal complement
to the verb. This will encourage you to say it together with the verb
as it should be said:

Wǒ chī-**guo** Yìndù fàn.	*I've eaten Indian food.*
Tā méi qù-**guo** Zhōngguó.	*He's never been to China.*
Nǐ shuō-**de** hěn màn.	*You speak very slowly.*
Tāmen xiě-**de** bú kuài.	*They don't write quickly.*

In general, we have written 'words' separately except where they are seen as being one idea:

hǎo	*good*	but	**hǎo deduō**	*much better*
		or	**hǎo duōle**	
tā	*he, she, it*	but	**tāde**	*his, hers, its*
xīngqī	*week*	but	**xīngqīyī**	*Monday*
yuè	*month*	but	**yīyuè**	*January*
běn	measure word for books	but	**běnzi**	*notebook*

However, verb-objects and so on are separate for clarity:

| **shuō** (verb) | **huà** (object) | *to speak* (speech) |
| **shuō** | **Fǎyǔ** | *to speak French* |

Pronunciation guide

Chinese sounds

🔊 CD 1, TR 1, 00:37

Vowels

Here is the list of the Chinese vowels with a rough English equivalent sound and then one or two examples in Chinese. There are single vowels, compound vowels or vowels plus a nasal sound, which will be listed separately.

	Rough English sound	Chinese examples
a	f<u>a</u>ther	b<u>a</u>b<u>a</u>, m<u>a</u>m<u>a</u>
ai	b<u>i</u>te	t<u>ai</u>, z<u>ai</u>
ao	c<u>ow</u>	h<u>ao</u>, zh<u>ao</u>
e	f<u>ur</u>	ch<u>e</u>, h<u>e</u>, g<u>e</u>
ei	pl<u>ay</u>	b<u>ei</u>, g<u>ei</u>, sh<u>ei</u>, f<u>ei</u>
i	t<u>ea</u>	d<u>i</u>d<u>i</u>, feij<u>i</u>, n<u>i</u>
i (after z, c, s, zh, ch, sh and r only)		z<u>i</u>, c<u>i</u>, sh<u>i</u>

The **i** is there more or less for cosmetic reasons – no syllable can exist without a vowel. Say the consonant and 'sit on it' and you have the sound.

ia	<u>y</u>arrow	j<u>ia</u>, x<u>ia</u>
iao	m<u>eow</u>	b<u>iao</u>, p<u>iao</u>, <u>yao</u>
ie	<u>ye</u>s	b<u>ie</u>, x<u>ie</u>, <u>ye</u>
iu	<u>yo</u>-yo	l<u>iu</u>, j<u>iu</u>, <u>you</u>

y replaces **i** at the beginning of a word if there is no initial consonant.

o	m<u>ore</u>	m<u>o</u>yim<u>o</u>, map<u>o</u>
ou	g<u>o</u>	d<u>ou</u>, z<u>ou</u>

u	m<u>oo</u>	b<u>u</u>, zh<u>u</u>
ua	s<u>ua</u>ve	g<u>ua</u>, h<u>ua</u>
uo	<u>war</u>	sh<u>uo</u>, c<u>uo</u>, <u>wo</u>
uai	s<u>wi</u>pe	k<u>uai</u>, <u>wai</u>
ui	<u>weigh</u>	d<u>ui</u>, g<u>ui</u>, z<u>ui</u>

w replaces **u** at the beginning of a word if there is no initial consonant.

| ü | pn<u>eu</u>monia | j<u>u</u>, q<u>u</u>, l<u>ü</u>, n<u>ü</u> |
| üe | pn<u>eu</u>matic + <u>air</u> (said quickly) | <u>yue</u>, <u>xue</u>, j<u>ue</u> |

Note that **ü** and **üe** can occur only with the consonants **n, l, j, q** and **x**. As **j, q** and **x** cannot occur as **j+u, q+u** or **x+u**, the umlaut (··) over the 'u' in **ju, qu** and **xu** has been omitted. N and l, however, can occur as both **nu** and **nü, lu** and **lü** so the umlaut (··) has been kept.

yu replaces **ü**, and **yue** replaces **üe** if there is no initial consonant.

Here are the **vowels with a nasal sound** formed with vowels followed by **n** or **ng**. Speak through your nose when you pronounce them and listen carefully to the recording.

	Rough English sound	**Chinese examples**
an	m<u>an</u>	f<u>an</u>, m<u>an</u>
ang	b<u>ang</u>	zh<u>ang</u>, sh<u>ang</u>
en	<u>un</u>der	r<u>en</u>, h<u>en</u>
eng	h<u>ung</u>	d<u>eng</u>, n<u>eng</u>
in	b<u>in</u>	n<u>in</u>, j<u>in</u>, x<u>in</u>
ian	<u>yen</u>	t<u>ian</u>, n<u>ian</u>, q<u>ian</u>
iang	<u>Yang</u>tse (River)	l<u>iang</u>, x<u>iang</u>
ing	f<u>ing</u>er	m<u>ing</u>, q<u>ing</u>, x<u>ing</u>
iong	<u>Jung</u> (the psychoanalyst)	<u>yong</u>, q<u>iong</u>, x<u>iong</u>
ong	<u>Jung</u>	t<u>ong</u>, c<u>ong</u>, h<u>ong</u>
uan	<u>wan</u>gle	w<u>an</u>, s<u>uan</u>, h<u>uan</u>
un	<u>won</u>	w<u>en</u>, l<u>un</u>, ch<u>un</u>
uang	<u>wr</u>o<u>ng</u>	<u>wang</u>, h<u>uang</u>, zh<u>uang</u>

üan	pneumatic + end (said quickly)	yuan, quan, xuan
ün	'une' in French	yun, jun, qun

Note that **ian** is pronounced '**yen**'.

The same rules about **y** replacing **i** and **w** replacing **u** at the beginning of a word if there is no initial consonant also apply to vowels with a nasal sound.

Yuan replaces **üan** and **yun** replaces **ün** if there is no initial consonant.

Consonants

Here is a list of the Chinese consonants, some of which are quite similar to English sounds, others less so. Those that are very different from the nearest English sound are explained.

	Rough English sound	**Chinese examples**
b	bore	bai, bei
p	poor	pao, pang
m	me	ma, mei, ming
f	fan	fan, feng
d	door	da, dou, duo
t	tore	ta, tai, tian
n	need	na, nü, nian
l	lie	lai, lei, liang
z	adds	zi, zai, zuo
c	its	ci, cai, cuo
s	say	si, sui, suan

The next four consonants are all made with the tongue loosely rolled in the middle of the mouth.

zh	jelly	zhao, zhong, zhu
ch	chilly	che, chi, chang
sh	shy	shi, shei, sheng
r	razor	re, ri, rong

The next three consonants are all made with the tongue flat and the corners of the mouth drawn back as far as possible.

j	genius	jia, jiao, jian
q	cheese	qi, qian, qu
	(as said in front of the camera!)	
x	sheet	xiao, xin, xue
	(rather like a whistling kettle)	

Arch the back of the tongue towards the roof of the mouth for the last three consonants.

g	guard	ge, gei, gui
k	card	kai, kan, kuai
h	loch	he, huan, hao

Tones

Chinese is a tonal language. Every syllable in Chinese has its own tone. **Pǔtōnghuà** has four distinct tones plus a neutral tone. This means that syllables which are pronounced the same but have different tones will mean different things. For example, **tang** pronounced in the first tone means *soup* but pronounced in the second tone means *sugar*! But don't worry – all the four tones fall within your natural voice range. You don't have to have a particular type of voice to speak Chinese.

The four tones are represented by the following marks which are put over the vowel such as **nǐ** *you* or over the main vowel of a syllable where there are two or three vowels, for example, **hǎo** *good*, but **guó** *country*:

¯	1st tone, high and level
´	2nd tone, rising
ˇ	3rd tone, falling – rising
`	4th tone, falling

The following diagrams will help to make this clearer.

Think of **1** as being at the bottom of your voice range and **5** at the top.

1st tone: Pitch it where **you** feel comfortable. Say 'oo' as in 'zoo' and keep going for as long as you can. You should be able to keep it up for maybe half a minute. When you have got used to that, change to another vowel sound and practise that in the same way and so on.

2nd tone: Raise your eyebrows every time you attempt a second tone until you get used to it. This is infallible!

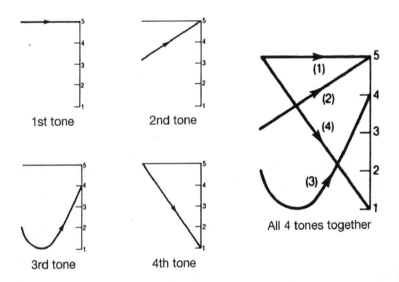

1st tone   2nd tone

3rd tone   4th tone

All 4 tones together

3rd tone: Drop your chin onto your neck and raise it again. Then practise the sound doing the movement at the same time.

4th tone: Stamp your foot gently and then accompany this action with the relevant sound.

Neutral tones: Some syllables in Chinese are toneless or occur in the neutral tone. This means they have no tone mark over the vowel. They are rather like unstressed syllables in English, such as *of a* in 'two of a kind'.

Tone changes

Occasionally syllables may change their tones.

- Two 3rd tones, one after another, are very difficult to say. Where this happens, the first one is said as a 2nd tone. We have still marked it as a 3rd tone in the book otherwise you may think that it is always a 2nd tone, which it isn't:

  Nǐ hǎo! (*How do you do?*) is said as **Ní hǎo.**

- If three 3rd tones occur together, the first two are normally said as 2nd tones:

  Wǒ yě hǎo (*I'm OK too*) is said as **Wó yé hǎo.**

- Note that in the phrase **yí ge rén** (*one* measure word *person*), the **ge** is said without a tone although it is actually 4th, but it still carries enough weight to change the **yì** into a 2nd tone.

You will find a few other tone changes in the book. These will be pointed out to you when they occur for the first time.

1

Nǐ hǎo! Nǐ hǎo ma?
Hello! How are you?

In this unit you will learn
- How to say *hello* and *goodbye*
- How to exchange greetings
- How to say *please* and *thank you*
- How to make a simple apology
- How to observe basic courtesies

Before you start

Read the **About the course** section. This gives useful advice on how to make the best of this course.

Everybody learns differently. You need to find the way which works best for you. You will find some useful learning tips in each unit.

Make sure you have your recording handy as you will need this to listen to the **Pronunciation guide** and **Dialogues**.

If you don't have the recording, use the **Pronunciation guide** at the beginning of the book to help you with the pronunciation of new words and phrases.

It's a good idea to listen to the **Pronunciation guide** all the way through and to practise the Chinese tones before starting Unit 1. This way you can make the most of the dialogues.

Remember that studying for 20 minutes regularly is much more effective than occasionally spending two hours in one go.

Try following this study guide and adapt it to your needs as you go along:

1 Listen to the **Dialogues** once or twice without the book (read them if you haven't got the recording).

2 Go over each one, bit by bit, in conjunction with the **Quick vocab** boxes and **Learning tips** underneath the dialogues.

3 Study the **Language notes** very carefully and make sure that you understand them.

4 Make sure you understand the **Learning tips** on how to pronounce and how to learn.

5 Read the **Insight** boxes.

6 Go back to the **Dialogues** and **Quick vocab** and listen and study for as long as it takes you to grasp them. This time use the pause button. Try reading a new word or phrase out loud after the speaker, then play it again to check your progress.

7 Do the **Practice** section and check your answers in **Key to the exercises** at the back of the book. Test yourself with the **Quick review**.

Now you are ready to start!

Rùkǒu
Entrance

bù	*not*
bú yòng xiè	*not at all* (lit. *no need thank*)
bú zài	*not at; to be not at/in*
duìbuqǐ	*excuse me/I'm sorry*
hǎo	*good, well*
. . . hǎo ma?	*How is/are . . . ?*
hěn	*very*
jīntiān	*today*
lái	*to come*
lǎoshī	*teacher*
ma	(question particle)
míngtiān	*tomorrow*
míngtiān jiàn	*see you tomorrow*
nǐ	*you* (sing)
Nǐ hǎo!	*Hello!* (sing)
nǐmen	*you* (pl)
Nǐmen hǎo!	*Hello!* (pl)
Qǐng jìn!	*Please come in.*
Qǐng wèn, . . . ?	*May I ask . . . ?*
Qǐng zuò!	*Please sit down.*
tā/tā	*she/he*
tàitai	*Mrs; wife*
xiānsheng	*Mr; husband; gentleman*
xiǎo	*little, young, small*
xièxie	*thank you; to thank*
zài	*at; to be at/in*
zàijiàn	*goodbye*

QUICK VOCAB

Learning tips

Read the words and expressions out loud. Concentrate on the pronunciation. Turn back to the **Pronunciation guide** and check anything you need to. Especially check out the four tones and the neutral tone. They're quite easy to get the hang of after a little practice.

If you have the recording, listen to the words and repeat them after the speaker using the pause button.

Dialogues

Listen to people saying *hello*, *thank you* and *goodbye* in Chinese. Press the pause button after each person has spoken and repeat out loud.

Dialogue 1   Saying 'hello'

◀) **CD 1, TR 2, 01:22**

Mr Wang is a tourist guide. He prefers to be called **Xiǎo Wáng** (*lit.* little Wang) as he is only 28 years old, although his full name is Wáng Jìjūn. When Mr and Mrs Green see Xiǎo Wáng, they greet him in Chinese.

Mrs Green	Nǐ hǎo, Xiǎo Wáng!
Mr Green	Xiǎo Wáng, nǐ hǎo!
Xiǎo Wáng	Gélín xiānsheng,
	Gélín tàitai,
	nǐmen hǎo!
Mrs Green	Nǐ tàitai hǎo ma?
Xiǎo Wáng	Tā hěn hǎo, xièxie.

Try saying two 3rd tones together. Difficult isn't it? Both **nǐ** (*you*) and **hǎo** (*good*) are 3rd tones but when said together **ni** is a 2nd tone. This was explained more fully in the **Pronunciation guide**.

Neutral tones
Some syllables or words in Chinese are toneless or have what is called a neutral tone. The -**sheng** of **xiānsheng**, the -**men** in **nǐmen**, and the question particle **ma** in **Dialogue 1** are good examples of this.

Dialogue 2 Saying 'goodbye'

◄) CD 1, TR 2, 01:47

When Mr and Mrs Green have finished their visit, they thank Xiǎo Wáng and say goodbye to him.

Mr Green	Xiǎo Wáng, xièxie nǐ.
Mrs Green	Xièxie nǐ, Xiǎo Wáng.
Xiǎo Wáng	Bú yòng xiè.
Mr Green	Zàijiàn.
Xiǎo Wáng	Zàijiàn.
Mrs Green	Zàijiàn.

How to pronounce q

This is not at all like a **q** in English as in *queen*. Q in Chinese is pronounced like the **j** in *jeans* but with air behind it. It is rather like the **ch** in *cheetah* but with the corners of the mouth drawn back as far as they can go. Refer back to the **Pronunciation guide** for more help.

Dialogue 3

◄) CD 1, TR 2, 02:10

Mr Green comes to see his Chinese visitor. He knocks at the door.

Lǐ	Qǐng jìn.
Green	(enters the room)
Lǐ	Gélín xiānsheng, nǐ hǎo!
Green	Nǐ hǎo, Lǐ xiānsheng.
Lǐ	Qǐng zuò.
Green	Xièxie.
Lǐ	Gélín tàitai hǎo ma?
Green	Tā hěn hǎo. Xièxie.

Dialogue 4

◀)) CD 1, TR 2, 02:40

Frank goes to the teachers' office to look for his teacher.

Frank	Qǐng wèn, Zhāng lǎoshī zài ma?
Lǐ lǎoshī	Duìbuqǐ, tā bú zài.
Frank	Tā jīntiān lái ma?
Lǐ lǎoshī	Bù lái. Tā míngtiān lái.
Frank	Xièxie nǐ.
Lǐ lǎoshī	Bú yòng xiè. Míngtiān jiàn.
Frank	Míngtiān jiàn.

How to practise tones

1 When you are practising words individually, pay attention to the tone and try to reproduce it. Go back and look at the **Tones** section at the beginning of the book, where you will find some useful hints on how to say each of the four tones.

2 When you are repeating phrases or sentences as in the dialogue, pay more attention to the shape of the whole sentence and copy that rather than each individual tone.

3 Don't worry if you find the idea of tones rather daunting at first – you will soon get used to them!

Language notes

1 Mr and Mrs

In Chinese, the surname or family name always comes first. Traditionally this is the most important thing about your identity. The Chinese have always placed much emphasis on the family. Your title appears after your surname:

Gélín xiānsheng	*Mr Green*
Gélín tàitai	*Mrs Green*
Wáng lǎoshī	*Teacher Wang*

2 Greetings

Nǐ hǎo can be used at any time to say *Hello* or *How do you do?*. You will come across other greetings which refer specifically to the morning or the evening, such as when wishing somebody goodnight.

3 Asking somebody to do something

Qǐng is used when you want to ask somebody to do something. You use the verb **qǐng** (*to invite/request*) plus the word for whatever you want them to do. Of course **qǐng** could be translated as **please** in such cases.

Qǐng jìn.	*Please come in.*
Qǐng zuò.	*Please sit down.*

You use the verb **wèn** (*to ask*) when you want to ask a question.

Wèn wèntí	*Ask (a) question(s)*
Qǐng wèn	*May I ask . . . ?*

4 *Hǎo* Adjective or verb?

The answer is both! **Hǎo** is both an adjective (a word that describes a noun) and a verb (a word that tells you what a person, animal or thing does, or is). However, Chinese adjectives can also act as verbs so: **hǎo** means *to be good, to be well*, as well as *fine, good, OK*:

Nǐ **hǎo**.	*How do you do./How are you?*
Tā hěn **hǎo**.	*He/she is (very) well./*
	He/she is (very) good.

But:

| **hǎo** tàitai | *a good wife* |
| **hǎo** lǎoshī | *a good teacher* |

The use of **hěn** in **hěn hǎo** is *not* optional. If you do not use it, a comparison is implied. **Hěn** carries a lot less weight than the English 'very' unless you stress it.

5 You like me? I like you!

Pronouns (words used in place of nouns to refer to a person) are very easy in Chinese: **Wǒ** means *me* as well as *I*. **Tā** means *him, her, it* as well as *he, she* or *it*. To make them plural you simply add -**men**. The following table will make this clearer:

wǒ	*I, me*	**wǒmen**	*we, us*
nǐ	*you* (sing)	**nǐmen**	*you* (pl)
tā	*he, she, it, him, her*	**tāmen**	*they, them*

Although *he, she* and *it* are all pronounced **tā**, each of them is written with a different character. This only affects the written language (see Unit 11), so there is absolutely nothing to worry about.

6 Simple questions with *ma*?

To make a question from any statement you just put **ma** at the end of it.

| Tā míngtiān lái. | *She will come tomorrow.* |
| Tā míngtiān lái ma? | *Is she coming tomorrow?* |

| Wáng lǎoshī zài. | *Teacher Wang is around.* |
| Wáng lǎoshī zài ma? | *Is Teacher Wang around?* |

7 How to say 'no'!

To make a verb negative in Chinese all you have to do is put **bù** in front of it. There is only **one** exception to this rule, which you will meet in Unit 2.

Nǐ hǎo.	*You're well/good.*
Nǐ bù hǎo.	*You are not well/not good.*
Tā zài.	*He/she's here.*
Tā bú zài.	*He/she's not here.*

8 Word order that's different but not difficult!

Basic Chinese word order is the same as in English:

| I | like | you |
| Subject | Verb | Object |

but in English, you say: *He is coming tomorrow.* Whereas in Chinese, you say:

| Tā míngtiān lái. | *He **tomorrow** comes.* |

To sum up, timewords like *today, tomorrow, Wednesday, 6 o'clock* come **before** the verb in Chinese. Other words that come before the verb are the negative **bù**, and words such as yě (*also*) and hěn (*very*).

Greetings

Traditionally (i.e. before 1949) the Chinese neither shook hands nor kissed when they met or said goodbye. The custom was to clasp your hands together at chest height and as you move them very slightly backwards and forwards you bow your head over them. The lower you bow your head, the higher the status of the other person. With the growing influence of the west, however, shaking hands is becoming more common.

Practice

1 What do you say? Choose the most appropriate response for **a** from the first four boxes. Do the same for **b** and **c**.

a When you greet a friend, you say:

Nǐ hǎo	Zàijiàn	Bú yòng xiè	Xièxie

b When you thank someone, you say:

Zàijiàn	Nǐ hǎo	Xièxie	Bú yòng xiè

c When someone thanks you for your help, you respond by saying:

Nǐ hǎo	Bú yòng xiè	Zàijiàn	Xièxie

2 Responding to a Chinese person. To help you out, the first letter of the correct response is already put in.

Example: Qǐng jìn. – Xièxie.

a Nǐ hǎo!   N_____ _____!
b Xièxie nǐ.   B_____ _____ _____.
c Qǐng zuò.   X_____.
d Zàijiàn!   Z_____!

3 This time you begin and the Chinese person responds. Now you're on your own.

10

a _____ _____ .　　　Nǐ hǎo!
b Lǐ tàitai _____ _____ ?　　　Ta hěn hǎo. Xièxie nǐ.
c Lǐ xiānsheng _____ _____ ?　　　Duìbuqǐ, tā bú zài.
d _____ _____ .　　　Bú yòng xiè.

4 What would you put in each of the gaps to make them into words or phrases?

Example: Duì_____qǐ. – Duì<u>bu</u>qǐ.

a Xiè _____ .　　　　　　e Qǐng _____ .
b _____ _____ xiè.　　f _____ zuò.
c _____ jiàn!　　　　　g _____ _____ hǎo.
d _____ jiàn!　　　　　h _____ hǎo _____ ?

5 Match the sentences on the left to those on the right.

a Tāmen hěn hǎo.　　　　i They won't be in tomorrow.
b Tāmen jīntiān bú zài.　　ii They will come today.
c Tāmen jīntiān lái.　　　iii They are not in today.
d Tāmen míngtiān bú zài.　iv They are very well.

Quick review

◆) CD 1, TR 2, 03:58

Now you've arrived at the end of Unit 1. What would you say in the following situations:

a You meet your Chinese friend, Mr Li, and you want to say hello.
b Then you ask how his wife is.
c You are a little bit late and you say you are sorry.
d Thank your friend (for his/her help).
e When he/she thanks you, say *You are welcome*.
f When you take your leave, what do you say?

Vocabulary and pronunciation

a Is the tone for 'you' in Chinese 1st, 2nd, 3rd or 4th tone?
b Is the Chinese for 'teacher' 'lǎoshī' or 'xiānsheng'?
c Which word means 'tomorrow'? Is it 'míngtiān' or 'jīntiān'?
d Which syllable in 'míngtiān jiàn' and 'zàijiàn' means 'to see'?

You'll find the answers to the **Quick review** in the **Key to the exercises** at the end of the book. If you got them correct, you are ready to move on to Unit 2. If you found the review difficult, spend more time revising this unit.

欢迎 **Huānyíng**
Welcome

再见 **Zàijiàn**
Goodbye

2

....

Nǐ jiào shénme?
What's your name?

In this unit you will learn
- How to say who you are
- How to make simple introductions
- How to ask who other people are
- How to address people correctly
- How to deny something

Before you start

There is a lot of practice with asking questions in this unit. Try to learn some of the questions by heart as they will be very useful. Remember what was said about tones in Unit 1 in the section **How to practise tones** and at the beginning of the book.

Let's try

🔊 **CD 1, TR 3**

A Chinese visitor has knocked on the door of your office.

a   What would you call out?
b   How would you greet him when he comes through the door?
c   How would you ask him to sit down?
d   At the end of your talk you show him to the door. What do you say to him? (You have arranged to see him again tomorrow.)

Learning tips

Here are some hints for learning vocabulary. See which one works best for you:

1   Practise saying the words out loud as you read them.

2   Cover up the English and see if you can remember what any of the Chinese words mean.

3   Cover up the Chinese and see if the English words jolt your memory.

4   Listen to the recording over and over again.

5   Write the words out several times.

6   Study the new words from beginning to end then start from the bottom and work back up again.

7   Group the words in a way that will help you to remember them, such as all the verbs together, all the countries, and the language which is spoken in each one.

8   Copy the words with their tone marks on to one side of a small card with their English equivalent on the other. Go through them looking at the Chinese first and giving the English word and then vice versa. If you get one wrong, put it back in the pile and have another go at it. You can also mix up the English and Chinese.

dāngrán	*of course*
guì	*expensive, honourable*
Nín guì xìng?	*What's your (honourable) name?*
háizi	*child/children*
huì	*can, to be able to*
jiào	*to call/be called*
méi	*no, not, (have not)*
méi guānxi	*it's OK/it doesn't matter*
míngzi	*name*
nà/nèi (used interchangeably)	*that*
nán	*male*
Nǐ ne?	*And you?*
nín	*you* (polite form)
péngyou	*friend*
piàoliang	*beautiful*
rènshi	*recognize, know* (people)
shéi/shuí?	*who?*
shénme?	*what?*
shì	*to be*
shuō	*to speak, to say*
wǒ	*I, me*
wǒde/nǐde/nínde/tāde	*my, your, his/her*
xiǎojie	*Miss*
xìng	*surname*
yě	*also*
yìdiǎn(r)	*a little*
Yīngwén	*English* (language)
yǒu	*to have*
zhè/zhèi (used interchangeably)	*this*
zhēn	*real/really*
Zhōngwén	*Chinese* (language)
Nǐ/tā jiào shénme (míngzi)?	*What is your/his/her name?*
Wǒ/tā jiào . . .	*I am/he is/she is called . . .*
Wǒ/nǐ/tā (bú) shì . . .	*I am/you are/he is/she is (not) . . .*
Zhè/nà (bú) shì . . .	*This/that is (not) . . .*

QUICK VOCAB

Tā shì shéi?
Tā shì bu shì . . . ?

Who is he/she?
Is he/she . . . (or not)?

Common Chinese surnames

◄) CD 1, TR 3, 02:59

Zhāng 张   Wáng 王   Lǐ 李   Zhào 赵   Liú 刘

Chén 陈   Lín 林   Wú 吴   Guō 郭   Zhèng 郑

Learning tips

1 Refer back to the **Pronunciation guide** to help you pronounce the surnames above. Repeat them out loud several times.

2 If you have the recording, listen to the names and repeat them after the speaker.

Dialogues

Dialogue 1

◄) CD 1, TR 3, 03:31

Listen to or read the dialogue and see how you ask what another person's name is in Chinese.

Jane	Nín guì xìng?
Chén	Wǒ xìng Chén. Nín ne?
Jane	Wǒ xìng Lord. Zhè shì nínde háizi ma?
Chén	Bú shì. Wǒ méi yǒu háizi. Zhè shì Lǐ tàitai de háizi.
Jane	(to the boy) Nǐ jiào shénme míngzi?
Child	Wǒ jiào Pàn Pan.

Dialogue 2   At a conference

🔊 CD 2, TR 3, 05:04

White	Zhèng xiānsheng, nǐ hǎo!
Cháng	Wǒ xìng Cháng, bú xìng Zhèng. Wǒ jiào Cháng Zhèng.
White	Duìbuqǐ, Cháng xiānsheng.
Cháng	Méi guānxi. White xiānsheng, nǐ yǒu mei yǒu Zhōngwén míngzi?
White	Yǒu. Wǒ jiào Bái Bǐdé.
Cháng	Bái xiānsheng, nǐ huì bu huì shuō Yīngwén?
White	Dāngrán huì. Cháng xiānsheng, nǐ yě huì shuō Yīngwén ma?
Cháng	Huì yìdiǎnr.

Tone of *bù*

Bù (*not*) is normally a 4th tone, but it becomes a 2nd tone before another 4th tone. When this happens it is marked as such in the book, such as **bú xìng** not **bù xìng**. It is toneless in such expressions as **huì bu huì** (see **Dialogue 2**).

Dialogue 3

◀) CD 1, TR 3, 05:50

How do you introduce yourself and somebody else? Find out in this dialogue.

Bái	Nà shì shéi? Nǐ rènshi bu rènshi tā?
Wú	Rènshi. Tā shì Guō xiǎojie.
Bái	Tā zhēn piàoliang. *(walks over to the girl)*
Bái	Nǐ hǎo! Wǒ jiào Bái Bǐdé. Nǐ ne?
Guō	Nǐ hǎo! Wǒ jiào Guō Yùjié. *(A man walks over to her and hands her a drink.)*
Guō	Zhè shì wǒde nán péngyou. Tā jiào Liú Wénguāng. Zhè shì Bái xiānsheng.
Liú	Bái xiānsheng, nǐ hǎo!
Bái	O, nǐ hǎo!

Language notes

1 How to be courteous

In Chinese, when you don't know somebody very well (or at all) or you wish to show respect (usually for older people, teachers, etc.), you use **nín** instead of **nǐ**. It is, however, used less frequently than it used to be and it cannot be used in the plural. This means that the plural form of both **nǐ** and **nín** is **nǐmen**, **nǐmen** being both heard and read frequently in daily life.

2 'You' and 'yours'!

Nǐ means *you* (sing). If you add the little word **de** to it, it means *your* or *yours*:

nǐ**de** háizi	*your child*
wǒ**de** xiānsheng	*my husband*
zhè shì nǐ**de**	*this is yours*
Lǐ tàitai **de** háizi	*Mrs Li's child*
tā**de** háizi	*her/his child*

In close personal relationships: **nǐ tàitai** (*your wife*), **wǒ māma** (*my mum*), the **de** may be omitted (**Unit 1, Dialogue 1,** where Mrs Green asks Xiǎo Wáng, **Nǐ tàitai hǎo ma?**).

3 How to say 'No' with *yǒu*!

To say *do not have* in Chinese, you put **méi** in front of the verb **yǒu** *to have*.

For present or future actions all other verbs are negated by putting **bù** in front of them.

Wǒ **méi yǒu** háizi.	*I have no children.*
Tā **méi yǒu** Zhōngwén míngzi.	*She doesn't have a Chinese name.*

4 Another way of asking questions

If you put the positive and negative forms of the verb together (in that order) you can make a question:

Nǐ **yǒu mei yǒu** háizi?	*Do you have children?*
Nǐ **shì bu shì** lǎoshī?	*Are you a teacher?*

This is a popular alternative to the question form with **ma** (see **Language note 6** in Unit 1). The negative form of the verb is normally unstressed when it is used to make a question in this way. It is stressed, however, if the question is said slowly or with emphasis.

5 'Yes' and 'no' in replies

Yes and *no* don't exist as such in Chinese. If you are asked a question the answer is either the positive form of the verb (to mean *yes*) or the negative form of the verb (to mean *no*):

Nǐ yǒu méi yǒu háizi?	*Do you have children?*
Yǒu.	*Yes, I do.*
Méi yǒu.	*No, I don't.*
Nǐ rènshi tā ma?	*Do you know her?*
Rènshi.	*Yes, I do.*
Bú rènshi.	*No, I don't.*

6 To be or not to be?

Shì, the verb *to be* in English, is used much less in Chinese than in English. This is because adjectives in Chinese can also act as verbs as you saw in Unit 1. For example, **hǎo** means *to be good* as well as *good* so there is no need for the verb *to be*.

Zhè **shì** nǐde háizi ma?	*Is this your child?*
Bú **shì**. Zhè **shì** Lǐ tàitai de háizi.	*No, it's Mrs Li's.*
Tā **shì** nǐde nǚ péngyou ma?	*Is she your girlfriend?*
Bú **shì**. Tā **shì** wǒ tàitai.	*No, she is my wife.*

7 Who and what?

In Chinese, question words such as **shéi** (*who*) and **shénme** (*what*) appear in the sentence in the same position as the word or words which replace them in the answer:

Nǐ jiào **shénme** míngzi?	*What are you called?*
	(*lit.* You are called what?)
Wǒ jiào **Pàn Pan.**	*I'm called* Pàn Pan.
Nà shì **shéi?**	*Who is that (young lady)?*
	(*lit.* That [young lady] is who?)
Tā shì **wǒ (de)** péngyou.	*She is my friend.*

This is different from the word order in English, where the question word is at the beginning of the sentence.

8 Follow-up questions

To avoid having to ask a question in full or to repeat the same question you can use the little word **ne** at the end of a phrase to take a short cut!

Nǐ jiào shénme míngzi?	*What's your name?*
Wǒ jiào Wú Zébì. Nǐ **ne?**	*I'm called/My name is Wu Zebi.*
	What about you?
	(i.e. what's your name?)
Wǒ jiào Bái Bǐdé. Tā **ne?**	*My name's Peter White.*
	What's hers?

Insight

As you saw in Unit 1, the surname or family name comes before your title in Chinese. This means that your given name (first name) comes **after** your surname:

Cháng (family name) **Zhèng** (given name)
Bái (family name) **Bǐdé** (given name)

The use of first names is generally reserved for family members and close friends. Colleagues or people in your peer group are addressed on an informal basis by their surnames prefaced by **lǎo** (*old*) or **xiǎo** (*young*), largely depending on whether the person in question is older or younger than you.

Practice

1 Complete the following exchanges by filling in the blanks in the sentences below:

a Tā jiào _____ míngzi?   Tā _____ Fāng Yuán.
b Nǐ _____ shuō Zhōngwén ma?   Huì. Wǒ huì _____ yìdiǎnr.
c Tāde nán péngyou _____ shéi?   Wǒ bú _____ tā.

2 Look at the pictures and answer the following questions in Chinese:

Lǐ Jīnshēng

Yīng Zìpéng

    a Tāmen shì shéi?
← b Tā jiào shénme?
    c Tā xìng Yīng ma? →
← d Tā yě xìng Yīng ma?
    e Nǐ rènshi tāmen ma?

◀) CD 1, TR 3, 07:10

3 Listen to the recording and answer the following questions about the Chinese woman in the passage. If you don't have the recording, read the passage below and then answer the questions.

a What's her surname?
b What's her first name?
c How much English does she speak?
d What is her occupation?
e Does she know you?
f What does she look like?
g Does she have a boyfriend?

Wǒde Zhōngwén lǎoshī jiào Wáng Lányīng. Tā hěn piàoliang. Tā yǒu nán péngyou. Tāmen bú rènshi nǐ. Tāmen huì shuō yìdiǎnr Yīngwén.

4 Who is who? State the name and the occupation of each person pictured below. You can get more practice if you use both of the patterns given in the example:

Tā jiào Yán Lóng. Tā shì xuésheng (*student*).
Zhè/nà shì Yán Lóng. Tā shì xuésheng.

a Zhào Huá	b Liú Guāng	c Guō Jié
jǐngchá	sījī	dàifu
d Lǐ Mínglì	e Zhōu Jiābǎo	f Wú Zébì
lǎoshī	xuésheng	chúshī

5 According to the pictures in Exercise 4, are the following statements true or false? If it's true, say **duì** meaning *correct*. If it's not true, say **bú duì**, meaning *not correct*. Tick the right box in each case.

Example: Zhào Huá xìng Huá. (bú duì)

	duì	bú duì?
a Zhào Huá shì lǎoshī.	☐	☐
b Liú Guāng bú shì sījī.	☐	☐
c Nà ge dàifu jiào Wú Zébì.	☐	☐

d Zhōu Jiābǎo xìng Jiābǎo. ☐   ☐
e Lǐ lǎoshī jiào Lǐ Míng. ☐   ☐
f Wú Zébì shì chúshī. ☐   ☐

6 You have learnt two ways to ask questions. With each set of words use these different question forms to make up two questions. The example will make this clear.

Example: Tā/huì shuō/Fǎwén (*French*)
           – Tā huì shuō Fǎwén ma?
           – Tā huì bú huì shuō Fǎwén?

a Nǐ/huì shuō/Yīngwén
b Nǐmen/shì/lǎoshī
c Xiǎo Zhèng/zài
d Lǐ xiānsheng/jīntiān/lái

e Wáng Fāng/yǒu/Yīngwén míngzi
f Lín lǎoshī/jiào/Lín Péng

Quick review

◄）CD 1, TR 3, 07:43

How would you say the following?

a Ask what a person's surname is.
b Say *My name is xxx*.
c Say that you haven't got a Chinese name.
d Say that you don't know her.
e Say *That's OK* when someone apologizes to you.
f Say that your friend is not a teacher.

Vocabulary and pronunciation

a Is the pronunciation for 'of course' 'dānrán' or 'dāngrán'?
b What is the Chinese for 'to speak/to say'? Is it 'shuō' or 'shōu'?
c The Chinese for 'who' can be pronounced in two ways: 'shuí' or _____?

d The Chinese for 'English (language)' and 'Chinese (language)' is 'Yīngwén' and 'Zhōngwén' respectively. What syllable in these two words means 'language'?

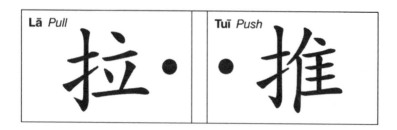

Lā *Pull*

Tuī *Push*

3

Nǐ shì nǎ guó rén?
Where are you from?

In this unit you will learn
- How to say where you come from and
  what nationality you are
- How to ask for and give an address
- The numbers 0–10
- How to ask for, and give,
  a telephone number
- How to fill out a form

Before you start

Talking about where you come from, what nationality you are, where you live and what your telephone number is in Chinese is straightforward with the necessary vocabulary and a few of the basic rules about word order. Chinese numbers are very easy as you will discover in this unit.

It is important to have short-term goals to encourage yourself. In this unit keep practising how to ask other people where they come from, where they live and what their telephone number is. Make sure you can answer these questions yourself! Aim at answering them without thinking.

Let's try

You are at a party where you know hardly anyone.

a How do you introduce yourself and how do you ask somebody his/her name?
b If you find out that one of the guests is married, how do you ask if they have any children?

🔊 **CD 1, TR 4**

diànhuà	*telephone* (lit. *electric speech*)
duì	*yes, correct*
Dōngchéng (Qū)	*Eastern City (District)*
duōshao?	*what's the number of?*
fàndiàn	*hotel*
fángjiān	*room*
fēijī	*plane*
Guǎngdōng	*Canton* (Province)
guó	*country*
hào	*number*
hàomǎ	*number* (often used for telephone, telex, fax numbers and car registration plates)
hépíng	*peace*
jǐ hào?	*which number?*
lù	*road, street*
Lúndūn	*London*
míngpiàn	*namecard*
nǎr?	*where?*
piào	*ticket*
qū	*district*
rén	*person*
Xīchéng (Qū)	*Western City (District)*
xǐhuan	*to like*
yìsi	*meaning*
zhù	*to live*
zhù zài	*to live in/at a place*

Learning tips

1 Try pronouncing the names of the countries on the maps that follow later in this unit. Repeat them out loud over and over again.

2 Every time you stumble over the pronunciation of a word or syllable go back to the **Pronunciation guide** and check it out.

3 Foreign names, such as the names of countries and cities, can be expressed in Chinese in three main ways:

- Based on the original sound, such as **Yìdàlì** (*Italy*)
- Based on the meaning, such as **Niújīn** (*Oxford*) (*lit.* ox/cow ford)
- A mixture of the orginal sound and its meaning, such as **Xīn** (*new*) **Xīlán** (*New Zealand*)

Dialogues

Dialogue 1

◀) **CD 1, TR 4, 01:16**

Mr Peter White (Bái Bǐdé) meets a Chinese person, Lín Jiànmù, at a conference.

Lín	Nín shì nǎ guó rén?
Bái	Wǒ shì Yīngguó-rén. Zhè shì wǒde míngpiàn.
Lín	Xièxie. O, Bái xiānsheng, nín zhù zài Lúndūn?
Bái	Duì. Nín shì Zhōngguó-rén ba?
Lín	Shì, wǒ shì Guǎngdōng-rén.

Dialogue 2

◀) **CD 1, TR 4, 02:45**

Bái xiānsheng goes to collect his plane ticket at a Chinese travel agency.

Assistant	Zhè shì nínde fēijī piào.
Bái	Xièxie. Wǒ zhù zài shénme fàndiàn?
Assistant	Nín zhù zài Hépíng Fàndiàn.
Bái	Hépíng shì shénme yìsi?
Assistant	Hépíng shì *'peace'* de yìsi.
Bái	Hěn hǎo. Wǒ xǐhuan hépíng.

Numbers 0–10

◄)) CD 1 , TR 4, 03:25

líng	0	sān	3	liù	6	jiǔ	9
yī	1	sì	4	qī	7	shí	10
èr	2	wǔ	5	bā	8		

yī　èr　sān　sì　wǔ　liù　qī　bā　jiǔ　shí

- Practise saying 1 to 5: yī èr sān sì wǔ. Then say 6 to 10: liù qī bā jiǔ shí. Then put them altogether: yī èr sān . . . jiǔ shí.
- Now say: yī sān wǔ qī jiǔ. Then say: èr sì liù bā shí.
- Now try this: yī èr sān, sān èr yī, yī èr sān sì wǔ liù qī.

Dialogue 3

◄)) CD 1 , TR 4, 03:56

Mr White and Mr Lin decide to further their business association.

Lín	Nǐ zhù zài nǎr?
Bái	Wǒ zhù zài Hépíng Fàndiàn.
Lín	Jǐ hào fángjiān?
Bái	Wǔ-líng-bā hào fángjiān. Nǐ zhù zài nǎr?
Lín	Wǒ zhù zài Píng'ān Lù qī hào.

Bái	Píng'ān Lù zài nǎr?
Lín	Píng'ān Lù zài Xīchéng Qū.
Bái	Hépíng Fàndiàn yě zài Xīchéng Qū shì bu shi?
Lín	Bú zài. Zài Dōngchéng Qū.
Bái	Nǐde diànhuà hàomǎ shì duōshao?
Lín	Liù-wǔ-wǔ-èr jiǔ-sān-èr-sì. Nǐde ne?
Bái	Wǒde shì liù-liù-qī-sān bā-bā-sān-líng.

Language notes

1 Where are you from?

To give your nationality you say the name of the country and then add -rén *person* after it:

Zhōngguó	*China, Chinese*
Zhōngguó-rén	*Chinese person*
Měiguó	*America (US)*
Měiguó-rén	*American*

Look at the two maps and the table between them to see exactly how this works.

Country	Nationality	Country/Nationality
Ài'ěrlán	Ài'ěrlán-rén	Ireland/Irish
Déguó	Déguó-rén	Germany/German
Fǎguó	Fǎguó-rén	France/French
Měiguó	Měiguó-rén	USA/American
Rìběn	Rìběn-rén	Japan/Japanese
Sūgélán	Sūgélán-rén	Scotland/Scottish
Yīngguó	Yīngguó-rén	Britain/British
Yuènán	Yuènán-rén	Vietnam/Vietnamese
Wēi'ěrshì	Wēi'ěrshì-rén	Wales/Welsh
(Xiānggǎng)	(Xiānggǎng-rén)	(Hong Kong/from HK)
Zhōngguó	Zhōngguó-rén	China/Chinese

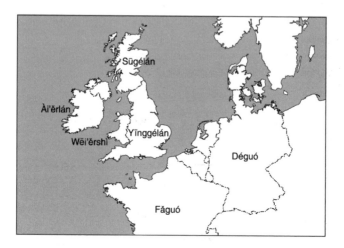

You do exactly the same thing when you wish to say which province or town you come from:

Wǒ shì Lúndūn-rén.	*I'm a Londoner.*
Nǐ shì Luómǎ-rén ma?	*Are you from Rome?*
Tā shì bu shì Běijīng-rén?	*Is he from Beijing?*
Wǒmen shì Fújiàn-rén.	*We're from Fujian Province.*
Tāmen shì Guǎngdōng-rén.	*They're from Canton Province.*

2 Question tag: *ba*

Ba is placed after a verb or phrase to make a suggestion or to ask for confirmation of a supposition:

Nǐ shì Zhōngguó-rén **ba**?   *You're Chinese, I take it?*
Hǎo **ba**?   *Is that all right then?*

3 Linking word *de*

You have to reverse the word order in Chinese to translate a phrase such as: *the meaning of peace.* The two words **hépíng** (*peace*) and **yìsi** (*meaning*) are linked by the little word **de**.

hépíng **de** yìsi   *the meaning of* hépíng

Some people call this the possessive **de** to distinguish it from another **de** you will meet in Unit 8.

Look carefully at the following examples:

Fàndiàn **de** yìsi shì *hotel*.   *The meaning of **fandian** is hotel.*

Bái xiānsheng **de** diànhuà hàomǎ   *Mr White's telephone number*

Mǎ tàitai **de** háizi   *Mrs Ma's child*

4 Room 508

Room 508 is said as *508 Room* in Chinese (the reverse of English word order) with the addition of the word **hào** (*number*) after 508. More examples of this are given below:

10 (shí) **hào**   *No. 10*
5 (wǔ) **hào** fángjiān   *Room 5*

Room numbers up to 100 are generally said as one number. You will meet numbers from ten to 100 in the next unit.

Numbers over 100 are broken down into single digits:

374 (sān-qī-sì) hào fángjiān   *Room 374*
896 (bā-jiǔ-liù) hào fángjiān   *Room 896*

5 Question tag: *shì bu shi?*

Making a question by putting **shì bu shi** at the end of a sentence in Chinese conveys the idea of *Am I right?* or *Is it true?*:

Hépíng Fàndiàn yě zài
   Xīchéng Qū **shì bu shi?**

The Peace Hotel is also in the Western City District, isn't it?

Nǐ shì Yīngguó-rén **shì bu shi?**

You're English/British, aren't you?

6 Telephone numbers

Telephone numbers are often made up of seven or eight digits each of which is usually said separately:

551 8274   wǔ-wǔ-**yāo** bā-èr-qī-sì
8228 9436   bā-èr-èr-bā jiǔ-sì-sān-liù

Yāo is used instead of **yī** when telephone numbers or large numbers for rooms, buses, trains, and so on, are broken down into single digits. This avoids any confusion with **qī** (seven).

Learning tips

1 Have imaginary conversations with yourself in Chinese using the material in the dialogues and the structures you have covered.

2 Think of somebody and say everything you can about them in Chinese: what their name is, what nationality they are, where they live, what their telephone number is, whether they have children, if you like them, and so on. Then do the same thing with

somebody else, and so on, until you can go through the whole routine without hesitation.

3 Don't worry about making mistakes!

Anybody who has successfully learnt a foreign language knows that the way to make progress is to listen and speak as much as possible. Don't worry if you don't understand a lot of what is said to you in the beginning – just respond to what you do understand.

You will find the following two sentences very useful. Practise them over and over again:

Qǐng nǐ shuō màn yìdiǎn.	*Please speak more slowly.*
	(*lit.* invite you say slow a little)
Qǐng nǐ **zài** shuō yí biàn.	*Please say it again.*
	(*lit.* invite you again say one time)

This **zài** is not the **zài** which means *to be in/at*; it is the **zài** which means *again* as in **zàijiàn** (*goodbye*) (*lit.* again see). Words like **zài** (*again*) are called adverbs. They come before the verb in Chinese.

Insight

Chinese people are very direct with their questions. It is not considered rude to ask how old you are, how much you earn, how much your house cost to buy or what the rent is, how much the clothes you are wearing cost, and so on.

Even questions as to why you are so fat or so thin or why you haven't married or why you got divorced (have you got a bad temperament?!) are all considered perfectly legitimate. Things are changing, however, as those people who have increasing contact with westerners realize that the latter are uncomfortable with such questions.

Practice

1 Answer the following questions. If you don't know, say **Wǒ bù zhīdao** (*lit.* I not know.):

    a Nǐ shì Měiguó-rén ma?
    b Nǐ māma (*mum*) shì Fǎguó-rén ma?
    c Nǐde lǎoshī shì Zhōngguó-rén ba?
    d Nǐ bàba (*dad*) bú shì Déguó-rén ba?
    e Dèng Xiǎopíng shì Zhōngguó-rén ma?
    f Shāshìbǐyà (*Shakespeare*) shì bu shì Yīngguó-rén?

◄) **CD 1, TR 4, 05:43**

2 You are going to hear three people introducing themselves. Listen to the recording twice and take notes while you are doing so. Then fill in as many details about each of the three speakers as you can. Listen again paying particular attention to the bits you have not been able to catch. Listen for a fourth time to check what you have written.

	Speaker 1	Speaker 2	Speaker 3
Surname:	....	....	....
Given name:	....	....	....
Nationality:	....	....	....
Telephone no:	....	....	....
Address:	....	....	....
– city:	....	....	....
– street:	....	....	....
– number:	....	....	....

If you're still not sure of what you've heard, have a look at what the three people say in the **Key to the exercises**.

NB: Chinese addresses are written in the reverse order to the way addresses are written in English. In English, you give the number of your flat/house first, then the street or road and then the town or city. In Chinese, it is city, street, number, as you can see from the chart above.

3 a Follow the same pattern as the passage you heard in exercise 2 and say something about yourself. Fill in your details on the chart below as you did in exercise 2. You can do this exercise even if you don't have the recording.
   b Think of one of your friends and fill in his/her details.
   c If you are doing this with another person, ask him/her questions and fill in his/her details.

	Yourself	Friend A	Friend B
Surname:	....		
Given name:	....		
Nationality:	....		
Telephone no:	....		
Address:	....		
– city:	....		
– street:	....		
– number:	....		

4 You often see Chinese addresses written in English, as in the following examples. How would these addresses be said (or written) in Chinese?

a *Mingli Li*
   (Lecturer)
   2, Chaoyang Lu
   BEIJING

b *Mr. Hua Zhao,*
   Room 384, Dongfang
   Hotel, 9 Longhai Lu,
   Suzhou

c *Miss Jiabao Zhao,*
   5, Heping Lu,
   Xicheng Qu
   Nanjing

5 Match the words in the left-hand column with the ones on the right to make words you've already seen. (We've done one for you.)

a	fēijī	i	Fàndiàn
b	Lúndūn	ii	jiàn
c	Hépíng	iii	piào
d	èr-líng-wǔ	iv	Qū
e	míngtiān	v	fángjiān
f	Dōngchéng	vi	hàomǎ
g	diànhuà	vii	rén

Quick review

◀) **CD 1, TR 4, 07:30**

a You meet someone you don't know. How do you ask your friend who he is?

b How do you ask someone where he/she lives?

c Tell someone that you don't live in London.

d Ask someone to give you his/her telephone number.

e Ask what the meaning of **diànhuà** is.

f Say to the Chinese air hostess that this is your (plane) ticket.

Vocabulary and pronunciation

a The Chinese for 'good' is 'hǎo'. What is the Chinese for 'number'?

b Put the tone marks on 'Lundun'.

c Is the sound for 'country' 'guó' or 'góu'?

d What is the meaning of 'yìsi'?

You'll find the answers in the **Key to the exercises**. How have you done? If most of them are correct, you will be ready to go on to Unit 4. Congratulations! Before you do so, spend some time revising Units 1, 2 and 3. Regular revision will help to consolidate what you have learnt and give you more confidence.

4

Nǐ yǒu xiōngdì、 jiěmèi ma?
Do you have brothers and sisters?

In this unit you will learn
- How to talk about yourself and your family
- How to ask other people about their family
- How to ask someone if they are married and/or have children
- How to say how old you are
- How to ask how old somebody is
- How to count up to 100

Before you start

You'll find that speaking about yourself and your family in Chinese is very easy. Remember how to say *I have* or *I don't have* (**wǒ yǒu**, **wǒ méi yǒu**)? Using this and the basic vocabulary you will learn in this unit, you have all you need!

You will also be able to count up to 100 by the end of this unit. Having mastered one to ten in Unit 3 you will be surprised how easy it is. 11 is 10 + 1, 12 is 10 + 2, 20 is 2 × 10, 30 is 3 × 10, all the way up to 99 which is 9 × 10 + 9. There is a special word **băi** for *hundred* so 100 is **yìbăi** (*one hundred* – you have to use yī *one*).

Let's try

You have just been introduced to a Chinese business associate who is on a week's visit to London.

a Ask her which hotel she is staying in and what the number of her room is.
b What do you say when you give her your card?

bú kèqi	*you are welcome* (lit. *not guest air*)
dà	*big*
. . . duō dà?	*How old . . . ?*
. . . duō dà niánjì?	*How old . . . ?* (respectful) (lit. *how old year record*)
gè	(measure word)
hé	*and*
jié hūn	*marry*
. . . jié hūn le ma?	*. . . married?*
. . . jĭ suì?	*How old . . . ?* (for children)
jīnnián	*this year*
le	*grammatical marker*
liăng	*two* (of anything)
. . . suì	*. . . years old; age*
xiàng	(to look) *like*
bú xiàng	*not to look* (like) *it*
xiăo	*small*
yí ge . . . yí ge	*one . . . , the other*
zhēnde	*really*

Family members

◄» CD 1, TR 5

bàba	*dad, father*
māma	*mum, mother*
érzi	*son*
nǚ'ér	*daughter*
gēge	*elder brother*
jiějie	*elder sister*
dìdi	*younger brother*
mèimei	*younger sister*
xiōngdì	*brothers*
jiěmèi	*sisters*
dà dìdi	*the older one of the younger brothers*
xiǎo dìdi	*the younger one of the younger brothers*

Numbers 11–100

◄» CD 1, TR 5, 00:46

shíyī	11	shíliù	16	sānshí	30	bāshí	80
shí'èr	12	shíqī	17	sìshí	40	jiǔshí	90
shísān	13	shíbā	18	wǔshí	50	yìbǎi	100
shísì	14	shíjiǔ	19	liùshí	60		
shíwǔ	15	èrshí	20	qīshí	70		

Dialogues

Dialogue 1

◄» CD 1, TR 5, 01:37

Dīng Fèng is carrying out a family planning survey and Liú Fúguì (from the Miáo national minority) has agreed to answer a few questions:

Dīng	Nín jiào shénme míngzi?
Liú	Wǒ jiào Liú Fúguì.
Dīng	Liú xiānsheng jié hūn le ma?
Liú	Jié hūn le.
Dīng	Yǒu mei yǒu háizi?
Liú	Yǒu liǎng ge, yí ge érzi, yí ge nǚ'ér.
Dīng	Tāmen jǐ suì?
Liú	Érzi liǎng suì, nǚ'ér wǔ suì.

Learning tips

Practise saying 11 to 15: **shíyī, shí'èr, shísān, shísì, shíwǔ**. Then say 16 to 20: **shíliù, shíqī, shíbā, shíjiǔ, èrshí**. Then put them together: **shíyī, shí'èr, shísān, . . . èrshí**. Do the same for 21 to 25, 26 to 30, and so on.

Tones on yī

Yī (*one*) is a 1st tone when it is part of a number, such as yī (*one*), shíyī (*eleven*), èrshíyī (*twenty-one*). When it occurs before a measure word it is normally a 4th tone, for example yì tiān (*one day*), yì běn shū (*one book*), but it turns into a 2nd tone before another 4th tone, for example yí suì (*one year old*). In yí ge háizi, gè is said without a tone, although it is actually 4th, but it still carries enough weight to change yī into a 2nd tone.

Suì (*year of age*), tiān (*day*) and nián (*year*), all act as measure words and nouns combined (refer to **Language note 2** for an explanation of what a measure word is). Note that yìbǎi is *one hundred*.

Dialogue 2

◀) CD 1, TR 5, 02:54

Dīng Fèng asks Liú Fúguì some more questions. By reading/listening to the dialogue can you find out whether Liú Fúguì has any brothers or sisters? How old are they?

Dīng	Nín yǒu xiōngdì jiěmèi ma?
Liú	Yǒu liǎng ge dìdi、yí ge mèimei. Méi yǒu gēge hé jiějie.
Dīng	Nín dìdi, mèimei duō dà?
Liú	Dà dìdi èrshíliù, xiǎo dìdi èrshísì.
Dīng	Mèimei ne?
Liú	Mèimei èrshíbā.
Dīng	Hěn hǎo, xièxie nín.
Liú	Bú kèqi.
Dīng	Zàijiàn.
Liú	Zàijiàn.

Dialogue 3

◄» CD 1, TR 5, 03:38

Wú and Lù are looking at a photo of Lù's family.

Wú	Nǐ bàba、māma duō dà niánjì?
Lù	Bàba wǔshísān, māma sìshíjiǔ.
Wú	Bú xiàng, bú xiàng. Zhè shì nǐ mèimei ba. Tā zhēn piàoliang.
Lù	Tā jīnnián èrshí'èr.
Wú	Zhēnde? Tā jié hūn le ma?
Lù	Méi yǒu. Kěshì yǒu nán péngyou le.
Wú	O.

Language notes

1 Sentences ending in ... *le*

If you put the little word **le** at the end of a sentence, it shows that something has happened or has already taken place:

Wǒ jié hūn **le**.	*I'm married.*
Wǒ qǐng tā **le**.	*I invited him.*
Wǒ wèn tā **le**.	*I asked her.*

If you want to make a question, simply add **ma** or **méi you** to the end of a sentence. **Yǒu** is unstressed.

Nǐ jié hūn le **ma**?	*Are you married?*
Nǐ jié hūn le **méi you**?	*Are you married?*

If you want to say something has not happened, you use **méi yǒu** (*not have*) plus the verb:

Wǒ **méi yǒu** jié hūn.	*I'm not married.*
Wǒ **méi** qǐng tā.	*I didn't invite him.*
Wǒ **méi** wèn tā.	*I haven't asked her.*

The **yǒu** can be omitted.

2 One or two

In Chinese, something called a measure word (MW) or classifier has to be used between a number and the noun following it.

In English, you can say:

two children
three daughters
four books

But in Chinese, you have to put the measure word/classifier in between the number and the item:

two measure word/classifier children
three measure word/classifier daughters
four measure word/classifier books

liǎng **ge** háizi	*two children*
sān **ge** nǚ'ér	*three daughters*
sì **běn** shū	*four books*

Different measure words are used with different categories of nouns. For example, **běn** is used for books and magazines whereas **zhāng** is used for rectangular or square, flat objects such as tables, beds, maps and so on, but it is not a true measure as to length or anything else:

wǔ **běn** zázhì	*five magazines*
liù **zhāng** zhuōzi	*six tables*
qī **zhāng** chuáng	*seven beds*

Gè is by far the most common measure word. It is used with a whole range of nouns which do not have their own specific measure word. When in doubt, use **gè**! The noun accompanying the number and measure word is often omitted when it is clear from the context what this is:

Nǐ yǒu mei yǒu háizi?	*Have you any children?*
Yǒu liǎng **ge** (háizi), yí **ge** érzi, yí **ge** nǚ'ér.	*Two, a son and a daughter.*

3 Two for tea!

Liǎng meaning *two of a kind* is used with measure words instead of **èr** (*two*), so *two children* is **liǎng ge háizi** and not **èr ge háizi**.

4 How old are you?

When asking small children how old they are, you use **jǐ** (*how many*) when you are expecting a small number (generally less than 10) as an answer plus the word for years (of age) **suì**:

| Háizi jǐ suì? | How old is/are the children? |
| Tā wǔ suì. | He/she's five years old. |

Note that no verb is necessary in such sentences. When asking teenagers or young adults how old they are you use **duō** (*how*) together with **dà** (*old/big*):

Nǐ **duō dà?**	How old are you
	(of teenager/young adult)?
Wǒ èrshí suì.	I'm twenty.

Again, note that no verb is necessary.

When asking older(!) adults how old they are, the phrase **duō dà niánjì** (*lit.* how big year record) is used:

Nǐ bàba、 māma **duōdà niánjì?**	How old are your Mum
	and Dad?
Bàba wǔshísān, māma sìshíjiǔ.	Dad is 53, Mum is 49.

Bàba (*dad*) comes before **māma** (*mum*) in Chinese word order, as does **fùqin** (*father*) before **mǔqin** (*mother*)!

5 Punctuation – when is a comma not a comma?

When it's a pause-mark! In Chinese, if two or more items are listed together, a pause-mark 、 is used between the items and not a comma. A comma is reserved for longer pauses:

Wǒ yǒu liǎng ge dìdi、 yí	I have two younger brothers
ge mèimei.	and a younger sister.
Nǐ bàba、 māma duō dà niánjì?	How old are your Mum
	and Dad?

6 Apostrophe for clarity

To prevent you saying **nǚér** instead of making a pause between the two syllables **nǚ** and **ér**, the Chinese insert an apostrophe (') between the two, so it is:

nǚ'ér
shí'èr (*not* shíèr)
èrshí'èr (*not* èrshíèr)

7 Brothers and sisters

The collective term for *sisters* (without saying whether they are older or younger) is **jiěmèi**, combining half of **jiějie** with half of **mèimei**. Similarly there is a collective term **xiōngdì** for *brothers*, although in this case a more literary term for elder brother is used:

Wǒ méi yǒu xiōngdì、jiěmèi. *I don't have any brothers or sisters.*

8 Polite talk

In Unit 1, when Mrs Green thanked Xiǎo Wáng he responded by saying:

Bú yòng xiè *Don't mention it/Not at all.*

He could also have said **Bú xiè**.

An equally appropriate response to thanks would be:

Bú kèqi. (*lit.* not guest *It's nothing, not at all.*
air/polite)

Chinese people tend to say 'thank you' rather less than in the west so they feel obliged to respond when somebody says 'thank you' to them.

Learning tips

Create opportunities to speak Chinese as much as you can.

1 Try to find other learners of Chinese to practise with. Find out about classes in your local area or where you work. (Your public library will usually be able to help you.)

2 If you have the recording, listen to it as much as you can – in the car, on public transport.

3 Advertise a language exchange in your local newspaper – offer to give English conversation lessons in return for Chinese ones. Make sure that you say you are learning Modern Standard Chinese (or Mandarin, as it is called by many overseas Chinese) as many Chinese people in the UK are Cantonese speakers who have come from Hong Kong.

Insight
The Chinese zodiac

The Chinese zodiac works in a 12-year cycle rather than in months as the western one does. You probably know whether you are a Capricorn or a Leo or whatever but do you know which **animal year** you belong to? The order is as follows:

Rat (*shǔ*)	1996	1984	1972	1960	1948	1936
Ox (*niú*)	1997	1985	1973	1961	1949	1937
Tiger (*hǔ*)	1998	1986	1974	1962	1950	1938
Rabbit (*tù*)	1999	1987	1975	1963	1951	1939
Dragon (*lóng*)	2000	1988	1976	1964	1952	1940
Snake (*shé*)	2001	1989	1977	1965	1953	1941
Horse (*mǎ*)	2002	1990	1978	1966	1954	1942
Sheep (*yáng*)	2003	1991	1979	1967	1955	1943
Monkey (*hóu*)	2004	1992	1980	1968	1956	1944
Cockerel (*jī*)	2005	1993	1981	1969	1957	1945
Dog (*gǒu*)	2006	1994	1982	1970	1958	1946
Pig (*zhū*)	2007	1995	1983	1971	1959	1947

Can you work out which animal you are?! For instance if you were born in 1976 you are a dragon, if you were born in 1971 you are a pig (but make sure you take the Lunar New Year into account in Unit 20). Each animal year is said to possess certain characteristics. It might be fun to get hold of a book on Chinese astrology and read up on your particular animal. Such books are now relatively easy to obtain at any reputable bookshop.

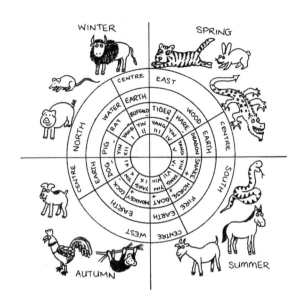

Practice

1 Choose the right number:

   a Which is the smallest number?
      wǔshíbā
      èrshíjiǔ
      sìshíliù

   b Which is the odd one out?
      qīshíyī
      bāshíbā
      jiǔshíjiǔ

   c Which number is the largest?
      sānshí'èr
      èrshísān
      sānshíyī

2 Now try the following calculations. Find the number to replace the question marks and say it out loud in Chinese.

a $7 \times 3 = ?$ **c** $10 + ? = 76$
b $? - 40 = 30$ **d** $98 \div 2 = ?$

You can also say equations in Chinese:

+	**jiā**	*plus*	×	**chéng**	*times*
−	**jiǎn**	*minus*	÷	**chú**	*divide*

What would you say to fill these blanks?

e Shíwǔ chéng èr shì _____.
f _____ jiǎn wǔshí shì shí.
g Èrshí jiā _____ shì sānshíwǔ.
h Jiǔshíjiǔ chú sān shì _____.

◀) **CD 1, TR 5, 04:24**

3 Listen to the recording (or read the following passage if you haven't got the recording) and say or write down the names and ages of Dīng's children. If you're still not sure of what you've heard, check it out in the **Key to the exercises**.

Dīng Fèng jié hūn le. Tā yǒu liǎng ge háizi, yí ge érzi, yí ge nǚ'ér. Érzi jiào Dīng Níng, jīnnián shí'èr suì. Nǚ'ér jiào Dīng Yīng, jīnnián shísì suì.

4 You are an only child and you are neither married nor have any children. Your father is a doctor (**yīsheng**), and your mother a teacher. How would you answer the following questions in Chinese?

a Nǐ yǒu gēge ma?
b Nǐ jié hūn le ma?
c Nǐ bàba shì lǎoshī ma?
d Nǐ yǒu jǐ ge háizi?
e Nǐ dìdi jiào shénme?

5 Match the questions in the left-hand column with the answers on the right.

a Nǐ jié hūn le ma?
b Tā jǐ suì?
c Wáng lǎoshī jiào shénme míngzi?
d Nǐmen yǒu háizi ma?
e Lǐ tàitai yǒu nǚ'ér ma?

i Wáng Yìfū.
ii Tā méi yǒu nǚ'ér.
iii Ta wǔ suì.
iv Wǒ jié hūn le.
v Wǒmen méi háizi.

◀ CD 1, TR 5, 05:02

6 The following is what Hēnglì (Henry) said about himself, his brother and his sister. Imagine you are Hēnglì's sister and talk about yourself and your brothers.

Wǒ jiào Hēnglì, jīnnián èrshí suì. Wǒ méi yǒu gēge, méi yǒu jiějie. Wǒ yǒu yí ge dìdi, yí ge mèimei. Wǒ dìdi jiào Bǐdé (*Peter*). Tā shíwǔ suì. Wǒ mèimei jiào Mǎlì (*Mary*). Tā jīnnián shíqī suì. Wǒmen dōu (*all*) shì xuésheng (*student*).

Quick review

◀ CD 1, TR 5, 06:01

You see a little Chinese girl and say the following to her:

a Hello!
b What's your name?
c How old are you?
d Have you got any brothers and sisters?
e Thank you.
f Goodbye!

Vocabulary and pronunciation

a   When you count two of something, do you use 'èr' or 'liǎng'?
b   What is the opposite of 'dà'?
c   Who is older? Is it 'dìdi' or 'gēge'?
d   The Chinese for 'and' is pronounced: 'hē', 'hé' or 'hè'?

5

···

Jǐ diǎn le?
What time is it now?

In this unit you will learn
- The days of the week
- The months of the year
- How to tell the time
- How to ask what time it is
- Some useful expressions of time
- How to give the date
- How to make arrangements

Before you start

In China, or any Chinese-speaking environment, you'd need to be able to find out when shops and banks are open. You also need to be able to recognize the Chinese characters for opening times **Yíngyè shíjiān** 营业时间 and the numbers 1 to 12 (plus the characters for *o'clock*) and the days of the week. You will be able to do all this by the end of the unit.

Let's try

1   You are at a reception where you meet a Chinese acquaintance of a friend of yours. He does not speak any English so you take the

opportunity to try out your Chinese. You know he is called Chén. Think of at least ten questions you can ask him in Chinese. Go back to Units 1 to 4 if you need to review vocabulary.

2 Revise the following numbers and say them out loud. 64 – 29 – 57 – 38 – 12 – 95 – 40 – 2 – 73 – 10. Check your answers with the section in Unit 4.

bàn	*half*
bāng	*help*
chà	*lacking, short of*
Chūnjié	*the Spring Festival*
dào	*to*
dì	(for ordinal numbers)
dōu	*all, both*
guān (mén)	*close* (door)
hái	*still*
hái yǒu	*still have, there are still*
huì	*meeting*
huǒchē	*train*
jǐ?	*how many?* (usually less than ten)
jiù shì	*to be precisely; to be nothing else but*
kāi huì	*to have a meeting*
kāi (mén)	*open* (door)
kāishǐ	*start*
kàn(yi)kàn	*to have a look*
kěxī	*it's a pity*
míngnián	*next year*
qù	*go*
shàng	*on*
shēngrì	*birthday*
yǐjīng	*already*
yǐwéi	*thought, assume*
zhàntái	*platform*
zhīdào	*know*
zhù (ni)	*wish* (you)
Zhù nǐ yílù shùnfēng!	*Have a safe journey!*

QUICK VOCAB

Time expressions

diǎn	*o'clock*
fēn(zhōng)	*minute*
jǐ diǎn?	*what time . . . ?*
(Xiànzài) jǐ diǎn le?	*What time is it now?*
Jǐ yuè jǐ hào?	*What's the date?*
	(lit. how many month, how many numbers?)
shàngwǔ	*morning*
shíjiān	*time*
wǎnshang	*evening*
xiànzài	*now*
xiàwǔ	*afternoon*
xīngqī	*week*
Xīngqī jǐ?	*What day is it?*
yíkè	*a quarter* (time)
yuè	*month*
zǎoshang	*morning*
zhōngwǔ	*noon*
zhōumò	*weekend*

一月 yīyuè January	二月 èryuè February	三月 sānyuè March	四月 sìyuè April
五月 wǔyuè May	六月 liùyuè June	七月 qīyuè July	八月 bāyuè August
九月 jiǔyuè September	十月 shíyuè October	十一月 shíyīyuè November	十二月 shí'èryuè December

Liǎng diǎn bàn   **Sān diǎn yí kè**   **Chà wǔ fēn sì diǎn**   **Chà yí kè liù diǎn** / **Wǔ diǎn sān kè**

Learning tips

CD 1, TR 6

1 Months of the year are very easy to say in Chinese. You already
know the numbers 1 to 12. All you then need is the word for **yuè**
月 (*moon*). January is **yī-yuè**, February is **èr-yuè** and so on. Be
careful not to confuse **yí ge yuè** *one month* with **yīyuè** *January*,
liǎng ge yuè *two months* with **èryuè** *February*.

yīyuè	January	**qīyuè**	July
èryuè	February	**bāyuè**	August
sānyuè	March	**jiǔyuè**	September
sìyuè	April	**shíyuè**	October
wǔyuè	May	**shíyīyuè**	November
liùyuè	June	**shí'èryuè**	December

◀) CD 1, TR 6, 00:43

2 Days of the week are also easy to say in Chinese. They all start
with **xīngqī** 星期 (*week*) (*lit.* star period) and then you use the
numbers 1 to 6 for Monday to Saturday. Sunday is special! You
add the word **rì** 日 (*sun*) or **tiān** 天 (*day*) to **xīngqī** to make it into
Sunday.

xīngqīyī	Monday	**xīngqīwǔ**	Friday
xīngqī'èr	Tuesday	**xīngqīliù**	Saturday
xīngqīsān	Wednesday	**xīngqītiān**	Sunday
xīngqīsì	Thursday	(or **xīngqīrì**)	

3 Repeat the days of the week and the months of the year several
times out loud until you have mastered them or listen to them on
the recording and say them after the speaker.

Unit 5 **What time is it now?**   55

Dialogues

◀) CD 1, TR 6, 01:15

Dialogue 1

A customer is ringing a shop to find out the opening hours.

营业时间

星期一至星期五　8:30 – 19:30
星期六、星期日　9:00 – 18:30

Yíngyè shíjiān
Opening hours

Customer	Qǐng wèn, nǐmen jǐ diǎn kāi mén?
Assistant	Shàngwǔ bā diǎn dào xiàwǔ wǔ diǎn bàn.
Customer	Zhōngwǔ guān mén ma?
Assistant	Bù guān.
Customer	Zhōumò kāi bu kai?
Assistant	Xīngqīliù kāi, xīngqītiān bù kāi.

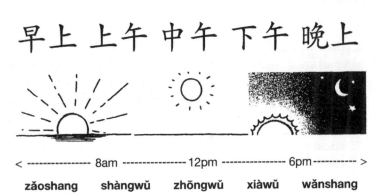

早上　上午　中午　下午　晚上

< ---------------- 8am ---------------- 12pm ---------------- 6pm ---------- >

zǎoshang　　shàngwǔ　　zhōngwǔ　　xiàwǔ　　wǎnshang

56

Dialogue 2

Two colleagues, Xiǎo Xú and Lǎo Wàn, are in the office when Xiǎo Xú suddenly remembers something.

Xiǎo Xú	Xiànzài jǐ diǎn le?
Lǎo Wàn	Liǎng diǎn yí kè le.
Xiǎo Xú	O, huì yǐjīng kāishǐ le.
Lǎo Wàn	Shénme huì? Nǐ bú shì míngtiān kāi huì ma?
Xiǎo Xú	Jīntiān xīngqī jǐ?
Lǎo Wàn	Xīngqīsān.
Xiǎo Xú	O, wǒ hái yǐwéi shì xīngqīsì ne.

Insight

In Chinese-speaking environments, other than in China, you may well hear the word **lǐbài 礼拜** used instead of **xīngqī**. So Monday would be **lǐbàiyī** instead of **xīngqīyī**, Tuesday would be **lǐbài'èr** and so on. The word **lǐbài** has certain Christian connotations as 'to go to church' is **zuò** (*do*) **lǐbài**.

Dialogue 3

◀) CD 1, TR 6, 03:13

Departure
LIVERPOOL
Platform 6
15.15
16.20

At a train station, Jane sees a Chinese person looking at the departure and arrivals board, obviously very perplexed. She decides to help him if she can.

Jane	Nǐ qù nǎr?
Chinese	Wǒ qù Lìwùpù.
Jane	Jǐ diǎn de huǒchē?
Chinese	Wǒ bù zhīdao. Piào shang méi yǒu shíjiān.
Jane	Wǒ bāng nǐ kànkan. (looks at the notice board)
	Ah, sān diǎn yí kè, zài dì-liù zhàntái.
Chinese	Xiànzài sān diǎn chà wǔ fēn, hái yǒu èrshí fēnzhōng.
Jane	Zhù nǐ yílù shùnfēng.
Chinese	Xièxie nǐ. Zàijiàn.

Dialogue 4

◀) CD 1, TR 6, 03:59

Ann wants to find out whether her birthday happens to fall on Chinese New Year. Read the dialogue and see if you can find the answer.

Ann	Míngnián Chūnjié shì jǐ yuè jǐ hào?
Friend	Èryuè shí'èr hào.
Ann	Zhēn kěxī. Wǒde shēngrì shì èryuè shíyī hào.
Friend	Méi guānxi. Yīngguó shíyī hào de wǎnshang jiù shì
	Zhōngguó shí'èr hào de zǎoshang.

Language notes

1 Telling the time

Xiànzài jǐ diǎn (zhōng) le?   *What time is it/now?* (lit. now how many points clock)

To reply to this question you use the 12-hour clock in Chinese. **Zhōng** is normally left out except when asking the time or (as in English) on the hour where it is optional. The use of **xiànzài** is also optional.

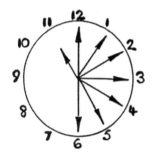

11.00 (Xiànzài) shíyī diǎn (zhōng) le.
11.05 (Xiànzài) shíyī diǎn (líng) wǔ fēn le. **Líng** (*zero*) is optional.
11.10 Shíyī diǎn shí fēn.
11.15 Shíyī diǎn shíwǔ fēn *or* shíyī diǎn yí kè (*one quarter*).
11.20 Shíyī diǎn èrshí fēn.
11.25 Shíyī diǎn èrshíwǔ fēn.
11.30 Shíyī diǎn sānshí *or* shíyī diǎn bàn (*half*).

1.35 Yì diǎn sānshíwǔ *or* chà (*lack*) èrshíwǔ (fēn) liǎng diǎn.
1.40 Yì diǎn sìshí *or* chà èrshí (fēn) liǎng diǎn.
1.45 Yì diǎn sìshíwǔ fēn *or* yì diǎn sān kè (*three quarters*) *or* chà yí kè liǎng diǎn *or* liǎng diǎn chà yí kè.
1.50 Yì diǎn wǔshí fēn *or* chà shí fēn liǎng diǎn.
1.55 Yì diǎn wǔshíwǔ fēn *or* chà wǔ fēn liǎng diǎn.

Formal announcements of time are given using the 24-hour clock.

2 Dates

Months of the year, days of the week and parts of the day are easy (see earlier in this unit) but you still need to learn dates. In Chinese, the order for a date is the reverse of that used in English:

It is year, month, day, time of day (morning, afternoon, etc.), hour.

In Chinese, you move from the general to the particular.

The year is read as single numbers followed by the word **nián** 年 (*year*):

| yī-jiǔ-yī-sì nián | 1914 |
| yī-jiǔ-sì-wǔ nián | 1945 |

You ask what the date is by saying: **Jǐ yuè jǐ hào?** (*lit.* how many months how many numbers).

Jīntiān jǐ yuè jǐ hào?	*What's the date today?*
Jīntiān bāyuè shí hào.	*Today's August the 10th.*
Xīngqīsān jǐ hào?	*What's the date on Wednesday?*
(Xīngqīsān) èrshíbā hào.	*It's the 28th (on Wednesday).*

You can now work out how to say 12 noon on Tuesday, 23 July 1989:

Yī-jiǔ-bā-jiǔ nián qīyuè èrshísān hào xīngqī'èr zhōngwǔ shí'èr diǎn.

Note that when you're telling the time and giving dates no verb is necessary. You have already met this in Unit 3 when dealing with ages.

3 Another type of *le*

You will have noticed the little word le appearing after **Xiànzài jǐ diǎn?** and **Liǎng diǎn yí kè** in **Dialogue 2**. It is used to indicate that a new state of affairs or situation has appeared. It is used at the end of such sentences as:

| Nǐmen yǐjīng hěn dà **le**. | *You're already pretty grown up* (whereas previously you weren't). |
| Ta xiànzài (hěn) piàoliang **le**. | *She's very good looking now* (whereas previously she wasn't!). |

The Chinese stretch this idea of a change of state to its limits by often using it with questions and answers about age and time:

| Háizi jǐ suì **le**? | *How old is the child?* (*lit.* child how many years become) |
| Xiànzài jǐ diǎn **le**? | *What time is it?* (*lit.* now how many o'clock become) |

4 Linking word *de*

This is the same **de** you looked at in Unit 3. The main idea – what you are talking about – comes after the **de**, and what describes this main idea or tells you more about it, comes before the **de**:

Jǐ diǎn **de** huǒchē?	*The train at what time?*
Xīngqītiān kāi **de** shāngdiàn	*Shops which open on Sundays*
Zài Lúndūn kāi **de** huì	*The meeting held in London*

5 Ticket on – on the ticket

Piào shang (*lit.* ticket on) *on the ticket.* Again the reverse of the English word order. Do the Chinese do everything back to front, you may be tempted to ask? No wonder they used to write from top to bottom and from right to left (and still do in Taiwan and Hong Kong)! Thus in Chinese you say:

shāngdiàn **lǐ**	*inside the shop*
lù **shàng**	*on the road/on the way*
huǒchē **xià**	*underneath the train*

Words such as **lǐ, shàng** and **xià** are normally unstressed when used in this way.

6 Repeating the verb: *kànkan*!

Repeating the verb has the effect of softening the suggestion, question or statement. Thus the repeated verb is often unstressed. It conveys the idea of *having a little go* at doing the action of the verb in both the sense of a trial and in not making a big fuss about doing something. Verbs of one syllable often have **yi** inserted in the middle when they are repeated.

Kànyikàn.	*Have a little look.*
Shuōyishuō.	*Try saying* or *talk briefly* (about something).

Verbs of two syllables cannot have **yi** inserted in this way; so you cannot say **rènshiyirènshi** or **kāishǐyikāishǐ**.

7 First or second

To make the numbers one, two, and so on into *the first*, *the second*, and so on, you only have to put the word **dì** in front of the number. **Èr** does not change into **liǎng** in such cases as there are not two seconds! An expression that used to be very common in China when any form of competition was involved is:

Yǒuyì dì-yī, bǐsài dì-èr.　　*Friendship first, competition second.*

Learning tips

Have fun while you're learning!

1 What have you learnt about the Chinese language so far? How is it different from any other language you've learnt? Take some time to reflect on this and jot down your thoughts. See if your ideas change as you learn more.

◀) CD1 , TR 6, 04:39

2 Tongue-twisters are fun in any language. Try the following. Repeat them until you can say them off by heart:

Sì shì sì.	*4 is 4.*
Shí shì shí.	*10 is 10.*
Sì bú shì shí.	*4 is not 10.*
Shí yě bú shì sì.	*10 is not 4 either.*
Shísì bú shì sìshí.	*14 is not 40.*
Sìshí yě bú shì shísì.	*40 is not 14 either.*

The last one is the hardest of all:

Sìshísì ge shí shīzi   *44 stone lions*

Practice

◀) CD 1, TR 6, 05:30

1 Can you say the dates of the following festivals (**jié**) in Chinese?

   a New Year's Day (**Xīnnián**)
   b Christmas Day (**Shèngdàn jié**)
   c International Women's Day (**Guójì Fùnǚ jié**)
   d National Day of China (**Zhōngguó de Guóqìng jié**)
   e National Day of your country (**X X Guóqìng jié**)

2 Give the birthdays of five people using the following structures:

   Sòng lǎoshī de shēngrì shì sìyuè shísì hào.
   Sìyuè shísì hào shì Sòng lǎoshī de shēngrì.

You can use these structures to talk about dates when you have learnt more words such as those in Exercise 1.

◀) CD 1, TR 6, 06:19

3 You will hear some dates and times. Repeat them and write them down. If you haven't got the recording, read the dates and times below and write them down in English.

   a jiǔyuè jiǔ hào
   b xīngqītiān shàngwǔ
   c shíyīyuè èrshíbā hào xīngqīsì
   d xīngqīliù shàngwǔ shí diǎn sìshíwǔ
   e qīyuè liù hào xīngqīwǔ xiàwǔ sān diǎn bàn
   f shí'èryuè sānshíyī hào xīngqīyī shàngwǔ shíyī diǎn

4 Based on the assumption that the time is now 5.05 in the afternoon (**wǔ diǎn líng wǔ fēn**), answer the following questions in Chinese:

    a What will the time be in ten minutes?
    b What time was it ten minutes ago?
    c How long is it before it is 5.45?
    d What time is it in 12 hours' time?
    e The train is leaving in two minutes. What time is the train scheduled to leave?

5 Answer the following questions in Chinese, based on the day of the week it is when you are doing this exercise.

    a What day is it tomorrow?
    b And yesterday?
    c Five days from today?
    d How many days is it before next Tuesday?

6 We don't know the answers to the following questions, but you do:

    a Which months are spring in the part of the world you are living in?
    b When is summer (i.e. what months)? Autumn? Winter?
    c How many months is it before your next birthday?
    d How many months is it before the New Year? (**Hái yǒu X ge yuè.**)

Quick review

Answer the following questions in Chinese, according to the information on the boards.

a What's the date today?
b What day is it today?
c What's the time now?

d When does the train from Oxford (**Niújīn**) arrive? At which platform?

e When does the train to Cambridge (**Jiànqiáo**) leave? From which platform?

Thursday March 30th
16.27
Departure
CAMBRIDGE
Platform 1
16.50

Thursday March 30th
16.27
Arrival
OXFORD
Platform 3
16.45

Vocabulary and pronunciation

a What's the pronunciation for 'all' or 'both'? Is it 'dōu' or 'duō'?

b Which word means 'morning'? Is it 'xiàwǔ' or 'shàngwǔ'?

c 'Xīngqīsān' is Wednesday. What does 'sān ge xīngqī' mean then?

d What is the difference between 'sānyuè' and 'sān ge yuè'?

e Do you know the meaning of 'zhīdào'?

6

··

Nǐ jīntiān xiǎng
zuò shénme?
What do you want to do today?

In this unit you will learn
• How to say what you want to do
• How to understand and ask for advice
• How to express similarities
• How to compare and contrast

Before you start

Word order is very important in Chinese, so there's plenty of help
with some of the basic rules in this unit. You'll also learn different
ways of making comparisons.

Let's try

1 It is often very difficult to get train tickets in China. You are in
   Běijīng and want to go to Tiānjīn in a couple of days' time. A
   Chinese friend offers to get your ticket for you as he knows you
   are very busy. Tell him you want a train ticket for the 9.30am
   train on Thursday.

2 Say the following dates in Chinese:

  a 6 January 1997
  b 21 March 2000 (líng = *zero*)
  c 15 August 1943

3 When is your birthday?
4 When were your parents born?

Běihǎi Gōngyuán	*Beihai Park*
bǐ	*compared to*
chē	*vehicle* (bus, bike, car)
dìng (piào)	*to book* (a ticket)
dōngxi	*thing, object*
fúwùyuán	*assistant, housestaff* (lit. *service person*)
gěi	*for; to give*
gēn	*and*
háishi	*or* (used in question forms)
huàn qián	*to change money*
kàn	*to watch, to look at*
mǎi	*to buy*
nàme	*in that case, then*
nán	*difficult*
qián	*money*
ránhòu	*afterwards*
róngyì	*easy*
tīng	*to listen to*
wèntí	*question, problem*
méi wèntí	*no problem*
xiān	*first*
xiǎng	*would like to; to think*
Xīfāng	*the west, western*
xiūxi	*to rest, rest*
yào	*to want, to need, will*
yínháng	*bank*
yíyàng	*same*
yǒu yìsi	*interesting* (lit. *have meaning*)
zài	(indicating continuing action)

QUICK VOCAB

Leisure activities

dǎ tàijíquán	*to do Tai Chi*
(kàn) diànyǐng	*film, movie*
(kàn) jīngjù	*Peking opera*
(tīng) yīnyuè	*music*
yīnyuèhuì	*concert*
tīng yīnyuèhuì	*to attend a concert*
(kàn) zájì	*acrobatics*
zuò	*to do*
zuò qìgōng	*to do qigong*

Questions and phrases

shénme shíhou?	*When?*
Zǎoshang hǎo!	*Good morning!*
Zhōngguó Yínháng	*Bank of China*
zuò chē	*to take the bus* (lit. *sit vehicle*)
A bǐ B nán/róngyì	*A is more difficult/easier than B*
A gēn B (bù) yíyàng	*A is the same as (different from) B*
Nǐ xiǎng zuò shénme?	*What do you want to do?*
Tā zài zuò shénme?	*What's he/she doing?*
Tài hǎo le!	*Excellent!*

Learning tips

1 Go back to the **Pronunciation guide** and read the notes there. The best way of learning this selection of sounds is in pairs, as follows:

b and p	zh and ch
d and t	j and q
z and c	g and k

2 Take a sheet of A4 paper and hold it vertically in front of you. Say **b** . . . If you are saying it correctly the sheet will not move. Then say **p** and the top of the sheet should be blown away from you. The same should happen with **d** and **t**, i.e. the sheet should not

move when you say **d** but it should move with **t**! Repeat this with each remaining pair. The sheet should not move with **z**, **zh**, **j** and **g** but it should move with **c**, **ch**, **q** and **k**.

Dialogues

Dialogue 1

🔊 **CD 1, TR 7**

Frank is attending a conference in China. Today he has a free day. His Chinese host, Xiǎo Wú, is asking him about his plans. Listen to or read the dialogue and note down his plans:

Frank's plans
Shàngwǔ:
Xiàwǔ:
Wǎnshang:

Xiǎo Wú	Jīntiān xiūxi. Nǐ xiǎng zuò shénme?
Frank	Wǒ xiǎng qù mǎi dōngxi. Kěshì wǒ yào xiān huàn qián.
Xiǎo Wú	Hǎo. Wǒmen xiān zuò chē qù Zhōngguó Yínháng huàn qián, ránhòu qù shāngdiàn mǎi dōngxi.
Frank	Hǎo. Xiàwǔ wǒ xiǎng qù Běihǎi Gōngyuán.
Xiǎo Wú	Méi wèntí. Wǎnshang ne?
Frank	Wǎnshang wǒmen qù kàn zájì hǎo bu hǎo?
Xiǎo Wú	Tài hǎo le. Wǒ qǐng fúwùyuán gěi wǒmen dìng piào.

Dialogue 2

🔊 **CD 1, TR 7, 01:06**

Frank has changed his money, done the shopping and been to Beihai Park. Unfortunately there are no tickets for the acrobatics this evening. So Frank and Xiǎo Wú are planning what to do instead.

Xiǎo Wú	Jīntiān wǎnshang nǐ xiǎng kàn diànyǐng háishi kàn jīngjù?
Frank	Wǒ bù xǐhuan jīngjù.
Xiǎo Wú	Nàme wǒmen kàn diànyǐng ba. Diànyǐng bǐ jīngjù yǒu yìsi.
Frank	Yǒu mei yǒu yīnyuèhuì?
Xiǎo Wú	Nǐ xiǎng tīng Zhōngguó yīnyuè háishi tīng Xīfāng yīnyuè?
Frank	Zài Zhōngguó dāngrán tīng Zhōngguó yīnyuè.

Dialogue 3

🔊 CD 1, TR 7, 02:58

A whole range of activities goes on in Chinese parks in the early morning. Tai Chi is especially popular. Frank decides to go and see for himself.

Frank	Zǎoshang hǎo!
Passer-by	Zǎoshang hǎo!
Frank	(*pointing to someone doing Tai Chi*) Tā zài zuò shénme?
Passer-by	Tā zài dǎ tàijíquán.
Frank	Nèi ge rén yě zài dǎ tàijíquán ma?
Passer-by	Bù. Tā zài zuò qìgōng.
Frank	Qìgōng gēn tàijíquán yíyàng ma?
Passer-by	Bù yíyàng.
Frank	Qìgōng bǐ tàijíquán nán ma?
Passer-by	Bù yídìng. Wǒ shuō qìgōng bǐ tàijíquán róngyì.

北海公园   Běihǎi Gōngyuán

Language notes

1 Word order again!

In some ways the Chinese language is less flexible than English in its word order. In English, you can say:

> *First* I want to change some money.
> *or*
> I want to change some money *first*.

In Chinese the position of **xiān** (*first*) is not changeable. It comes after **Wǒ yào** (*I want*) but before **huàn diǎnr qián** (*change some money*):

> Wǒ yào **xiān** huàn diǎnr qián.

This is because **xiān** is connected with what you want to do, not with what you want; and adverbs like **xiān** precede the verb to which they refer.

2 Time before manner before place (TMP)

In Chinese you say:

I *tomorrow at 9am* (time) *by plane* (manner) go *to China* (place).

You can't say:

I'm going to China by plane at 9am tomorrow.
or I'm going by plane to China at 9am tomorrow.

In Chinese the word order is logical: first you establish *when* you're going to do it, then *how* you're going to do it, and then *where* you're going to do it. So the rule to remember is **Time (T)** comes before **Manner (M)** and **Manner (M)** comes before **Place (P)**; TMP for short:

Wǒmen xiān (**T**) zuò chē (**M**) qù Zhōngguó Yínháng (**P**) huàn qián.	*We'll go to the Bank of China in the car to change money first* (lit. we first sit car go China Bank change money).
Wǒmen shí'èr diǎn zhōng (**T**) zài Hépíng Fàndiàn (**P**) chī wǔfàn.	*We'll have lunch at the Peace Hotel at 12.*

As you can see from the second example sometimes only two out of the three elements (TMP) are present but the rule still applies.

3 Either . . . or?

Do you want to go to a film *or* to the opera?
To express the *or* in the sentence above you use **háishi** in Chinese. Of course, you don't have to reverse the subject/verb order to make a question as in English.

All you do is put **háishi** between two statements thereby making them alternatives from which the listener must choose *one*:

Nǐ xiǎng kàn diànyǐng **háishi** kàn jīngjù?	*Would you like to go to a film or to the Peking opera?* (lit. you fancy see film or see Peking opera)

Nǐ xiǎng tīng Zhōngguó
  yīnyuè **háishi** (tīng)
  Xīfāng yīnyuè?

*Would you like to listen to
  Chinese music or western
  music?*

If the subject or object in both halves is the same you don't need to repeat it (this holds true for any two clauses, not just ones using **háishi**, and is a feature of Chinese), but there should be a verb in both halves even if it is the same one. However, in colloquial Chinese the second verb is sometimes left out if it is the same as the first one. This is shown in the two examples above.

An exception to this rule is if the verb is **shì** (*to be*). In this case, the second **shì** may be left out. Here is an example of this:

Tā shì nǐde péngyou **háishi**
  nǐde lǎoshī?

*Is he your friend or your
  teacher?*

Try saying **háishi shì** and you'll understand why!

4 To be in the middle of doing something

To show that an action is in progress the word **zài** is put in front of the verb:

Tā **zài** dǎ tàijíquán.
Wǒ **zài** zuò qìgōng.
Nǐ **zài** kàn diànshì.

He's doing Tai Chi.
I'm doing qigong.
You're watching TV.

You will sometimes find the words **zhèng** or **zhèng zài** used in exactly the same way instead of **zài**. They are simply alternatives. **Ne**, at the end of a sentence, can also convey the idea that the action is in progress; or you might find **ne** occurring with any of the above. Here are a few examples to illustrate this:

Xiǎo Liú **zhèngzài** tīng
  yīnyuè (**ne**).
Tāmen **zhèng** chī wǔfàn **ne**.

*Xiao Liu is listening to
  music.*
They're in the middle of lunch.

Wǒmen kāi huì **ne**. Qǐng
nǐ míngtiān zài lái.

We're in the middle of a meeting.
Please come again tomorrow.

Note that this action in progress can take place in the past, present
or future and it is the use of time-words (plus context) which tells us
when the action actually takes place:

Míngtiān shàngwǔ tā yídìng
zài yóuyǒng (**ne**).
Zuótiān wānshang wǒ **zài**
kàn xì (**ne**).

She'll certainly be swimming
tomorrow morning.
I was at the theatre yesterday
evening.

5 The same or not the same?

In Chinese, to express that one
thing is the same as another, or
A is the same as B you say A
gēn (*with*) **B yíyàng** (*the same*).

A **gēn** B **yíyàng** gāo.
A is as tall as B.

Wáng tàitai **gēn** Lǐ xiǎojie
yíyàng gāo.
Mrs Wang is as tall as Miss Li.

Zhāng xiānsheng **gēn** tā jiějie
yíyàng pàng.
Mr Zhang is as fat as his elder
sister.

To say that A is *not* the same as B you simply put **bù** in front of
yíyàng:

A **gēn** B **bù** yíyàng gāo.
A is not as tall as B.

6 Making comparisons

To say that something is *more . . . than* use **bǐ**:

A **bǐ** B nán. *A is more difficult than B.*
Qìgōng **bǐ** tàijíquán nán. *Qigong is more difficult than Tai Chi.*

Kàn diànyǐng **bǐ** kàn jīngjù *Going to the cinema (lit. see/watch*
  yǒu yìsi.   *film) is more interesting than*
       watching Peking opera.

It is important to note that **bù bǐ** does not mean *less . . . than*. Look carefully at the following examples:

Tā **bù bǐ** wǒ dà.   *He is no older than I.*
Wǒ jiějie **bù bǐ** nǐ gāo. *My elder sister is no taller than you.*

7 Helping verbs

Verbs such as *want, ought to, must, can* occur before action verbs or verbal expressions:

Nǐ **xiǎng** zuò shénme? *What would you like to do?*
Wǒ **xiǎng** qù mǎi dōngxi. *I'd like to go shopping.*

Wǒ **gāi** qù.   *I ought to go.*
Tā **yào** zǒu.   *She wants to leave.*
Nǐ **huì** shuō Hànyǔ ma? *Can you speak Chinese?*

Tāmen **xǐhuan** mǎi dōngxi. *They like shopping.*

Note the difference between **xiǎng** (*would like to do, fancy doing something*) and **xǐhuan** (*like*).

Unlike other types of verbs which can take endings to indicate, for example, that something has taken place or to show direction, these 'helping' or auxiliary verbs cannot have anything added to them.

8 To give or not to give

Gěi basically means *to give*, but it can be used with a noun or pronoun (referring to a person or living thing) *before* the verb to mean *to do something for someone or something*.

Wǒ gěi nǐ kànkan.	*I'll take a look for you.*
Tā gěi wǒ kāi mén.	*He opened the door for me.*
Wǒ qǐng fúwùyuán gěi wǒmen dìng piào.	*I'll ask the attendant to book tickets for us.*

Insight

Chinese traditional music sounds very different from western music. If you ever have the chance to see Peking opera, do take it. You may decide never to go again but it is certainly worth trying once, just for the experience! The make-up and costumes are very elaborate and give you all sorts of information about the characters being portrayed, so try to go with somebody who knows something about Peking opera. Most people enjoy the battles and the acrobatics if not the singing!

Examples of Peking opera masks

You might have heard of **tàijí** (often written **Tai Chi** in the west) or of **qìgōng** which are forms of exercise practised for hundreds of years in China. Some forms of **qìgōng** are thought to be beneficial to cancer sufferers and people are encouraged to go to regular classes (usually in the local park early in the morning around 6am) as part of their treatment and recovery programme.

Why not try out a **tàijí** or **qìgōng** class yourself? Ask at your local library for information. You are likely to meet other people in the class who are interested in learning Chinese and with whom you can practise, chat and exchange ideas.

Practice

1 Tā/tāmen zài zuò shénme? *What is he/she doing? What are they doing?*

Look at the pictures below and say what the people are doing using the pattern above.

a mǎi dōngxi   **b kàn zájì**   **c huàn qián**

d dǎ tàijíquán   **e kàn diànyǐng**   **f tīng yīnyuè**

2 Look at the pictures in Exercise 1. Suppose these are the things you plan to do at the weekend. Draw up a plan and say when you are going to do what. Expressions of time can either occur before the verb, or at the beginning of the sentence if you want to give them more emphasis. Look at these examples:

Xīngqīliù shàngwǔ wǒ yào qù zuò qìgōng.
Xīngqītiān wǎnshang wǒ xiǎng qù kàn diànyǐng.

3 Tāmen yíyàng ma? *Are they the same?*

gāo	*tall*
dà	*old*
xiǎo	*young* (used when comparing ages)
zhòng	*heavy*

Answer the following questions using **yíyàng** or **bù yíyàng**.

a Qū gēn Xǔ yíyàng gāo ma?
b Xǔ gēn Hú yíyàng dà ma?
c Qū gēn Hú yíyàng zhòng ma?
d Xǔ gēn Hú yíyàng gāo ma?
e Qū gēn Xǔ yíyàng zhòng ma?
f Hú gēn Qū yíyàng dà ma?

Qū   Hú   Xǔ

AGE 70   AGE 25   AGE 25
60 kg   76 kg   60 kg
1.66 m   1.75 m   1.76 m

4 According to the information in Exercise 3, are the following statements true or false? If true, say **duì**. If false, say **bú duì** and say what is true.

		duì	bú duì
a	Hú bǐ Xǔ gāo.	☐	☐
b	Hú bù bǐ Qū zhòng.	☐	☐
c	Xǔ bǐ Hú dà.	☐	☐
d	Qū bǐ Xǔ dà.	☐	☐
e	Hú gēn Xǔ bǐ Qū xiǎo.	☐	☐

5 The following is what Mr Jones (Qióngsī xiānsheng) has put in his diary. Answer the questions below according to what is written in the diary.

Monday evening - learn Chinese
Tuesday morning - meeting
Wednesday evening - go to a concert
Thursday afternoon - meet a friend
Friday evening - see a film
Saturday - shopping
        - change money
Sunday - learn Tai Chi

a Qióngsī xiānsheng xīngqīliù háishi xīngqītiān xué tàijíquán?
b Tā shénme shíhou qù kàn péngyou?
c Tā xīngqīsān shàngwǔ qù tīng yīnyuèhuì háishi xīngqīsì wǎnshang qù?
d Tā xīngqī'èr shàngwǔ kāi huì háishi xiàwǔ kāi huì?
e Tā shénme shíhou qù mǎi dōngxi?

Quick review

CD 1, TR 7, 03:45

a Ask your Chinese friend what she would like to do tomorrow.
b Say Xiǎo Mǎ and her elder sister are as tall as each other.
c Say you find acrobatics more interesting than Peking opera.
d Ask Xiǎo Zhào where he would like to go this evening.
e Ask Miss Lǐ whether she would like to see a film or go to a concert.

The following signs should come in useful.

Gentlemen

男 厕 所

Nán cèsuǒ

Ladies

女 厕 所

Nǚ cèsuǒ

Vocabulary and pronunciation

a   You learnt 'hé' meaning 'and' in Unit 4. What is another Chinese word for 'and' in this Unit?

b   'Háishi' means 'or' only in: a) question forms or b) statements?

c   Which phrase means: 'there is a problem': a) 'méi wèntí' or b) 'yǒu wèntí'?

d   What is the opposite of 'róngyì'?

e   Is the Chinese for 'music': 'jīngjù', 'yīnyuè' or 'diànyǐng'?

7

Duōshao qián?
How much is it?

In this unit you will learn
- How to ask for things (in shops)
- How to ask the price
- How to state quantities
- Numbers 100–1000
- How to express the distance between two points

Before you start

You will get to grips with Chinese money in this unit and be able to comment on the prices of things. You will also master basic colours and learn how to make more complex comparisons.

Let's try

Tomorrow evening it is your turn to entertain your business colleagues from China.

a You don't know whether to take them to a concert or to a play (**kàn xì**) so what do you ask them?
b They want to go to a concert. How do you ask them whether they like western music?
c They assure you that in the west they want to listen to western music so what do **they** say to you?

bǎi	*hundred*
búcuò	*pretty good, not bad*
cái	*not . . . until, only then*
dào	*to arrive, to go to*
-deduō	*much (more)*
-duōle	*much (more)*
jǐ	*crowded*
jiàn	(measure word for clothes)
jīn	*half a kilogram*
jìn	*near, close*
jiù	*just; only*
kěshì	*but*
kuài	(unit of money)
lí	*distance from*
lóu	*floor*
mài	*to sell*
máoyī	*woollen pullover*
něi/nǎ?	*which?*
nèi/nà	*that*
shìchǎng	*market*
shìhé	*to suit*
shìshi	*to try*
tài . . . le!	*too . . . !*
tián	*sweet*
xīnxiān	*fresh*
yuǎn	*far*
zánmen	*we/us* (including listener)
zhàn	(bus) *stop, station*
zhèi/zhè	*this*
zhèr	*here, this place*
zhème (guì)	*so* (expensive)
zìyóu	*free, freedom*
zǒu lù	*to walk, on foot*
zuì	*the most*

Fruits

cǎoméi	*strawberry*
píngguǒ	*apple*

82

| pútao | grape |
| xiāngjiāo | banana |

Questions and phrases

A lí B duō yuǎn?	*How far is A from B?*
A lí B hěn jìn/yuǎn.	*A is close to/far from B.*
duō cháng?	*how long?*
duō yuǎn?	*how far?*
duōshao?	*how much? how many?*
Duōshao qián yì jīn?	
Yì jīn duōshao qián?	*How much is it for half a kilo?*
. . . kěyǐ ma?	*Can I . . . ? Is it allowed . . . ?*
Nín mǎi shénme?	*What would you like (to buy)?*
Wǒ yào . . .	*I want . . .*
shénme yánsè (de)?	*what colour?*
. . . xíng ma?	*Is it OK? Can I . . . ?*
X zěnme mài?	*How much is X?*

Colours

hóng(sè) (de)	*red*	lán(sè) (de)	*blue*
huáng(sè) (de)	*yellow*	bái(sè) (de)	*white*
lǜ(sè) (de)	*green*	hēi(sè) (de)	*black*

Learning tips

Here are two more pairs: **lu** and **lü**, **nu** and **nü**.

Go back to the **Pronunciation guide** and read the notes there. You will need a mirror for the next exercise.

First of all push out your lips and say *oo*. Then tighten them and say *you*. Repeat this but put *l* in front of the *oo*. Now you have the sound **lu**. To say **lü** say the word *lewd* without the d. For **nu** and **nü** say the *noo* of *noodles* and the *nu* of *nude*! Now look in the mirror and say the sounds again. What do you notice about your lips when you say the two different sounds?

You have to tighten them to say the ü sound don't you? For those of you who know a little French or German, the ü in Chinese is like the *u* in *tu* (French) or the *ü* in *über* (German).

Ju, qu and **xu** are also pronounced as though they were written with **ü**. Don't confuse them with **zhu, chu,** and **shu** where the **u** is the *oo* sound.

Numbers 100–1000

◀) **CD 1, TR 8**

100	yìbǎi	300	sānbǎi
200	èrbǎi *or* liǎng bǎi	308	sānbǎi líng bā
202	èrbǎi líng èr	410	sìbǎi yīshí
210	èrbǎi yīshí	794	qībǎi jiǔshísì
225	èrbǎi èrshíwǔ	1000	yìqiān

Think of a number as being made up of units, tens and hundreds. If there is a zero in the tens column, you have to say **líng** (*zero*) in Chinese.

Ten is **shí** in Chinese but when it occurs with *one hundred, two hundred*, and so on you have to say *one ten:* **yīshí**, so 110 is **yìbǎi yīshí**.

Dialogues

Dialogue 1

◀) **CD 1, TR 8, 00:44**

It may not be easy to get what you want in a shop despite the polite service you get. This customer knows what she wants and what she doesn't want, as this dialogue shows:

	(at the information point)
Customer	Qǐng wèn, zài nǎr mǎi máoyī?
Assistant	Zài èr lóu.
	(at knitwear counter)
Assistant	Nín mǎi shénme?
Customer	Wǒ xiǎng mǎi yí jiàn máoyī.
Assistant	Yào něi jiàn? Nín xǐhuan shénme yánsè de?
Customer	Nèi jiàn hóngsè de gěi wǒ kànkan xíng ma?
Assistant	Zhèi jiàn hěn hǎo.
Customer	O, tài dà le. Nèi jiàn huángsè de wǒ shìshi kěyǐ ma?
Assistant	Zhèi jiàn yě búcuò.
Customer	O, tài xiǎo le.
Assistant	Zhèi jiàn lánsè de hěn shìhé nǐ.
Customer	Tài hǎo le. Duōshao qián?
Assistant	Wǔbǎi kuài.
Customer	Ēn, tài guì le. Duìbuqǐ, xièxie nǐ.
Assistant	......

五星 超级市场

Wǔxīng chāojí shìchǎng
Five star supermarket

Insight

In Chinese, the ground floor is **yī lóu**, (*lit.* one floor), the first floor is **èr lóu** (*lit.* two floor), the second floor **sān lóu** (*lit.* three floor), the third floor **sì lóu** (*lit.* four floor) and so on.

Dialogue 2

🔊 **CD 1, TR 8, 01:55**

If you can't get what you want in one shop, you can try somewhere else. This is what Xiǎo Fāng is suggesting to Ann.

Fāng	Wǒmen qù zìyóu shìchǎng kànkan ba.
Ann	Hǎo. Zìyóu shìchǎng lí zhèr duō yuǎn?
Fāng	Hěn jìn. Zuò chē liǎng、 sān zhàn jiù dào le.
Ann	Chē tài jǐ le. Zánmen zǒu lù qù ba.
Fāng	Kěshì zǒu lù tài yuǎn le.
Ann	Zǒu lù yào duō cháng shíjiān?
Fāng	Zǒu lù èr、 sānshí fēnzhōng cái néng dào.
Ann	Hǎo ba. Nàme zánmen zuò chē qù ba.

Dialogue 3

🔊 **CD 1, TR 8, 03:21**

There are markets throughout China where you can probably bargain. This is what you might hear at a fruit stall.

Buyer	Píngguǒ zěnme mài?
Seller	Sì kuài yì jīn.
Buyer	Zhēn guì! Tāmende píngguǒ sān kuài bā yì jīn.
Seller	Kěshì wǒde píngguǒ bǐ tāmende dà yìdiǎnr.
Buyer	Pútao duōshao qián yì jīn?
Seller	Sì kuài liǎng máo wǔ yì jīn.

Buyer	Zhème guì! Tāmen de sì kuài yì jīn.
Seller	Kěshì wǒde pútao bǐ tāmende tián duōle.
Buyer	Cǎoméi yì jīn duōshao qián?
Seller	Bā kuài èr.
Buyer	Tài guì le!
Seller	Kěshì wǒde cǎoméi bǐ tāmen de xīnxiān deduō.
Buyer	Nǐde dōngxi zuì guì.
Seller	Kěshì wǒde dōngxi zuì hǎo!

Chinese proverb: 斤斤计较 **Jīn jīn jìjiào**
Haggle over every ounce, quibble over small differences

Language notes

1 More on measure words

You have already met the measure words **běn** (for books and magazines) and **zhāng** (for rectangular or square flat objects) in Unit 4, together with the most common measure word of all, **gè**.

Some measure words like **jīn** (*half a kilogram*) and **bēi** (*cup*) are actually indicators of quantity. The following table lists some of the more common of these:

Pinyin	Category	Examples
bǎ	objects with a handle, chairs	*knife, umbrella, toothbrush, chair*
bāo	parcel, packet	*cigarettes, noodles*
bēi	cup, glass	*tea, coffee, wine*
běn	volume	*book, dictionary*
fēng		*letter*

(Continued)

gè	people, things which do not fall into other categories; substitute MW	*person, student*
jiàn	piece, article	*clothes, luggage*
jīn	indicator of quantity (0.5 kilogram)	*fruit, vegetables*
kuài	piece	*soap, land*
lǐ	indicator of length (1/3 mile, 0.5 km)	*road*
liàng	things with wheels	*car, bicycle*
píng	bottles, jars	*beer, wine, jam*
tiáo	long and winding; carton (e.g. 200)	*towel, trousers, fish; cigarettes*
wèi	people (*polite*)	*teacher, lady, gentleman*
zhāng	flat, rectangular objects	*ticket, blanket, table, paper, map*

Note that **gōngjīn** (*lit.* public pound) is a *kilogram*, **gōnglǐ** (*lit.* public li) is a *kilometre* and **yīnglǐ** (*lit.* English li) is a *mile*.

2 Money, money, money . . . !

Chinese money is based on the decimal system and the currency in China is known as **rénmínbì** (*the people's currency*). Foreign currency is known as **wàibì** (*lit.* external/outside currency).

The largest single unit is the **yuán** 元 (written as ¥ in many transactions). There are ten **jiǎo** 角 in one **yuán** and ten **fēn** 分 in one **jiǎo**. These are the words (and Chinese characters) used in the written language and printed on banknotes, tickets, etc. so it is important to recognize them.

You saw how the characters for 1 to 10 were written in Unit 3. Don't be put off by the more complex characters you will see on Chinese banknotes. This also goes for the character 元 which is written 圆 on banknotes. These prevent confusion (and forgery!) when numbers are being written out in financial transactions.

In spoken Chinese, **kuài** 块 *piece/lump* is used for **yuán** and **máo** 毛 for **jiǎo** but **fēn** remains unchanged.

RMB	Spoken	Written
0.01 yuán	yì fēn (qián)	yì fēn
0.1 yuán	yì máo (qián)	yì máo
1.00 yuán	yí kuài (qián)	yì yuán
5.5 yuán	wǔ kuài wǔ *or* wǔ kuài bàn	wǔ yuán wǔ jiǎo
14.32 yuán	shísì kuài sān máo èr	shísì yuán sān jiǎo èr fēn
30.09 yuán	sānshí kuài líng* jiǔ fēn	sānshí yuán líng* jiǔ fēn

* If a sum of money involves **kuài** and **fēn** but no **máo** the absence of **máo** is marked by a **líng** (*zero*).

When two or more different units of currency are used together, the last one is often omitted:

| sì kuài liù | rather than | sì kuài liù máo | ¥4.60 |
| bā máo qī | rather than | bā máo qī fēn | ¥0.87 |

3 Too much?

Tài (*too*) is almost always with **le**:

tài xiǎo **le**	*too small*
tài guì **le**	*too expensive*
tài hǎo **le**	*excellent, great*

It is probably better just to accept this as a rule rather than try to analyze it!

4 How far is A from B?

To say A is a long way from B, where A and B are fixed points, use:

A **lí** (*separate*) B **hěn yuǎn** (*far*)

If you don't use **hěn** (*very*), some sort of comparison is implied, i.e. A is a long way from B (but near to C). Thus in Chinese, as we have said before, **hěn** is very weak.

| Lúndūn **lí** Àidīngbǎo **hěn yuǎn**. | *London is a long way from Edinburgh.* |

To say A is near B use: A **lí** B **hěn jìn** (*near*).

| Niújīn **lí** Lúndūn **hěn jìn**. | *Oxford is close to London.* |

To say exactly how far A is from B use: A **lí** B **yǒu** + the distance. **Yǒu** (*to have*) can also have the meaning *there is/there are*.

| Jiànqiáo (*Cambridge*) **lí** Niújīn **yǒu yìbǎiliùshí gōnglǐ**. | *Cambridge is 160 km from Oxford.* |

A and B can also be fixed points in time. To say how far A is from B *in time* use: A **lí** B **yǒu** + time difference.

> Nǐde shēngrì lí jīntiān hái   *There are still four days to go to*
>   yǒu sì tiān.   *your birthday. (lit. your birthday*
>   *separate today still have four days).*

5 Approximate numbers

If you want to say two or three (people) in Chinese, you put the words for two (of a pair) and three one after another with a pause-mark in between them:

> **liǎng、 sān ge rén**   *two or three people*
> **wǔ 、 liù běn shū**   *five or six books*

20 or 30 is **èr、 sānshí**: the **shí** is only said *once*.
45 or 46 is **sìshíwǔ、 liù**: the **sìshí** is only said *once*.

6 We, including you!

Both **zánmen** and **wǒmen** mean *we* and *us*. The difference is that **zánmen** specifically includes the listener(s) in what is being said.

A says to his sister:

> **Zánmen bàba、 māma duì**   *Our Mum and Dad were very*
>   wǒmen hěn hǎo shì bu shi?   *good to us, weren't they?*

Zánmen here has a more intimate feel to it than **wǒmen**.

7 More on comparisons

You have already met **bǐ** in Unit 6:

> Chī fàn **bǐ** hē jiǔ yǒu yìsi.   *Eating is more interesting than consuming alcohol.*

To say that A is *much* more . . . than B use:

A **bǐ** B adjective/verb **duōle**

or   A **bǐ** B adjective/verb **deduō**.

Zhè jiàn máoyī **bǐ** nèi jiàn dà **duōle**.	*This sweater is much bigger than that one.*
Cǎoméi **bǐ** píngguǒ guì **deduō**.	*Strawberries are much more expensive than apples.*

To say that A is a little more . . . than B use:

A **bǐ** B adjective/verb **yìdiǎnr**.

Wǒde shuǐguǒ (*fruit*) **bǐ** tāde (shuǐguǒ) xīnxiān **yìdiǎnr**.	*My fruit is a little fresher than his.*

8 Be the best!

You only have to put the little word **zuì** (*most*) in front of **hǎo** to make it into *the best*! Look carefully at the following examples using **zuì**:

zuì hǎo	*the best* (*lit.* most good)
zuì guì	*the most expensive*
zuì tián	*the sweetest*

You can put **de** + noun after the examples to make such phrases as:

zuì hǎo **de** pútao	*the best grapes*
zuì guì **de** cǎoméi	*the most expensive strawberries*
zuì tián **de** píngguǒ	*the sweetest apples*

9 *Cái* and *jiù*

Both **cái** and **jiù** are adverbs indicating something about time. **Cái** indicates that something takes place later or with more difficulty than had been expected. **Jiù**, by way of contrast, indicates that something takes place earlier or more promptly than expected:

Tā sì diǎn zhōng **cái** lái.   *He didn't come until four* (though I had asked him to come at 3.15).

Tāmen liù diǎn bàn **jiù** lái le.   *They were there by 6.30* (though we had invited them for seven).

Cái often translates as *not . . . until*. **Jiù** usually has a **le** at the end of the sentence to convey a sense of completion whereas **cái** does not. **Jiù** will sometimes have **zǎo** (*early*) in front of it as well as **le** at the end.

Both **cái** and **jiù** must come immediately before the verb whatever else there is in the sentence. Look carefully at the following examples:

Zuò chē liǎng、sān zhàn **jiù** dào le.   *It's only two or three stops on the bus.*

Zǒu lù èr、sānshí fēnzhōng **cái** néng dào.   *It will take as much as 20 or 30 minutes on foot* (if we walk).

Zuótiān hěn lěng dànshi jīntiān **cái** xià xuě.   *Yesterday was very cold but it didn't snow until today.*

Wǒ xiànzài **cái** zhīdao Fǎguó dōngxi guì.   *It's only now that I know things in France are expensive.*

Wǒ **zǎo jiù** zhīdao le.   *I knew ages ago* (that things in France are expensive).

Learning tips

What do you do if you don't understand?

1 Don't panic and don't give up listening.
2 Try to concentrate on what you do understand and guess the rest. If there comes a point where you really feel you can't understand

anything, isolate the phrase or word(s) that is causing you problems and say to the speaker:

. . . . shì shénme yìsi?   *What does . . . mean?*

Hopefully he or she will say it in another way that you will be able to understand. Remember the two useful sentences you learnt in Unit 3:

Qǐng nǐ zài shuō yí biàn.   *Please say it again.*
Qǐng nǐ shuō màn yìdiǎn.   *Please speak more slowly.*

....

Insight

Most Chinese people are expert bargainers. A lot of selling is done from street stalls or with articles laid out on a piece of cloth on the ground. In these circumstances it is possible to bargain. If you are interested in buying something, point to it and say:

Zhè ge duōshao qián?   *How much is this?*

Having got a price, one way is to start by halving it and to say:

Wǒ zhǐ néng gěi nǐ X kuài. *I can only give you X kuai.*

And then the fun starts with the two of you negotiating a price that you both find acceptable. It is a good policy to decide from the outset how much you are prepared to pay for something so that you have that in mind when bargaining. If neither of you can agree on a price, you can finish the bargaining by saying:

Xièxie, wǒ bù mǎi le.   *Thank you, I won't buy it then.*

and walking away. Sometimes if you are lucky, the vendor will rush after you and offer it to you for the last price you offered or one very similar.

Fruit and vegetables sold from stalls are normally offered at a certain price and if you think it's too expensive, you just don't buy them. Don't buy from anyone whose prices are not shown until you have ascertained how much they are. The Chinese are very good at charging fellow-Chinese one price and foreigners another (naturally more expensive). Unfortunately, it is very hard to check whether they are giving you the correct weight as they often use a pole with weights on one end and a pan (to hold the purchased fruit on) on the other. There is no bargaining in ordinary shops and department stores.

Practice

1 Say the following prices in Chinese.
Example: ¥ 4.03 sì kuài líng sān fēn

a ¥0.52   c ¥12.76   e ¥205.54
b ¥2.25   d ¥99.99   f ¥8.07

2 Duōshao qián? *How much is it?*

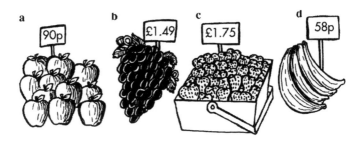

a 90p   b £1.49   c £1.75   d 58p

Tell your Chinese friend how much these fruits cost in your local town. You need to know the words **yí bàng** (*a pound in money*) and **biànshì** (*pence*).

Example: Píngguǒ wǔshíbā biànshì yì jīn.
Pútao yí bàng sì-jiǔ yì jīn.

Note that in prices over £1 which include pence, **shí** (*ten*) is left out where the number of pence is ten or more. The number of pence are treated as separate digits, for example, £1.45 is **yí bàng sì-wǔ**. One **jīn** (used all over China) is equivalent to half a kilogram or a little over a pound in weight.

3 You want to buy the following vegetables in a Chinese market, but they are not priced. Ask the greengrocer the prices by filling in the blanks in the questions below:

xīhóngshì (*tomato*)	¥0.65 a jin
báicài (*Chinese leaves*)	¥0.42 a jin
tǔdòu (*potato*)	¥0.28 a jin

a You _____ _____ mài?
    Greengrocer Liù máo wǔ yì jīn.
b You _____ yì jīn _____ qián?
    Greengrocer Yì jīn sì máo èr.

c **You** _____ _____ qián yì jīn?
Greengrocer Liǎng máo bā yì jīn.

🔊 **CD 1, TR 8, 04:37**

4 Listen to the recording and write down the items mentioned and their prices. We've done the first for you. If you get really stuck look at what is said in the **Key to the exercises**.

a yú (*fish*)   ¥7.09 jīn
b   ¥
c   ¥
d   ¥
e   ¥

5 What would you say in the following situations?

Example: Situation – It's freezing today.
             You could say – **Jīntiān tài lěng** (*cold*) **le.**

a You've tried on a pullover and found it too big.
b It is 30°C today. (**rè** = *hot*)
c She's got too much money!
d The ticket to a match costs £150.
e You have studied French for years and still cannot speak it. (i.e. *French is too difficult*).

6 Make comparisons with the information given using the pattern

A bǐ B adjective

or

A bǐ B adjective (yìdiǎnr, deduō or duōle):

Example: cǎoméi ¥8.50/jīn, pútao ¥6.30/jīn
             Cǎoméi bǐ pútao guì duōle.

a Nǎ ge guì? (bǐ)   Píngguǒ ¥4.00/jīn;
         Pútao ¥4.10/jīn

b Tāmen shéi gāo? (yìdiǎnr) Xiǎo Wáng 1.73m;
           Lǎo Lǐ 1.70m

c Nǎ ge dìfang rè? (duōle) Běijīng 29°C; Lúndūn 17°C

d Tāmen shéi dà? (deduō) Bái xiānsheng 58;
         Bái tàitai 48

7 Use either **cái** or **jiù** to fill in the blanks.

a Wǔ diǎn kāi huì, tā sì diǎn bàn _____ lái le.
b Nǐ hái bù zhīdao ma? Wǒ zuótiān (*yesterday*) _____ zhīdao le.
c Duìbuqǐ, Lǐ lǎoshī jīntiān bù néng lái. Tā míngtiān _____ lái.
d Tā bù xiǎng míngtiān qù, tā xiǎng xiànzài _____ qù.
e Yīnyuèhuì qī diǎn kāishǐ (*start*), tā qī diǎn yíkè _____ lái.

Quick review

🔊 **CD 1, TR 8, 05:41**

How do you say:

a It will take only five minutes to get there.
b It will take (as long as) 50 minutes to get there.
c In my family my father is the oldest.
d The cinema is not far from my home.
e Bananas cost 49p per pound.

Vocabulary and pronunciation

a What do the two words, 'jīn' and 'jìn', mean respectively?
b What do the two words, 'mǎi' and 'mài', mean respectively?
c What would be the measure word for a coat?
d Put the tone mark on the word 'bai' for 'hundred'.
e The pinyin for 'to try' is: (a) 'shìshi' or (b) 'shìshì'?

8

Zěnmeyàng?
What's it like?

In this unit you will learn
- How to ask about sizes
- How to talk about clothes and shoes
- How to describe things
- How to express likes and dislikes
- How to make comparisons

Before you start

This unit will give you the necessary vocabulary and structures to ask people their opinions about things **Nǐ kàn zěnmeyàng?** (*What's it like?*) and to make comparisons **Zhè ge méi yǒu nà ge hǎo** (*This one is not as good as that one*).

Let's try

Refer back to **Dialogue 1** and **Dialogue 3** in Unit 7 and answer the following questions:

1 Did the customer buy a pullover? Why?
2 How did the fruitseller justify his prices being higher than other people's? Give four reasons.

bù zěnmeyàng	*not so good*
dàxiǎo	*size*
fēicháng	*extremely*
gèng	*even more*
guò	*to pass or spend* (of time)
hái kěyǐ	*just so so*
héshì	*suitable*
jiàqī	*holiday, vacation*
juéde	*to feel, think*
kuài	*fast*
màn	*slow*
měi	*every*
měi tiān	*every day*
mō(mo)	*to feel, touch*
nǎli nǎli	*not really* (response to a compliment)
nánkàn	*ugly*
piányi	*cheap*
xià yǔ	*to rain*
xīn	*new*
xīn mǎi de	*newly bought*
xué(xí)	*to learn, study*
yánsè	*colour*
Yìdàlì	*Italy*
yǐhòu	*later, in future*
yǐqián	*before, in the past*
Yīngwén	*English language*
yǒu yìdiǎn(r)	*a little*
yòu ... yòu ...	*both ... and ...*
zǎo jiù	*ages ago, for ages*
zěnme le?	*what is/was the matter?*
zěnmeyàng?	*how is it? how about it?*

zhāng	(measure word for flat objects)	QUICK VOCAB
zhìliàng	*quality*	
zhǐ yào	*only need/cost*	
zhǔyì	*idea*	
zúqiú	*football*	

Learning tips

Here's another set of pairs:

> j and q
> zh and ch
> sh and r

Go back to the **Pronunciation guide** again and read the notes there.

The j in Chinese is the same as our own. Say *jeans*, in the same way as you would say 'cheese' to the camera, a few times and observe your mouth in a mirror. You will notice that the corners of your mouth are drawn back as far as they can go.

Q bears no resemblance to our q. It is pronounced *in exactly the same way as* j but you put air behind it to make the q. You have already done some practice on q in Unit 1, but as it is so different from q in English, it is worth looking at again.

For zh, ch, sh and r you must curl your tongue back in a loose sausage-roll. They are all pronounced with the tongue in this position. Zh and ch are identical sounds except the ch is said with air behind it.

R is the one to watch. Listen to the recording carefully and try to reproduce the sounds you hear as closely as possible. Recording your own voice and then comparing it with the original would be extremely helpful at this stage.

Dialogues

Dialogue 1

◀) CD 1, TR 9

Sùlán is showing her newly bought pullover to her boyfriend, Colin. She is very pleased with it as the price was reduced. But what does Colin think of it?

Sùlán	Zhè shì wǒ xīn mǎi de máoyī. Nǐ kàn zěnmeyàng?
Colin	Búcuò, búcuò.
Sùlán	Dàxiǎo héshì ma?
Colin	Ēn, yǒu diǎnr dà.
Sùlán	Yánsè hǎokàn ma?
Colin	Ēn, bù nánkàn.
Sùlán	Nǐ mōmo. . . . Nǐ juéde zhìliàng zěnmeyàng?
Colin	Ēn, hái kěyǐ. Duōshao qián?
Sùlán	Bú guì, zhǐ yào yìbǎi wǔshí kuài.
Colin	Shénme?! Yìbǎi wǔshí kuài wǒ kěyǐ mǎi sān zhāng zúqiú piào!

大减价

Dà jiǎn jià
Big reductions

Dialogue 2

◀) CD 1, TR 9, 01:30

Mr Li and Mrs Law are just back from holiday. How were their respective holidays?

Mrs Law	Jiàqī guò-de hǎo ma?
Mr Lǐ	Fēicháng hǎo, jiù shi dōngxi bù piányi.
Mrs Law	Wǒ zǎo jiù zhīdao le.
Mr Lǐ	Wǒ yǐqián juéde Yīngguó de dōngxi guì, xiànzài cái zhīdao Fǎguó de dōngxi gèng guì.

Mrs Law	Yìdàlì de dōngxi yě hěn guì shì bu shi?
Mr Lǐ	Yìdàlì de dōngxi yě bù bǐ Fǎguó de piányì. Nǐ de jiàqī guò-de zěnmeyàng?
Mrs Law	Bù zěnmeyàng.
Mr Lǐ	Zěnme le?
Mrs Law	Měi tiān dōu xià yǔ.

Dialogue 3

◀◉ CD 1, TR 9, 02:22

Martin is learning Chinese. He has met a Chinese girl who is studying English. What is their plan?

Bǎojié	Nǐde Zhōngwén shuō-de zhēn hǎo.
Martin	Nǎli, nǎli. Wǒde Zhōngwén méi yǒu nǐde Yīngwén hǎo.
Bǎojié	Bù. Nǐde Zhōngwén bǐ wǒde Yīngwén hǎo deduō.
Martin	Yǐhòu wǒ bāng nǐ xué Yīngwén, nǐ bāng wǒ xué Zhōngwén, zěnmeyàng?
Bǎojié	Hǎo zhǔyì. Kěshì wǒ xué-de bú kuài.
Martin	Méi guānxi, wǒ xué-de yě hěn màn.

Language notes

1 A bit . . . ?

To say something is *a little/bit* . . . use:

adjective + (yì)diǎnr

| hǎo (yì)diǎnr | *a bit better* |
| dà (yì)diǎnr | *a little older/bigger* |

(See also **Language note 7** in Unit 7, where adjective + **yìdiǎnr** is used in comparisons.)

When you wish to convey a negative feeling even if it is only subjective on your part, then **yǒu (yì)diǎnr** is put in front of the adjective:

Yǒu (yì)diǎnr guì.   *It's a bit on the expensive side.*
Yǒu (yì)diǎnr dà.   *It's a little on the big side.*

In all these examples, you can miss out the **yì** to sound more colloquial.

2 How well do you speak Chinese?

When you are describing how the action of a verb is carried out, such as *quickly, slowly, well,* you use **de** after the verb and *then* the word for *quick, slow, good,* and so on.

You do *not* have to change them into adverbs as in English – quick → quickly, good → well.

Nǐde Zhōngwén shuō-**de zěnmeyàng?**   *What's your Chinese like?*
Wǒde Zhōngwén shuō-**de bù hǎo.**   *I don't speak Chinese well.*
Wǒ xué-**de bú kuài.**   *I don't learn fast.*

This **de** is different from the **de** you met in Units 3 and 5 but they are written the same in pinyin and both are toneless. They are represented by two entirely different Chinese characters however.

When sentences of this kind have an object you can either repeat the verb after the object adding **de** to the second verb:

Wǒ   xué   Zhōngwén **xué-de** hěn màn.
subject   verb   object
(I'm learning Chinese very slowly.)

Tā kàn shū **kàn-de** hěn duō.   *He reads a lot.*

Or you can miss out the first verb and have the object coming straight after the subject followed by the verb with **de:**

Nǐ Rìyǔ shuō-de zěnmeyàng?   *What's your Japanese like?*
object

Wǒ Rìyǔ shuō-de bù hǎo.   *My Japanese is not very good.*

3 What's it like?

Zěnmeyàng *(What's it like? How?)* is a useful question word in Chinese. As you saw in Unit 2, with shéi *(who)* and shénme *(what)*, question words appear in the same position as the word or words which replace them in the answer:

Nǐ kàn zěnmeyàng?   *What do you think?*
Nǐ mōmo. Nǐ juéde   *Feel it. What do you think of*
  zhìliàng zěnmeyàng?   *the quality?*
Jiàqī guò-de zěnmeyàng?   *How was your holiday?*
(Guò-de) bù zěnmeyàng.   *Not very good/not up to much.*

Note the neat expression bù zěnmeyàng *(not up to much)* in response to a question containing the question word zěnmeyàng.

4 Even more!

To say *even more expensive* in Chinese, you only have to put the little word gèng in front of guì:

gèng guì   *even more expensive*
gèng piányi   *even cheaper, still cheaper*
gèng kuài   *even quicker, even more quickly*
Tā bǐ wǒ xué-de gèng màn.   *He learns even more slowly than*
   I do.

You will sometimes find hái *(still)* used instead of gèng, but the meaning remains exactly the same:

Nǐ bǐ tā xiě-de hái hǎo.   *You write even better than she*
   does.

5 Even more on comparisons!

You have already met **bǐ** in Units 6 and 7. If you wish to say that something (A) is not up to a certain standard as represented by another person, living thing or object (B) use:

A **méi yǒu** B *adjective/verb*

Wǒde Zhōngwén (A) **méi**
  yǒu nǐde Yīngwén (B) **hǎo**.
Nǐde qìchē **méi yǒu** wǒde
  (qìchē) **kuài**.

My Chinese is not as good as
  your English.
Your car is not as fast as mine.

You will sometimes find **nàme** or **zhème** (*so*) in front of the adjective:

Zhè jiàn máoyī de dàxiǎo
  méi yǒu nà jiàn (máoyī
  de dàxiǎo) **nàme héshì**.

This sweater doesn't fit as well
  as that one. (*lit.* This MW
  sweater's size not up to that MW
  (sweater's size) so suitable).

This construction can also be used in the positive form by omitting **méi**, but it is not nearly so common as the negative form:

Wǒ jiějie **yǒu** nǐ gēge **gāo**.

My elder sister is as tall as your
  elder brother.

6 Each and every!

Měi (*each/every*) is often reinforced by putting **dōu** (*both/all*) before the verb:

Měi tiān **dōu** xià yǔ.
Tā **měi** nián **dōu** qù Zhōngguó.

It rains/rained every day.
He goes to China every year.

In the example above, it is clear that **dōu** has to refer back to **měi nián** rather than to **tā**, which is singular.

Tiān and **nián** don't need a measure word between **měi** and themselves because they act as measure words as well as nouns, but other nouns do:

měi ge jiàqī *every holiday*   měi **jiàn** máoyī *every sweater*

Note that the measure word between **měi** and **rén** is optional.

Learning tips

Don't worry about making mistakes!

The important thing is to keep talking. People quickly lose interest in talking to you if you look at them blankly and don't respond. Say something. Use gestures to help you out and don't worry about the mistakes. Don't be too ambitious in the initial stages – use vocabulary you know even if it means you have to keep the conversation simple. If all else fails, use a word in English (the foreign language most likely to be known by Chinese speakers), clearly pronounced, to keep things moving.

The Chinese are normally so delighted that someone has made the effort to learn their language that they are very patient and make enormous allowances for your accent and poor tones (or lack of them!), and are always very complimentary about your efforts.

Chéngjī   **Quēdiǎn**   **Cuòwù**
Achievements   *Shortcomings*   *Mistakes*

Insight

Following on from the above, even if your Chinese is very poor you will usually be told how good it is! The correct response to such compliments is either **Guòjiǎng, guòjiǎng** (*you praise me too much*), or **Nǎli, nǎli** lit. *where, where?* (meaning that you don't see it the way they do!). Self-deprecation is definitely a Chinese art – you are invited to somebody's house and the table is groaning with delicious food and you are told that it is only **biànfàn** (*simple/convenience food*). The cook asks you to forgive his/her poor cooking when you can see that the opposite is the case. Examples such as these are endless and come under the general heading of **kèqi huà** (*polite talk*). You will find more examples of **kèqi huà** later on in the book. Why not start making a list of them for your own interest? Note people's self-deprecatory remarks and other people's responses to them.

Never give Chinese friends white flowers. White is the colour for mourning in China. Be circumspect with red, too – it's the colour associated with weddings (the bride's dress is traditionally red, although with western influence this is also changing). At Chinese New Year presents of money are given in little red envelopes (**hóng bāo**), and couplets expressing good luck and good fortune for the coming year are written on red paper and pasted on people's doors.

Practice

1 Match up the opposites:

a	yǐqián	i	nánkàn
b	dà	ii	màn
c	guì	iii	róngyì
d	hǎokàn	iv	piányi
e	kuài	v	yǐhòu

| f | zǎo | | vi | xiǎo |
| g | nán | | vii | wǎn |

Items of clothing

◄) CD 1, TR 9, 03:06

Item	Measure word	
chènyī	(jiàn)	*shirt*
dàyī	(jiàn)	*overcoat*
jiākè	(jiàn)	*jacket*
kùzi	(tiáo)	*trousers*
nèikù	(tiáo)	*underpants*
qúnzi	(tiáo)	*skirt*
shuìyī	(jiàn)	*nightdress, pyjamas*
xié	(shuāng)	*shoes* (a pair of)
xīfú	(tào)	*suit* (western)
yǔyī	(jiàn)	*raincoat*

2 Refer to the list of colours (Unit 7) and items of clothing above. How would you ask for the following things in Chinese? (Note the measure words.)

Example: a green jacket   yí jiàn lǜ jiākè

  a a white shirt
  b a yellow overcoat
  c a blue suit
  d a green skirt
  e a pair of black shoes
  f a pair of red trousers

◄) CD 1, TR 9, 03:56

3 Listen to the recording and answer the following questions. If you don't have the recording, read the passage and then answer the questions.

a Xiǎo Cài jīntiān chuān (*wear*) shénme?
b Xiǎo Zhào jīntiān chuān shénme?
c Lǎo Fāng jīntiān chuān shénme?

Materials

bù	*cotton/cloth*
bùxié	*cloth shoes*
pí	*leather*
píxié	*leather shoes*
sīchóu	*silk*
rénzào gé	*imitation leather*

Xiǎo Cài jīntiān chuān yí jiàn bái chènyī、yì tiáo lán qúnzi. Xiǎo Cài hěn xǐhuan chuān píxié. Jīntiān tā chuān yì shuāng hóng píxié.

Xiǎo Zhào jīntiān chuān yí jiàn lán de sīchóu chènyī、yì tiáo hēi kùzi. Xiǎo Zhào zuì bù xǐhuan chuān píxié. Tā jīntiān chuān yì shuāng lǜ bùxié.

Lǎo Fāng jīntiān chuān yí tào hēi xīfú、yí jiàn bái chènyī、yì shuāng hēi píxié. Xīngqīyī dào xīngqīwǔ tā dōu chuān xīfú hé píxié.

4 Describe what the following people are wearing with the information provided:

Example: Xiǎo Wáng/white shirt/black trousers/yellow shoes.
Answer: Xiǎo Wáng chuān yí jiàn bái chènyī, yì tiáo hēi kùzi, yì shuāng huáng píxié.

a Lǎo Mǎ/black leather shoes/blue shirt.
b Xiǎo Qián/red shirt/black trousers/cloth shoes.
c Liú xiānsheng/grey (**huī**) suit/yellow shirt/brown (**zōng**) leather shoes.

5 How well do they do the following things? Answer each of the following questions using the information given in brackets.

Example: Xiǎo Zhǔ Fǎyǔ shuō-de zěnmeyàng? (*not at all well*)
Answer: Tā Fǎyǔ shuō-de bù zěnmeyàng.

a Lǐ xiānsheng Déwén (*German*) shuō-de zěnmeyàng? (*very well*)
b Zhāng tàitai jiàqī guò-de hǎo bu hǎo? (*not very well*)
c Cháo xiǎojie Yīngwén xué-de kuài bu kuài? (*extremely quickly*)
d Mǎlì yòng kuàizi (*chopsticks*) yòng-de zěnmeyàng? (*not at all well*)
e Hēnglì shuō Rìyǔ (*Japanese*) shuō-de hěn qīngchu (*clearly*) ma? (*very clearly*)

6 Look carefully at the pictures of Zhāng Tóng and Mǎ Fēng's cars below and the sentences comparing their size and price. Then make up similar sentences comparing their height, age and weight, TVs (**diànshì**) and handwriting (**zì**) using **méi yǒu** . . . and the adjectives given in brackets.

Zhāng Tóng's car (dà, guì)   Mǎ Fēng's car

Example: Mǎ Fēng de chē **méi yǒu** Zhāng Tóng de chē **dà**.
Zhang Tóng de chē **méi yǒu** Mǎ Fēng de chē **guì**.

Zhāng Tóng   Mǎ Fēng

a (gāo, dà, zhòng)

Zhāng Tóng's TV   Mǎ Fēng's TV

b diànshì (*TV*) (dà, guì)

| 5 July 2010
Dear Jack,
Weather here sunny and warm. Having a great holiday, See you soon!
Zhang Tong | 8/C.
Hello Susan
Raining again today. Why did I have to come to Scotland for my holidays? Miss you —
MaFeng |

c zì (*handwriting*) (qīngchu *clear*)

Quick review

◀) CD 1, TR 9, 05:19

What do you say?

a Say to someone that she speaks English very well.
b Say that something, e.g. a shirt, is a bit small.
c Ask someone how her holiday was.
d Say that England (**Yīnggélán**) is bigger than Ireland (**Ài'ěrlán**).
e Say that Germany is not as big as France.

Bù gōngpíng *Unfair*

Vocabulary and pronunciation

a What do the two syllables stand for in the Chinese word 'dàxiǎo' meaning 'size' ?

b What is the opposite of 'piányi'?

c Which word means 'slow': (a) 'màn' or (b) 'kuài'?

d Is the tone for the word 'rain': (a) 'yú', (b) 'yǔ' or (c) 'yù'?

e You want to say 'later, in future'. Do you say: (a) 'yǐhòu' or (b) 'yǐqián'?

9

·····

Qù . . . zěnme zǒu?
How do I get to . . . ?

In this unit you will learn
- How to ask for and understand directions
- How to use public transport
- How to ask people if they have ever done something
- How to express how long something happens for

Before you start

You will be able to say all sorts of things about where you are going, where you are coming from and by what means of transport, by the time you have worked your way through this unit. You will also be able to say which order you are going to do things in and whether you have ever done them before.

Let's try

1 Refer back to **Dialogue 1** in Unit **8** and answer the following questions in Chinese:

a How much was the pullover?
b What could Colin have bought for the money instead?

2 **a** Somebody asks you whether French goods are more expensive than British ones. What do you reply?

   b The same person compliments you on your spoken Chinese. What is your response?

Àomén	*Macao*
biān	*side*
xībiānr	*west side*
chēzhàn	*bus/train stop or station*
chuán	*ship, boat*
cóng	*from*
dǎsuàn	*to plan*
dìfang	*place*
dù jià	*to take a holiday*
duìmiàn	*opposite*
-guo	*have ever* (verb suffix)
hái	*still*
háishi	*would be better*
huàn (chē)	*to change* (bus)
jià	*holiday*
jiù	(emphatic)
X lù (chē)	*the number X bus*
mǎlù	*road*
méi shénme	*it's nothing, don't mention it*
nàr/nàli	*there* (used interchangeably)
qián	*front, ahead*
tiān	*day*
Tiāntán	*Temple of Heaven*
tīngshuō	*I heard, I am told*
tuìxiū	*to retire*
wǎng	*in the direction of*
wǎng nán kāi de chē	*southbound bus*
xià chē	*to get off the bus*
Xiānggǎng	*Hong Kong*
xiànmu	*to envy*
xíng	*OK*
yǐhòu	*after*

QUICK VOCAB

yòng	to need, to use
zěnme	how
zhōumò	weekend
cóng A dào B	from A to B
. . . jiù dào le.	It takes only . . . to get there.
Qù X zěnme zǒu?	How do (I) get to X?
xiān . . . zài . . .	first . . . then . . .

Learning tips

1 z is pronounced like the -ds in *adds* or the z in *zoo*.

2 c is not at all like the c in English, so be very careful with it. It is pronounced like the -ts in *its*. It is useful to practise it together with z and to say them one after the other so that you can hear the difference clearly. Remember the top of your sheet of A4 (see Unit 6) should be blown away from you when you say c but not when you say z.

Dialogues

Dialogue 1

◀) CD 1, TR 10

Xiǎo Féng and Lǎo Qiáo are talking about taking their holidays. Where is Xiǎo Féng going and how will she get to those places? What about Lǎo Qiáo? How long is his holiday?

| Qiáo | Tīngshuō nǐ kuài yào qù dù jià le. |
| Féng | Duì. Wǒ yǒu sān ge xīngqī de jià, cóng liùyuè èrshíqī hào dào qīyuè shíbā hào. |

116

Qiáo	Nǐ dǎsuàn qù nǎr?
Féng	Xiānggǎng hé Àomén. Zhèi liǎng ge dìfang wǒ dōu méi qù-guo.
Qiáo	Nǐ zěnme qù?
Féng	Wǒ xiān zuò fēijī dào Xiānggǎng, zài nàr zhù wǔ tiān. Zài cóng Xiānggǎng zuò chuán dào Àomén.
Qiáo	Wǒ zhēn xiànmu nǐ.
Féng	Nǐ shénme shíhou dù jià?
Qiáo	Wǒ? O, shí'èryuè.
Féng	Duō cháng shíjiān?
Qiáo	Bù zhīdao.
Féng	Zěnme huì bù zhīdao?
Qiáo	Jīnnián shí'èryuè wǒ jiù yào tuìxiū le.
Féng	Wǒ zhēn xiànmu nǐ.

Insight

As China is situated in the east, to the Chinese the most important cardinal point is east rather than north. In the west we say *north, south, east, west* but the Chinese start with **dōng** (*east*) and say **dōng**、**nán** (*south*)、**xī** (*west*)、**běi** (*north*).

South-west in Chinese is **xīnán** (west, south), *north-east* is **dōngběi** (*lit.* east, north) and so on.

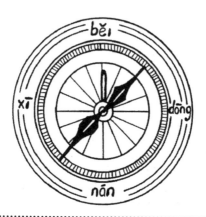

Dialogue 2

Ann is touring in Beijing. Today she is going to visit Tiantan. Can you follow the directions given to her by a passer-by?

Gōnggòng qìchēzhàn *Bus stop*

Ann	Qǐng wèn, qù Tiāntán zěnme zǒu?
Passer-by	Tiāntán zài xīnán biānr. Zuò chē sì zhàn jiù dào le.
Ann	Zuò jǐ lù chē?
Passer-by	Nǐ xiān cóng zhèr wǎng dōng zǒu, zài zuò wǎng nán kāi de chē, shíwǔ lù、èrshísān lù dōu xíng. Chēzhàn zài yínháng duìmiànr.
Ann	Yòng huàn chē ma?
Passer-by	Bú yòng. Xià chē yǐhòu wǎng qián zǒu yìdiǎnr. Tiāntán jiù zài mǎlù xībianr.
Ann	Xièxie nín.
Passer-by	Méi shénme.

Insight

When giving you directions, the Chinese (especially in the north) usually use the points of the compass rather than left and right. So it's good to know where north and south are when you ask somebody the way!

Dialogue 3

James is suggesting something adventurous to his friend, Huáng Zìlì. What is his suggestion and does Huáng accept it?

James	Nǐ qù-guo Tiānjīn ma?
Huáng	Méi qù-guo.
James	Xià ge zhōumò zánmen yìqǐ qù ba.
Huáng	Hǎo'a. Nǐ dǎsuàn zěnme qù? Zuò qìchē háishi zuò huǒchē?
James	Zánmen qí chē qù zěnmeyàng?
Huáng	Shénme? Nǐ fā fēng le! Qí chē qù Tiānjīn yào liǎng、sān tiān, yòu lèi yòu wēixiǎn.
James	Wǒ bú pà lèi, yě xǐhuan màoxiǎn!
Huáng	Fǎnzhèng wǒ bù gēn nǐ yìqǐ qù. Wǒ zài jiā kàn diànshì, yòu shūfu yòu ānquán.

ānquán	*safe*
diànshì	*TV*
fā fēng	*mad*
fǎnzhèng	*no way, in any case*
gēn	*with*
jiā	*home*
lèi	*tired, tiring*
màoxiǎn	*adventurous, to take the risk*
pà	*afraid*
qí	*to ride* (bicycle, motorbike, horse)
qìchē	*vehicle, bus, car*
shūfu	*comfortable*
wēixiǎn	*dangerous*
xià ge	*next*
yào . . .	*it takes . . .*
yìqǐ	*together*
yòu . . . yòu . . .	*both . . . and . . .*
zìxíngchē	*bicycle*

QUICK VOCAB

Language notes

1 About to

To say something is about to happen or is going to happen soon use:

yào (*want, will*) + verb . . . **le**

Nǐ **yào** qù dù jià **le**.	*You're going on holiday soon.*
Wǒ **yào** qù Xiānggǎng **le**.	*I'm about to leave for Hong Kong.*

Kuài (*quick*) or **jiù** (*then*) can also be put in front of **yào** to make the imminence of the action even clearer:

Jīnnián shí'èr yuè wǒ **jiù yào** tuìxiū **le**.	*I'll be retiring in December.*
Tā **kuài** yào kàn diànshì **le**.	*He's about to watch TV.*

2 From . . . to . . .

Simply use **cóng** (*from*) and **dào** (*to*).

cóng Xiānggǎng **dào** Àomén	*from Hong Kong to Macao*
cóng Běijīng **dào** Tiānjīn	*from Beijing to Tianjin*

And from one time to another:

cóng sānyuè shíbā hào **dào** sìyuè jiǔ hào   *from 18 March to 9 April*

There are only two small points to remember.

- The word order *cannot* be reversed in Chinese. You cannot say *I am going to* (**dào**) *China from* (**cóng**) *Japan*. So **cóng** must always precede **dào**.
- In the sentence *I am going to* (**dào**) *Macao from* (**cóng**) *Hong Kong by* (**zuò**) *boat*, 'from Hong Kong' must come first followed by the means of transport 'by boat' and then 'to Macao' last:

Wǒ **cóng** Xiānggǎng **zuò** chuán **dào** Àomén.

The Chinese are very logical – you cannot get to Macao unless you 'sit on the boat' **zuò chuán** first so that should come before 'to Macao' **dào Àomén**.

3 Have you ever . . . ?

If you put the little word **guo** after the verb it will emphasize a past experience:

Wǒ qù-**guo** Yìdàlì.	*I've been to Italy* (at some time or other).
Tā chī-**guo** Yìndù fàn.	*He has eaten Indian food* (at some time in the past).

You make the negative by putting **méi yǒu** in front of the verb:

Wǒ **méi** (yǒu) qù-**guo** Zhōngguó.   *I have never been to China.*

You make the question by putting **ma** or **méi you** at the end of the statement:

Nǐ qù-**guo** Tiānjīn **ma**?	*Have you (ever) been to Tianjin?*
Nǐ zuò-**guo** fēijī **méi you**?	*Have you (ever) travelled by plane?*
Hái **méi yǒu** (qù-guo).	*Not yet.*
Méi zuò-guo.	*No, never.*

Note the two possible ways of answering a question with -**guo**.

4 First . . . then . . .

By using **xiān** (*first*) + verb followed by **zài** (*then*) + verb you show that the two actions are linked:

Wǒ **xiān** zuò fēijī dào Xiānggǎng, **zài** zuò huǒchē qù Běijīng.	*First I'll go Hong Kong by plane then I'll go by train to Beijing.*

Nǐ **xiān** cóng zhèr wǎng dōng zǒu, **zài** zuò wǎng nán kāi de chē.	*You walk eastwards from here first. Then you get on a bus going south (lit.* then sit towards south drive on bus).

The **xiān** + verb and the **zài** + verb may occur in two separate sentences but the idea of sequence of actions is still there:

(Wǒ) **xiān** zuò fēijī dào Xiānggǎng . . . **Zài** cóng Xiānggǎng zuò chuán dào Àomén.	*First I'll go to Hong Kong by plane . . . Then from Hong Kong I'll go to Macao by boat.*

By the way, this **zài** is written like the **zài** in **zàijiàn** (*again*) not as in **zài** (*at, in*).

5 How long?

As you saw in Unit 1, time-words like *today, Wednesday, 6 o'clock* come before the verb in Chinese. However, when you want to say how long you do the action of the verb, the time-word comes after the verb:

Wǒ zài nàr zhù **wǔ tiān**.	*I'll stay there five days.*
Tā zài zhèr gōngzuò le **liǎng nián**.	*She worked here for two years.*

The **le** after the verb shows that the action of the verb has been completed.

6 Huì *Can*

You met **huì** (*can*) in Unit 6 with the meaning *to know how to do something* (having learnt to do it). Its other meaning is *to be likely to* or *to be possible*:

Tā xiàwǔ **huì** lái.	*He'll* (is likely to) *come in the afternoon.*

Zěnme **huì** bù zhīdao?   *How could* (you) *not know?*
                                              (*lit.* how possible not know?)

7 Both . . . and . . .

To express *both . . . and . . .* you put **yòu** in front of the two adjectives or verbs:

yòu lèi **yòu** wēixiǎn	*both tiring and dangerous*
yòu shūfu **yòu** ānquán	*both comfortable and safe*
yòu hǎo **yòu** bú guì	*both good and inexpensive*

8 Added 'r'

You will find **r** added to some words in this unit in order for you to get used to seeing and reading it. It is used a great deal by people in the north of China especially around Beijing. You certainly don't have to use it but it is important to know that it exists. It is to be found on the ends of words such as:

(yì)diǎn	(yì)diǎn<u>r</u>	*a little bit*
yì wǎn	yì wǎn<u>r</u>	*one bowl*
tiān	tiān<u>r</u>	*day*
duìmiàn	duìmiàn<u>r</u>	*opposite*
biān	biān<u>r</u>	*side*
xībian	xībian<u>r</u>	*west side*
wán (verb)	wán<u>r</u>	*to enjoy oneself*

Learning tips

Learn from your mistakes and keep trying

1 Everyone makes mistakes when learning a language. If you didn't make mistakes, you wouldn't have to learn it! Small children also make mistakes when learning their own language so accept that this is perfectly normal and natural.

2 Some mistakes affect the meaning of what you say more than others. For instance, it is important not to confuse **mǎi** (3rd tone) (*to buy*) with **mài** (4th tone) (*to sell*) for obvious reasons. But surprisingly enough, poor tones don't seem to affect the ability of most Chinese people to understand what you are saying. There is also a wide variety of pronunciation across the whole of China because it is so vast.

So concentrate on getting your message across rather than on not making any mistakes. Learning to speak a foreign language is one case where quantity (as long as it is comprehensible) is better than quality! That is the way you will learn.

Nevertheless when a standard speaker of Chinese corrects your Chinese, make a mental note of it and at the first opportunity write it down, learn it and try to use it.

3 It is good to deliberately try out new constructions and vocabulary. Practise them beforehand so that you won't be too hesitant the first time you try something. If it doesn't work as well as you'd hoped, look at them again and have another go. It's like learning to ride a bicycle. When you fall off you have to get on again straight away so that you don't lose confidence.

Insight

It is still sometimes very difficult to buy return tickets in China especially for trains and long-distance buses. Normally you have to think when you are going to leave a place as soon as you have arrived in it and organize your return (or ongoing) ticket accordingly. China's large population makes queuing inevitable unless you book your ticket through an agency (hotel, China Travel Service and so on), which may require plenty of notice and a commission charge.

Practice

1 Answer the following *Have you ever . . . ?* questions:

Example: Nǐ qù-guo Zhōngguó ma?
Qù-guo or **Méi qù-guo.**

a Nǐ qù-guo Rìběn ma?　　　　[ever been to Japan?]
b Nǐ zuò-guo fēijī ma?　　　　[ever travelled by plane?]
c Nǐ kàn-guo Déguó　　　　　 [ever seen German films?]
　 diànyǐng ma?
d Nǐ chī-guo Zhōngguó　　　　[ever had Chinese food?]
　 fàn ma?
e Nǐ hē-guo Měiguó　　　　　 [ever drunk American wine?]
　 pútáojiǔ ma?

◀) **CD 1, TR 10, 03:52**

2 Listen to the recording (or read the following passage) and draw
the way to the cinema (**diànyǐngyuàn**) on the plan below. Which
letter represents the cinema?

Xiān wǎng nán zǒu. Dào Dōnghǎi Lù zuò wǎng dōng kāi de chē.
Zuò liǎng zhàn. Diànyǐngyuàn jiù zài Dōnghǎi Lù de nánbianr,
shāngdiàn de duìmiànr.

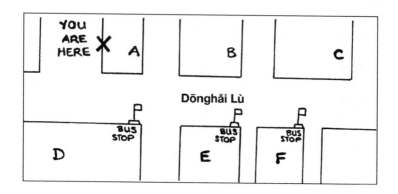

3 You are now in the cinema. You have just seen a film. Can you say in Chinese how you walk back to the hotel you are staying in (A)?

4 Read the directions below which tell you where various places are situated. Then go back to the sketch and identify the buildings represented by the letters (B), (C), (D) and (E).

  a **Zhōngguó Yínháng** zài diànyǐngyuàn de xībianr.
  b **Shāngdiàn** zài diànyǐngyuàn de duìmiàn.
  c **Dōnghǎi Gōngyuán** zài Zhōngguó Yínháng de xībian.
  d **Xuéxiào** (*school*) zài Zhōngguó Yínháng de běibian, fàndiàn de dōngbian.

5 Answer the following questions using (**cóng**) . . . **dào** . . . . If you don't know, say **Wǒ bù zhīdao.** (But you could find out.)

  Example: When is Mr Wang's next holiday?
                  (**Cóng**) wǔyuè sānshí hào **dào** liùyuè bā hào.

  a When is **your** next holiday?
  b What are the opening hours of **your** local (or school) library during the weekdays and weekends?
  c Which days of the week do **you** work? (e.g. from Monday to Friday)
  d What are **your** working hours during the week?

6 How do you get there?
Choose an appropriate means of transport from the list below to make complete sentences in Chinese, according to the information given in **a–e**. Take care with the word order!

zuò gōnggòng qìchē	*by bus*
zuò huǒchē	*by train*
zuò dìtiě	*by underground*
zuò fēijī	*by plane*

zuò chuán	*by ship*
qí (zìxíng)chē	*to cycle*
kāi chē	*to drive*
zǒu lù	*to walk*

Example: to go to work (qù shàng bān)
Wǒ **qí zìxíngchē** qù shàng bān.

a to go to work [qù shàng bān]
b to go to school [qù xuéxiào]
c to do shopping [qù mǎi dōngxi]
d to go to see a film [qù kàn diànyǐng]
(at your local cinema)
e to go to X train station [qù X huǒchē zhàn]

7 In the following Quick vocab box you will find some useful words to describe things. Which pair would you use to describe the following things? Try to use **yòu . . . yòu . . .**

Example: Zuò fēijī **yòu** guì **yòu** bù shūfu.
Zuò fēijī **yòu** kuài **yòu** shūfu.

guì	*expensive*	**bú guì**	*not expensive*
piányi	*cheap*	**bù piányi**	*not cheap*
fāngbiàn	*convenient*	**máfan**	*troublesome*
kuài	*fast*	**màn**	*slow*
wēixiǎn	*dangerous*	**ānquán**	*safe*

a Cóng Rìběn zuò chuán dào Zhōngguó
b Zài Lúndūn/Bālí (*Paris*) qí zìxíngchē
c Zuò gōnggòng qìchē qù shàng bān
d Cóng Yīngguó zuò fēijī dào Měiguó
e Kāi chē qù mǎi dōngxi

8 Listen to the recording and answer the following questions about Mr White's holiday.

See first if you can answer the questions in Chinese. If you find them too difficult, read the questions in English that follow and answer them either in English or in Chinese.

If you haven't got the recording, read the passage after the questions and then answer the questions. If you need to refer to it, the English script is in the **Key to the exercises.**

a Bái xiānsheng dǎsuàn qù shénme dìfang?
b Tā zài Bālí zhù jǐ tiān?
c Tā gēn shéi yìqǐ qù Yìdàlì? Tāmen zěnme qù Yìdàlì?
d Bái xiānsheng dǎsuàn zài Yìdàlì zhù jǐ tiān?
e Tā zěnme huí Yīngguó?
f Tā péngyou zěnme huí Fǎguó?

a *Where did Mr White plan to go?*
b *How long does he plan to stay in Paris?*
c *Who will he go to Italy with? How will they travel to Italy?*
d *How long does Mr White plan to stay in Italy?*
e *How will he get back to the UK?*
f *How will his friend get back to France?*

Bái xiānsheng de jiàqī *Mr White's holidays*

Bái xiānsheng yào qù dù jià le. Tā yào qù liǎng ge dìfang. Tā xiān cóng Lúndūn zuò huǒchē dào Bālí. Tā dǎsuàn zài Bālí zhù sì tiān. Ránhòu tā gēn tāde Fǎguó péngyou kāi chē qù Yìdàlì. Tāmen dǎsuàn zài Yìdàlì zhù yí ge xīngqī. Zuìhòu tā cóng Yìdàlì zuò fēijī huí Lúndūn. Tāde péngyou kāi chē huí Fǎguó.

Quick review

◀)) CD 1, TR 10, 06:39

a Ask how to get to the Bank of China (**Zhōngguó Yínháng**).
b Tell the Chinese person who has asked you the way to take the number 10 bus.
c Then tell her that it will be five stops (before she gets there).
d Say that your friend has never been to China.
e Say it's going to rain soon.

Jìnzhǐ xī yān
禁止吸烟

Vocabulary and pronunciation

a What is the Mandarin Chinese for Hong Kong?
b 'Nàli' means 'there'. What is the other way of saying it?
c What place is 'Àomén'?
d What does 'cóng' mean?
e Do 'change money' and 'change bus' share the same Chinese word for 'change'?

10

Nín xiǎng chī shénme?
What would you like to eat?

In this unit you will learn
- How to order a meal and drinks
- How to pay the bill
- How to say you have given up something (such as smoking)
- More about verb endings

Before you start

By the end of this unit, you will be able to get yourself various things to eat and drink and even to question the bill! There's lots of very useful vocabulary so take your time.

Let's try

1 You need to tell a Chinese friend your itinerary once you have left home so she can book your hotel in Beijing and arrange your programme.

   a Tell her that you are going by air to Hong Kong first and staying there two days.
   b Then you are going from Hong Kong to Shanghai by train.

c You plan to travel by air to Beijing on the morning of 10th August.

2 The same friend asks if you have ever been to Shanghai before. What does she say to you?

àiren	*husband/wife* (sometimes used in the People's Republic)
bēi	*a cup of; cup*
bié	*don't*
bīngqílín	*ice-cream*
cài	*dish*
càidān	*menu* (lit. *dish list*)
Chángchéng	*the Great Wall*
chī	*to eat*
chī-wán/chī-bǎo/chī-hǎo le	*to have finished eating/be full/satisfied*
chī sù	*to be vegetarian* (lit. *eat non-meat food*)
chōu (yān)	*to smoke* (a cigarette)
dòufu	*beancurd*
duì	*to, for*
duō	*more; many*
gēn wǒ lái	*follow me*
hǎochī	*delicious, tasty*
hē	*to drink*
jiè (yān)	*to give up* (smoking)
jié zhàng	*to ask for the bill*
júzizhī	*orange juice*
là (de)	*hot, spicy* (food)
lái	*I'll have* (colloquial)
mápó dòufu	*spicy beancurd/tofu*
pàng	*fat*
pútáojiǔ	*wine* (lit. *grape alcohol*)
qīngcài	*vegetables*
ràng	*to let, allow*
rè	*hot*

QUICK VOCAB

ròu	*meat*
shǎo	*less; few*
shēntǐ	*health*
shōu	*to accept, to receive*
tāng	*soup*
suānlà tāng	*hot and sour soup*
tiānqi	*weather*
xiànjīn	*cash*
xìnyòng kǎ	*credit card*
yú	*fish*
yùdìng	*to book* (a room)
zhī	(measure word for cigarettes)
zhǐ	*only*
zhīpiào	*cheque/check*
Nǐmen chī/hē diǎnr shénme?	*What would you like to eat/ drink?*
Jiǔ lái le	*Here comes the wine*

Learning tips

1 Practise the difference between **-uo** and **-ou** as in **duō** (*much/ many*) and **dōu** (*both/all*).

2 Practise the difference between **-an** and **-ang** as in **fàn** (*food*) and **fàng** (*to put*) and between **-en** and **-eng** as in **fēn** (*minute/smallest unit of Chinese currency*) and **fēng** (*wind*).

◄» CD 2, TR 1

3 Now go back and revise all the vowels with a nasal sound in the **Pronunciation guide**. Listen to the recording if you have it.

Hold your nose gently as you practise these sounds. You should be able to feel the vibration in it when you say **-ang**, **-eng**, **-iang**, **-ing**, **-iong**, **-ong** and **-uang**. This is particularly obvious when you say the sound in the 1st tone and hang on to it.

Dialogues

Sìchuān cāntīng
Sichuan restaurant

Dialogue 1

🔊 **CD 2, TR 1**

Mr Brown and his friend Yúqiáo are going to have a Chinese meal. What drinks and food have they ordered?

Waiter	Nǐmen yùdìng le ma?
Brown	Yùdìng le. Wǒ jiào John Brown.
Waiter	Wǒ kànyikàn. . . . Mr Brown, qī diǎn bàn, liǎng ge rén.
Brown	Duì, duì.
Waiter	Hǎo, qǐng gēn wǒ lái. . . .
Waiter	Zhè shì càidān. Nǐmen xiān hē diǎnr shénme?
Yúqiáo	Wǒ yào yì bēi júzizhī.
Brown	Nǐmen yǒu shénme pútáojiǔ?
Waiter	Wǒmen yǒu Chángchéng bái pútáojiǔ hé Zhōngguó hóng pútáojiǔ.
Brown	Lái yì bēi bái pútáojiǔ ba. . . .
Waiter	Jiǔ lái le. Nǐmen yào shénme cài?
Yúqiáo	Wǒ bù chī ròu.
Brown	Nǐ chī bu chī yú?
Yúqiáo	Bù chī. Wǒ zhǐ yào qīngcài hé dòufu.
Brown	Shénme? Nǐ xiànzài chī sù le.
Yúqiáo	Shì'a. Wǒ yǐjīng hěn pàng le.
Waiter	Nǐmen xǐhuan chī là de ma?
Yùqiáo	Xǐhuan. Kěshì bié tài là le.
Waiter	Lái yí ge mápó dòufu ba.
Brown	Hǎo'a. Xiān lái liǎng ge suānlà tāng.

Yúqiáo	Jīntiān tiānqi yǐjīng hěn rè le. Wǒmen yīnggāi shǎo chī là de.
Waiter	Méi guānxi. Chī-wán fàn yǐhòu, nǐmen duō chī diǎnr bīngqílín. Wǒmen dē bīngqílín fēicháng hǎochī.

Insight

The custom when eating Chinese food is that all the dishes are put in the middle of the table and shared. The host helps her/ his guest to the best titbits. Too bad if you don't share his/her taste! The soup is usually eaten last in China except for some areas in the south.

Dialogue 2

◀) CD 2, TR 1, 02:45

Mr Brown and Yúqiáo are chatting over the meal. Listen to or read their conversation and find out why Yúqiáo has given up smoking and Mr Brown hasn't.

Brown	Chōu zhī yān ba.
Yúqiáo	Wǒ bù chōu yān le.
Brown	Wèishénme?
Yúqiáo	Wǒ àiren bú ràng wǒ chōu le. Tā shuō chōu yān duì wǒde shēntǐ bù hǎo, duì tāde shēntǐ yě bù hǎo.
Brown	Wǒ yě bù xiǎng chōu le. Kěshì wǒ yǒu yí ge péngyou, jiè yān yǐqián bú pàng, jiè yān yǐhòu jiù pàng le. Wǒ pà pàng.
Yúqiáo	Wǒ yě pà pàng, kěshì jīntiān de cài tài hǎochī le.
Brown	Nǐ chī-bǎo le ma?
Yúqiáo	Chī-bǎo le.
Brown	Wǒmen jié zhàng ba. Fúwùyuán, qǐng jié zhàng.
Waiter	Nǐmen chī-hǎo le ma?
Yúqiáo	Chī-hǎo le, xièxie.
Brown	Nǐmen shōu bu shōu xìnyòng kǎ hé zhīpiào?
Waiter	Duìbuqǐ, wǒmen zhǐ shōu xiànjīn.

Dialogue 3

🔊 **CD 2, TR 1, 04:00**

Ann and Xiǎo Fāng have arrived at the street market (see **Dialogue 3, Unit 7**). What are they going to do next? Are they going to get a bargain this time?

Ann	Wǒ **è** le. Wǒmen **suíbiàn** chī diǎnr ba.
Fāng	Nàr yǒu ge xiǎo **tānzi**. Tāmen de **chǎomiàn** hǎochī-**jíle**.
	(At the food stall)
Ann	*(whispering)* Wǒ kàn zhèr bú tài **gānjìng**.
Fāng	Méi guānxi, tāmen huì gěi wǒmen **wèishēng kuàizi**.

* * *

Fāng	Qǐng lái liǎng **wǎnr** chǎomiàn、liǎng **tīng kěkǒukělè**.
Waitress	Qǐng xiān **fù qián**. Liǎng wǎnr chǎomiàn shí'èr kuài, liǎng tīng kěkǒukělè shísì kuài, **yígòng** èrshíliù kuài.
Fāng	Shénme? Nǐ **suàn-cuò** le ba. **Shàng cì** chǎomiàn wǔ kuài yì wǎnr.
Waitress	Méi suàn-cuò. Shàng cì shì shàng cì, xiànzài yì wǎnr liù kuài le.

Words in **bold** are listed in the Quick vocab box.

è	*hungry*
chǎomiàn	*fried noodles*
fù qián	*to pay* (money)
gānjìng	*clean*
-jíle	(suffix) *extremely*
kěkǒukělè	*Coca-Cola*
kuàizi	*chopsticks*
shàng cì	*last time*
suàn-cuò le	*to have calculated wrongly*
suíbiàn	*casually*
tānzi	*stall*
tīng	(measure word for cans (of drink))
wǎn(r)	*bowl*
wèishēng	*hygiene, hygienic*
yígòng	*altogether*

QUICK VOCAB

Language notes

1 Already and *le*

Remember using **le** in Unit 4 to show that something has happened or has already taken place? When **yǐjīng** (*already*) appears in front of a verb it reinforces this idea of something having happened so you will find **le** at the end of such sentences:

Wǒ **yǐjīng** hěn pàng **le**.	*I'm already very fat.*
Jīntiān **yǐjīng** hěn rè **le**.	*It's already very hot today.*

2 More before the verb!

To say *eat more*, put the little word **duō** (*much/many*) in front of the verb *to eat*:

duō chī	*eat more*

This works with all full verbs, i.e. verbs that cannot also act as adjectives such as **hǎo** (*good*), **pàng** (*fat*) and so on.

duō hē	*drink more*
duō yào	*want more*
duō gěi	*give more*

You do exactly the same thing if you want to say *eat less*, *drink less*, and so on but you put **shǎo** (*less/few*) in front of the verb instead of **duō**:

shǎo chī	*eat less*
shǎo hē	*drink less*
shǎo yào	*want less*
shǎo gěi	*give less*

3 Not any more!

To say that you don't do something any more use:

bù verb (+ object) **le**

Wǒ **bù** chōu yān **le**.	*I don't smoke any more/I've given up smoking.*
Wǒ tàitai **bú** ràng wǒ chōu **le**.	*My wife doesn't let me smoke any more.*
Tā **bù** hē jiǔ **le**.	*She's given up drinking.*
Tāmen **bù** niánqīng **le**.	*They're no longer young.*

If the verb is **yǒu** (*to have*), you have to use **méi** instead of **bù**:

You	Nǐ yǒu **mei** yǒu hóng chènyī?
	Do you have a red shirt?
Shop assistant	**Méi** yǒu **le**, mài-wán le.
	We're out of stock. They're sold out.
	(*lit.* not have any more, sell finish **le**).

4 Smoking is not good for your health!

As you know, **duì** means *right, correct*. In certain contexts it also means *to* or *for*. Learn the following useful phrases:

A **duì** shēntǐ (**bù**) hǎo.	*A is (not) good **for** the health/body.*
Y **duì** X (**bù**) hǎo.	*Y is (not) good **to** X.*

Thus **Chōu yān duì wǒde shēntǐ bù hǎo** means *Smoking is not good for my health*.

5 After...

In English, you say *after I've been to the restaurant* but in Chinese, you say *I've been to the restaurant after* – the reverse of the English word order:

Jiè yān **yǐhòu**	*After giving up smoking*
Chī fàn **yǐhòu**	*After eating*

The same happens with **yǐqián** (*before*) and **de shíhou** (*when*). (You will meet **de shíhou** later in Units 12–21):

Jiè yān **yǐqián**	*Before giving up smoking*
Fù qián **yǐqián**	*Before paying*
Jié zhàng **de shíhou**	*When working out the bill*

6 To eat your fill

To say that you *have eaten your fill* in Chinese you put **bǎo** (*full*) after the verb **chī** (*to eat*):

Wǒ chī-**bǎo** le.	*I'm full* (*lit.* I eat full **le**).

The **le** after the verb shows completed action. (See Unit 4.)

To make the verb negative, use **méi** not **bù** and drop the **le** as the verb is then no longer completed.

Other little words, or endings, which appear after the verb in this way have other meanings:

Nǐmen chī-**hǎo** le ma?	*Have you finished eating* (to your satisfaction)?
Chī-**hǎo** le.	*Yes, we have* (finished eating to our satisfaction).
Nǐ suàn-**cuò** le ba.	*You must have got it wrong* (*lit.* you calculate wrong **le**, haven't you).
Méi suàn-**cuò**.	*No, I haven't* (*lit.* not have calculate wrong).

Nǐmen hē-**wán** le ma?	*Have you finished your drinks* (*lit.* you drink finish le ma)?
Wǒmen hē-**wán** le.	*Yes, we have* (*lit.* we drink finish **le**).
Nǐ kàn-**jiàn** tā le ma?	*Did you see him/her* (*lit.* you look perceive him/her **le ma**)?
Wǒ méi kàn-**jiàn** ta.	*I didn't see him/her* (*lit.* I not have look perceive him/her).

If you put **bù** between the verb and **one** of these endings as in the examples below, you have the meaning of **cannot + verb + ending**:

Wǒ kàn-**bu**-jiàn.	*I can't see.*
Tā tīng-**bu**-dǒng.	*She can't understand.* (*lit.* she listen cannot understand).
Wǒmen hē-bu-wán.	*We can't finish* (our drinks).

If on the other hand you put **de** (yes, **de** again!) between the verb and one of these endings, you have the meaning of **can + verb + ending**:

Wǒ kàn-**de**-jiàn.	*I can see.*
Tāmen tīng-**de**-dǒng.	*They can understand.* (*lit.* they listen can understand)
Wǒmen hē-**de**-wán.	*We can drink up.*

This is the same **de** as the one used in Unit 8.

7 Cans, bowls and bottles

You should be familiar with measure words by now but did you spot the ones for *bottle*, *bowl* and *can* in this unit?

yì **píng** Fǎguó jiǔ	*a **bottle** of French wine*
liǎng **wǎn**(r) chǎomiàn	*two **bowls** of fried noodles*
liǎng **tīng** kě (kǒukě)lè	*two **cans** of Coke*

8 Don't . . . !

To tell somebody not to do something, all you have to do is put the word **bié** (*don't*) in front of what you don't want them to do:

| Bié shuō huà. | *Don't speak.* |
| Bié zǒu. | *Don't go.* |

Adding **le** at the end of such sentences helps to soften the idea of giving an order or command.

Learning tips

Do you feel comfortable with the grammar?

Having now got to the halfway mark in the book it is probably a good idea to see how well you're doing with grammar and how to revise and consolidate what you know.

1 Units 1 to 10 contain all the grammar you will need to know to study Units 12 to 21 so it is important that you feel comfortable with it before proceeding. Go back to the **Practice** sections of Units 1 to 9 and pick out one or two exercises from each unit and do them again. If you find any particular exercise difficult, revise the relevant **Language notes** carefully and try the exercise again.

2 By the time you have completed **Language tip 1** you should be feeling more confident. When you go on to study Units 12 to 21 look at the structures in the dialogues and fit them into the patterns you have already learnt. You might like to jot these down so that you have a list of examples under each structure. You will find this helps the consolidation process.

Practice

◄ CD 2, TR 1, 05:09

1 Listen to the dialogue and tick on the menu what Mr Jones has ordered for his meal. You will need to know the word for *beer*, which is **píjiǔ** in Chinese.

Fúwùyuán	Nín xiǎng chī diǎnr shénme?
Jones	Wǒ xǐhuan chī là de.
Fúwùyuán	Wǒmen yǒu yúxiāng ròusī hé mápó dòufu.
Jones	Wǒ yào yí ge yúxiāng ròusī ba.
Fúwùyuán	Nín yào tāng ma?
Jones	Nǐmen yǒu shénme tāng?
Fúwùyuán	Suānlà tāng hé zhàcài tāng.
Jones	Lái yí ge suānlà tāng ba.
Fúwùyuán	Yào jiǔ ma?
Jones	Yào yì píng píjiǔ.
Fúwùyuán	Wǔxīng píjiǔ háishi Qīngdǎo píjiǔ?
Jones	Lái yì píng Wǔxīng píjiǔ.
Fúwùyuán	Hǎo de.

Càidān

Mápó dòufu

Yúxiāng ròusī

....

....

suānlà tāng

zhàcài tāng

....

....

Wǔxīng píjiǔ

Qīngdǎo píjiǔ

2 How many? Put the correct number and measure word under each of the items in the following pictures. You may not be able to use all of these measure words: **píng, gè, bēi, zhāng, wǎn, jiàn, tīng, zhī**.

Example: yì **běn** shū (*a book*)

3 Have things changed?

If something has changed, you use . . . **le**.

If it has not changed, you say **méi yǒu**, or **gēn yǐqián yíyàng** (*the same as before*).

Example: Dōngxi guì **le** ma?
Guì **le** (yìdiǎnr).
Méi yǒu *or* **Gēn yǐqián yíyàng**.

a Dōngxi guì le ma?   (compared with five years ago)
b Nǐ pàng le ma?   (compared with five years ago)
c Tiānqi lěng le ma?   (compared with a month ago)
d Nǐ zhǎng (*to grow*)   (compared with five years ago)
gāo le ma?

4 The following dialogue is between you and a waitress. Complete your part.

a **You**	(*Waiter! The bill please.*)	
Fúwùyuán	Nǐmen chī-hǎo le ma?	
b **You**	(*Yes. Thank you.*)	
Fúwùyuán	Yígòng sānbǎi kuài.	
c **You**	(*I think you've got it wrong.*)	
Fúwùyuán	Wǒ zài kànkan (*let me look at it again*). Duìbuqǐ. Wǒ suàn-cuò le.	
d **You**	(*That's all right.*)	

5 Which is correct, **méi** or **bù**, in the following sentences?

a Tā yǐqián chōu yān, xiànzài **méi/bù** chōu yān le.
b Wǒ liùyuè qù dù jià le, xiànzài **méi/bù** yǒu jià le.
c Yǐqián wǒ yǒu yì tiáo gǒu (*dog*), xiànzài
méi/bù yǒu le.
d Tiānqi tài rè le, wǒ **méi/bù** chī là de le.

142

Halfway review

◄» CD 2, TR 1, 05:58

1 On the recording, you will hear different years being said.

Example: yī-jiǔ-jiǔ-qī nián *1997*

Repeat each one and write them down.

2 You have learnt two ways of asking *yes* or *no* questions. Can you try to turn the following statements into questions using both ways?

Example: Statement – Jīntiān tiānqi hěn hǎo.
Question 1 – Jīntiān tiānqi hǎo ma?
Question 2 – Jīntiān tiānqi hǎo bu hǎo?

a Tāmen shì jiěmèi.
b Tāde chǎomiàn zhēn hǎochī.
c Míngtiān tā tàitai qù mǎi dōngxi.
d Nǐ bú rènshi tā.
e Xiǎo Lǐ yǒu yì tiáo hóng kùzi.

3 Which of the following statements talk about habitual things one does or does not do (call these X), and which state things one has done at some point or has never done (call these Y)?

a Xiǎo Fāng chōu-guo yān.
b Tā měi tiān chōu yān.
c Tā méi chī-guo Yìdàlì fàn.
d Tā bù xǐhuan chī Yìdàlì fàn.

4 Pair up the question words in Chinese with their English equivalents.

a shéi   i *where*
b nǎr   ii *what*

c shénme
d zěnme
e nǎ
f jǐ

iii *which*
iv *how many*
v *who*
vi *how*

5 Can you answer the following questions about Jane?

JANE

Jane went to the USA in 1985. She studied German for one year in 1990 and visited France in 1992. In 1993, she had Vietnamese food for the first time, and she stopped smoking in 1994. She will visit China and Japan for the first time next year.

---

a Tā qù-guo Zhōngguó ma?
b Tā 1985 qù nǎr le?
c Tā huì shuō Déyǔ ma?
d Tā qù-guo Fǎguó ma?
e Tā xiànzài hái chōu yān ma?
f Tā chī-guo Yuènán fàn ma?
g Tā míngnián qù nǎr?

(tíng)
No stopping

Jìnzhǐ tíng chē
No parking (*lit.* forbid stop vehicle)

Good luck with the rest of the book!

11

Wǒmen kànkan Hànzì ba!
Let's look at Chinese characters!

In this unit you will be introduced to the Chinese writing system and learn

- The structure of Chinese characters
- The rules of writing
- How to write the numbers 1–99
- How to write the days of the week and the date
- How to write the time

Before you start

You will remember from the introduction that this unit is largely independent of the rest of the book, so if you have decided not to get involved with the Chinese script, you can miss it out. Alternatively, you can choose to come back to it later when you have finished the other units. Even if you don't do any of the exercises in this unit, it would be a good idea to read it through, so that at least you have some idea what the Chinese script is all about. This will help your understanding of the Chinese language as a whole and hence of the people who speak it.

The Chinese writing system

Chinese characters (**Hànzì**) are the symbols used to write the Chinese language. Written Chinese does not use a phonetic alphabet. This means that you cannot guess how a character (**zì**) is pronounced just by looking at it. The Chinese script is extremely old. Its earliest written records date back over 3500 years. These are the markings on oracle bones (tortoise shells and animal bones) on which the priests used to scratch their questions to the gods. The earliest characters were pictures representing easily recognizable objects, such as the sun, the moon, fire, water, a mountain, a tree, and so on.

火 fire　水 water　山 mountain　雨 rain

Such characters (**zì**) were known as *pictographs*. Some of them are still in use even today.

The next step was for *pictographs* to be combined to form new characters known as *ideographs* because they express an idea:

日 *sun* + 月 *moon* = 明 *bright*
女 *woman* + 子 *child* = 好 *good*
日 *sun* + 木 *tree* = 東 *east* (the sun coming up behind a tree)
人 *person* + 木 *tree* = 休 *to rest* (a person leaning up against a tree)

So far so good! Unfortunately, only a limited number of ideas could be expressed in this way so then characters were created which contained a *meaning* element (often known as the *radical*) and a *phonetic* element which was to help with the pronunciation of the character. Of course, pronunciation has changed over the centuries,

146

so that now this phonetic element is only of limited help. Let's look at a few of these *radical-phonetic* or compound characters. You can see how such characters came into being and what they look like today.

fēn *divide; separate*   **fěn** *powder*

Both the characters above are pronounced the same, although they have different tones. This is quite normal. The next pair have the same pronunciation and the same tone, but this is unusual.

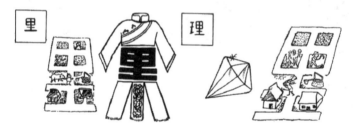

lǐ *village; mile; inside*   **lǐ** *polish; reason; principle*

At the opposite end of the spectrum we have the following three characters, which have a common phonetic element 母 **mu**, but are pronounced quite differently. This is the worst scenario!

mǔ *mother*   **měi** *every*   **hǎi** *sea*

The basic rules for writing Chinese characters

As you can imagine, there are some basic rules for writing Chinese characters which you need to master. This is important if you are to remember them, and so the brain needs to operate a kind of orderly filing system. To do this, it needs help. Chinese characters should always be written the same way, so that they become fixed in your imaginary filing system. Most characters are made up of two or more basic structural parts called 'character components', although of course some character components such as 日 **rì** (*sun*) can stand by themselves, as we have mentioned earlier. Although the total number of characters is quite large, the number of character components is limited. These components are written with a number of basic strokes, which are illustrated here:

Stroke	Name	
`	diǎn	*dot*
—	héng	*horizontal*
|	shù	*vertical*
)	piě	*left-falling*
＼	nà	*right-falling*
╱	tí	*rising*
ﾠJﾠLﾠﾠ	gōu	*hook*
┐┐	zhé	*turning*

These strokes are basically straight lines and were traditionally written in ink with a hair brush. The main directions are from top to bottom and from left to right. The arrows on the basic strokes opposite show how the characters are written by indicating the direction each stroke takes:

148

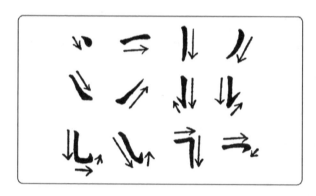

The rules of stroke order in writing Chinese characters and character components are as follows:

Example	Stroke order						Rule
十	一					十	First horizontal, then vertical
人	丿					人	First left-falling, then right-falling
三	一	二				三	From top to bottom
州	丶	丿	州	州	州	州	From left to right
月	丿	刀	月	月			First outside, then inside
四	丨	冂	冈	四	四		Finish inside, then close
小	亅	小	小				Middle, then the two sides

Numbers 1–10

Now let's try writing the numbers 1 to 10. We have shown the direction and sequence of each stroke to help you. It is helpful to think of each character, however simple or complex, as occupying a square of the same size.

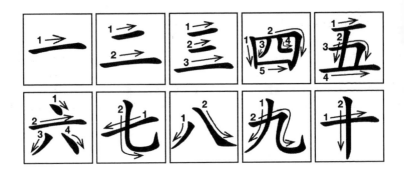

Numbers 11–99

11 is	10 + 1	=	十一
12 is	10 + 2	=	十二
20 is	2 × 10	=	二十
30 is	3 × 10	=	三十
65 is	6 × 10 + 5	=	六十五
99 is	9 × 10 + 9	=	九十九

It is worth noting that Arabic numerals are being used more and more in China. Newspapers and magazines in the People's Republic all use Arabic numerals for dates and (large) numbers. The traditional Chinese characters are still widely used in Hong Kong and Taiwan.

Practice

1 Which numbers do the following characters represent?

a 二   f 二十四
b 六   g 八十三
c 十   h 六十九
d 五   i 五十七
e 十一   j 三十六

2 Write out the following numbers in Chinese characters:
a 3   b 8   c 10   d 15   e 42   f 98   g 67

(The answers to all the exercises are in the **Key to the exercises** at the back of the book.)

Days of the week

All you need to know to write the characters for the days of the week are the two characters **xīng** (*star*) and **qī** (*period*) which, when combined together, form the word for *week*; plus the numbers 1 to 6 and the characters for *sun* (**rì**) or *day* (**tiān**). **Xīng** is made up of the radical 日 **rì** (*sun*) and 生 **shēng** (*to give birth*):

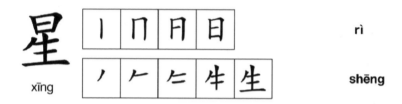

Qī is made up of the phonetic element 其 **qí** and the radical 月 **yuè** (*moon*).

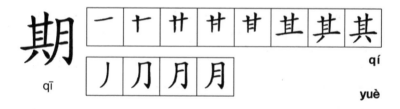

You have already met 日 **rì** (*sun*).

Tiān (*day*) is also a nice easy character:

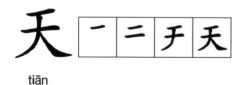

It is actually made up of one horizontal stroke plus the character 大 **dà** (*big*).

Revise the days of the week (see **Learning tip 2** in Unit 5) and then do the following exercises.

Practice

3 Which day of the week . . .

a do people go to church? 星期 ☐

b comes after Tuesday? 星期 ☐

c are many football matches played in the UK? 星期 ☐

d comes before Friday? 星期 ☐

4 Now fill in the missing characters for the days of the week:

a Sunday 星期 ☐ or 星期 ☐

b Tuesday 星 ☐ 二

c Friday 星 ☐ 五

d Thursday ☐ 期四

e Saturday ☐ 期六

How to write the date

For this you need to revise your numbers (1–31) and the characters for *moon* or *month* (**yuè** 月). Having done that, check up on how to say the date in Chinese (see Unit 5). In formal *written* Chinese **rì** 日 is used instead of **hào** 号. Thus, 21 February is:

二月二十一日   **èryuè èrshíyī rì**

Practice

5 Can you recognize the following dates?

a 十一月三日
b 六月十八日
c 七月十一日
d 十月十四日
e 八月二十九日

6 Can you write out the following dates in Chinese characters?

a Christmas Day (25 December)

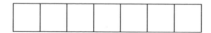

b International Women's Day (8 March) (see cartoon at the end of this unit)

c Your birthday (you might not fill all the squares in!)

d Your father's birthday

e Your mother's birthday

How to write the years

This is dead easy! Revise what you learnt in **Language note 2** in Unit 5.

1945 is 一九四五 **nián** (year)
Nián is written:

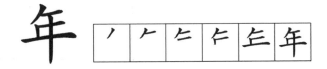

Practice

7 Write down the years represented by the Chinese characters in the spaces provided:

e.g.	一九一四年	1914
a	二〇*八年	_____
b	一九三七年	_____
c	一九四九年	_____
d	一八八五年	_____
e	一六四二年	_____

* 〇 is used for 'zero' in the People's Republic of China while the traditional character 零 **líng** is still widely used in Hong Kong and Taiwan.

How to write the time

For this you will need to learn to write the character for *minute* **fēn** 分 and the characters for *o'clock* **diǎn** (**zhōng**). Before you do this, revise how to tell the time (Unit 5). Now let's look at the two characters **diǎn** and **zhōng**.

点
diǎn

is made up of the radical for *fire* **huǒ** 灬 (also written 火) and the phonetic element 占 **zhàn**. Whoops! This one has moved a long way from its original pronunciation. **Diǎn** is written as follows:

| 丶 | 卜 | 卜 | 占 | 占 | 点 | 点 | 点 | 点 | **diǎn** |

钟
zhōng

is made up of the radical for *metal* **jīn** 钅 (also written 金) and the phonetic element 中 **zhōng**. Whew! This character is pronounced **zhōng** too! **Zhōng** is written as follows:

| 丿 | 𠂉 | 𠂉 | 钅 | 钅 | 钅 | 钅 | 钅 | 钟 | **zhōng** |

So 3.20 is 三点二十分 and 5.00 is 五点钟.

Insight

By the way, you should never give a Chinese person a clock for a present, as the character for 'clock' has exactly the same sound and tone (**zhōng**) as the character in classical Chinese meaning 'the end' or 'death'. So giving somebody a clock might send the wrong message!

You will also need to know the characters for *quarter* **kè**, for *half* **bàn**, and for *minus* or *to lack* **chà**.

刻
kè

is made up of the radical for *knife* **dāo** 刂 (also written 刀) and the phonetic element 亥 **hài**. **Kè** is written as follows:

| 丶 | 二 | 亠 | 歺 | 歺 | 亥 | 刻 | 刻 | **kè** |

半
bàn

is made up of the vertical line radical 丨 and the phonetic element 八 **bā** (often written 丷 as here), plus two horizontal lines. **Bàn** is written as follows:

| 丶 | 丷 | 丷 | 半 | 半 | **bàn** |

差

chà

is made up of the radical for *sheep* **yáng** 羊 (slanted here) and the phonetic element 工 **gōng**. No help here for pronunciation, unfortunately. **Chà** is written as follows:

丶	丷	丷	丷	兰	羊	差	差	差

chà

Practice

8 What time is it?

  a 九点一刻   *9.15*
  b 十二点二十五分
  c 六点半
  d 差十分四点
  e 八点差一刻

Can you write out the following times in Chinese characters? (One square represents one Chinese character, but there are alternatives.)

  a 6.20

  b 11.45

  c 10.10

  d 4.48

  e 7.30

Congratulations! If you have got this far you obviously have an aptitude for writing and recognizing Chinese characters. You will be able to build on your knowledge in the second half of the book.

Hopefully, some of the signs in the first half of the book will also make a bit more sense to you.

The different style of writing Chinese characters is an art form known as calligraphy, which is highly valued by the Chinese. You have just had a little taste of it!

If you have enjoyed learning something about Chinese characters, why not go on to *Read and write Chinese Script*, which will allow you to explore the Chinese script even more?

International Women's Day (March) and the day after . . .

12

Zài lǚguǎn
At the hotel

In this unit you will learn
- How to check into a hotel
- How to say if something is wrong
- How to make requests
- How to make complaints

Revise before you start

The numbers in brackets refer to the unit in which the item first appears.

- use of possessive **de**   (3)
- measure words   (4)(7)
- making comparisons   (6)(7)
- room numbers   (3)
- new situation **le**   (5)
- verb endings   (10)
- helping verbs   (6)
- how long   (9)
- when . . .   (10)
- **tài . . . le**   (7)
- not any more   (10)
- to do something for somebody   (6)
- to be in the middle of doing something   (6)

长城饭店	和平宾馆	东风旅馆
CHÁNGCHÉNG FÀNDIÀN	**HÉPÍNG BĪNGUǍN**	**DŌNGFĒNG LǙGUǍN**

In Chinese, there are several words for something that has just one word in English. Read the following passage and find out what those words are and what they mean. Furthermore, if you go to China as a foreigner can you stay in just any hotel so long as you can afford it? (Words in *italics* are explained in the box below the passage.)

Fàndiàn *Hotel*

Xuǎnzé lǚguǎn   *Choosing a hotel*

'Hotel' zhèi gè *cí* de Zhōngwén kěyǐ shì *bīnguǎn、fàndiàn、lǚguǎn* hé *lǚdiàn*. Fàndiàn hé bīnguǎn *yìbān* hěn dà, lǚguǎn hé lǚdiàn yìbān bú dà. *Guǎn* hé *diàn* dōu shì 'house' de yìsi. *Bīn* de yìsi shì 'guest', *lǚ* de yìsi shì 'travel'. *Fàn* shì 'food' de yìsi.

Zài Zhōngguó yǐqián hěn duō lǚguǎn hé lǚdiàn bú ràng wàiguó-rén zhù. *Wèishénme?* Yǒu *gèzhǒng gèyàng de yuányīn*. Yǐqián hěn duō dà fàndiàn、dà bīnguǎn yě bú ràng Zhōngguó-rén zhù, xiànzài ràng le. Dà fàndiàn、bīnguǎn de *tiáojiàn* bǐ lǚguǎn、lǚdiàn de tiáojiàn hǎo duōle. Dāngrán tāmen yě bǐ lǚguǎn、lǚdiàn guì duōle.

bīnguǎn/fàndiàn/lǚguǎn/lǚdiàn	*hotel*
cí	*word*
fàn	*food; meal*
gèzhǒng gèyàng de	*all kinds of*
tiáojiàn	*condition*
wèishénme?	*why?*
xuǎnzé	*to choose*
yìbān	*usually*
yuányīn	*reason*

QUICK VOCAB

Exercise 1 Read the opening passage twice. Then answer the following questions in Chinese. You may need to read the passage a few more times to answer all the questions.

a What are some of the Chinese words for *hotel*?
b What do they mean?
c Can foreigners stay in any hotel in China?
d Does the passage tell you why this is the case?
e What is the position for Chinese people themselves?

ānjìng	*quiet*
Bāo zǎocān ma?	*Is breakfast included?*
-zǎocān/zǎofàn	*breakfast*
biǎo	*form*
biéde	*other*
bǐjiào	*relatively*
búguò	*but, however*
cèsuǒ	*toilet*
chǎo	*noisy*
cì	*time, occasion*
dǎ diànhuà	*to telephone*
dānrén/shuāngrén fángjiān	*single/double room*
. . . de shíhou	*when*
diànshì	*television*
fúwù	*service*
fúwùtái	*reception* (lit. *service platform*)
gàosu	*to tell*
hái yǒu	*another thing* (lit. *still have*)
huán	*to return something to*
hùzhào	*passport*
jiān	*(measure word for rooms)*
jīnglǐ	*manager*
línyù	*shower*
měiyuán	*US dollar*
néng	*to be able to, can*
rúguǒ	*if*
shénme shíhou?	*when?/what time?*
shuǐ	*water*

160

tián	*to fill in* (a form)
wǎnfàn	*dinner, supper*
xiǎng yào	*would like*
xiǎoshí	*hour*
xǐzǎojiān	*bathroom*
xiū	*to repair*
yàoshi	*key*
yídìng	*certainly, definitely*
yǒu wèntí	*to have problems*
zhǎo	*to ask for, to want to see*
zhèngzài	*at this moment*
zǒu	*to leave*

Dialogues

Dialogue 1

◆ CD 2, TR 2

Frank is checking into a hotel. Listen to or read the dialogue between Frank and the **fúwùyuán** (*attendant*), and then do **Exercise 2**.

Fúwùyuán	Nín hǎo!
Frank	Nǐ hǎo! Wǒ xiǎng yào yì jiān dānrén fángjiān.
Fúwùyuán	Nín yùdìng le ma?
Frank	Méi yǒu.
Fúwùyuán	Nín yào zhù jǐ tiān?
Frank	Sān、sì tiān. Wǒ míngtiān gàosù nǐ wǒ shénme shíhou zǒu, kěyǐ ma?
Fúwùyuán	Kěyǐ.
Frank	Yì tiān duōshao qián?
Fúwùyuán	Dānrén fángjiān měi tiān wǔshí měiyuán.
Frank	Bāo zǎocān ma?
Fúwùyuán	Dāngrán bāo.
Frank	Yǒu xǐzǎojiān ma?
Fúwùyuán	Yǒu. Búguò zhǐ yǒu línyù hé cèsuǒ.

Frank	Hǎo ba.
Fúwùyuán	Qǐng xiān tián **yíxiàr** zhèi zhāng biǎo.... Qǐng gěi wǒ nínde hùzhào. Nín zǒu de shíhòu huán gěi nín.
Frank	Zhè shì wǒde hùzhào.
Fúwùyuán	Nínde fángjiān shì èr-líng-yāo, zài èr lóu. Zhè shì yàoshi.
Frank	Xièxie.
Fúwùyuán	Rúguǒ nín yǒu wèntí, qǐng gěi fúwùtái dǎ diànhuà.
Frank	Bú huì yǒu wèntí ba.

Yíxià(r) placed after the verb softens the meaning; it is often used after instructions or advice as in the earlier example.

Exercise 2 Are these statements about **Dialogue 1 duì** or **bú duì**?

	duì	bú duì?
a The price does not include breakfast.	☐	☐
b The guest can take a bath in his room.	☐	☐
c The hotel keeps the guest's passport during his stay.	☐	☐
d The guest's room is on the first floor.	☐	☐
e The guest is asked to ring reception if he has any problems.	☐	☐

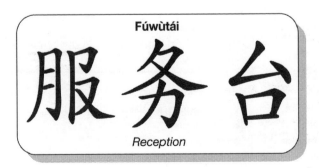

Fúwùtái

服务台

Reception

Dialogue 2

◆ CD 2, TR 2, 03:50

Frank is ringing reception from his hotel room to make some complaints. What are his complaints and how are they resolved?

Fúwùyuán	Nín hǎo. Fúwùtái.
Frank	Wǒ shì (zhù) èr-líng-yāo fángjiān de Frank. Wǒde fángjiān tài chǎo le. Néng bu néng huàn yì jiān ānjìng yìdiǎnr de?
Fúwùyuán	Duìbuqǐ, méi yǒu biéde dānrén fángjiān le. Zhǐ yǒu shuāngrén fángjiān.
Frank	Shuāngrén fángjiān yì wǎnshang duōshao qián?
Fúwùyuán	**Bǐ** dānrén fángjiān **guì èrshí měiyuán.**
Frank	Tài guì le.
Fúwùyuán	Rúguǒ míngtiān wǒmen yǒu biéde dānrén fángjiān, yídìng gěi nín huàn.
Frank	Hǎo ba. Ò, hái yǒu, wǒde línyù zěnme méi yǒu rè shuǐ?
Fúwùyuán	Duìbuqǐ, xiànzài zhèngzài xiū. Wǔ ge xiǎoshí yǐhòu jiù yǒu le.
Frank	Wǔ ge xiǎoshí yǐhòu? Bù xíng. Wǒ yào zhǎo nǐmende jīnglǐ.

You know how to say A is much more expensive than B:

A **bǐ** B **guì** deduō/duōle.

If you want to say exactly by how much A is more expensive than B, you use:

A **bǐ** B **guì** + (*by how much*)

Shuāngrén fángjiān **bǐ** dānrén fángjiān **guì** èrshí měiyuán.	*A double room is US$20 more expensive than a single.*

Exercise 3 You are staying in a hotel in China. The following dialogue is between you and the hotel *receptionist* (**fúwùyuán**). You are ringing to complain:

	Fúwùyuán	Nín hǎo. Fúwùtái.
a	**You**	(*Say your name and that you are in room 301 and your room is too small. Ask if it is possible to change to a bigger one.*)
	Fúwùyuán	Duìbuqǐ, méi yǒu biéde dānrén fángjiān le. Zhǐ yǒu shuāngrén fángjiān.
b	**You**	(*Ask how much a double room costs.*)
	Fúwùyuán	Bǐ dānrén fángjiān guì èrshí měiyuán.
c	**You**	(*Say that's too much. Another thing. Ask why there is no television in your room.*)
	Fúwùyuán	Duìbuqǐ, diànshì xiànzài zhèngzài xiū. Liǎng ge bàn xiǎoshí yǐhòu jiù xiū-hǎo le.
d	**You**	(*Say the football match will be starting in half an hour!*) (Use *after half an hour*)

cāntīng	*restaurant, canteen*
chī de	*something to eat*
hē de	*something to drink*
huǒtuǐ	*ham*
jiā	*to add*
jiàoxǐng	*to (call to) wake up*
jīròu	*chicken* (meat)
kāfēi	*coffee*
máfan	(*to*) *trouble*
nǎi	*milk*
nǎilào	*cheese*
niúròu	*beef*
qǐ	*to get up*
sānmíngzhì	*sandwich*
shénme yàng de?	*what kind?*
sòng lái	*to send over* (to the speaker)

QUICK VOCAB

164

sòng qù	to *send over* (away from the speaker)
táng	*sugar*
Wǎn'ān!	*Good night!*
xiànzài	*now*
yìhuǐ(r)	*a short while*
yǐnliào	*drink(s)*

Dialogue 3

Frank gets back to his hotel very late and finds the bar (**jiǔbā**) closed. Read the dialogue and find out what Frank does next.

Fúwùyuán	Nín hǎo. Fúwùtái.
Frank	Wǒ shì èr-líng-yāo fángjiān de Frank. Néng bu néng máfan nǐmen gěi wǒ sòng **lái** yìdiǎnr chī de? Wǒ è le.
Fúwùyuán	Duìbuqǐ, cāntīng xiànzài guān mén le. Wǒmen zhǐ yǒu sānmíngzhì hé yǐnliào.
Frank	Kěyǐ. Nǐmen yǒu shénme yàng de sānmíngzhì?
Fúwùyuán	Wǒmen yǒu nǎilào de、huǒtuǐ de、jīròu de hé niúròu de.
Frank	Wǒ yào yí ge nǎilào de、yí gè niúròu de、hé yì bēi kāfēi.
Fúwùyuán	Hǎo de. Kāfēi yào jiā nǎi, jiā táng ma?
Frank	Yào jiā nǎi, bù jiā táng.
Fúwùyuán	Xíng. Wǒmen yìhuǐr jiù sòng **qù**.
Frank	Hái yǒu. Míngtiān zǎoshang wǒ yào qǐ-de hěn zǎo. Nǐmen néng bu néng dǎ diànhuà jiàoxǐng wǒ?
Fúwùyuán	Kěyǐ. Jǐ diǎn?
Frank	Qī diǎn bàn.
Fúwùyuán	Méi wèntí.
Frank	Xièxie nǐ. Wǎn'ān.
Fúwùyuán	Wǎn'ān.

Jiǔbā

The Chinese language is much more specific about the direction in which things are said or done by the speaker than English. This means that you will often find the little words **qù** (*go*) or **lái** (*come*) at the end of a sentence: **qù** indicates *away* from the speaker and **lái** indicates *towards* the speaker:

Néng bu néng máfan nǐmen
    gěi wǒ sòng **lái** yìdiǎnr chī de?
Wǒmen yìhuǐr jiù sòng **qù**.

*Could I trouble you to send
    me up something to eat?
We'll send it up as soon as
    we can (lit. in a moment).*

Qǐng wù dǎrǎo!   *Do not disturb!*

Insight

Rooms in small hotels in China are usually equipped with thermos flasks containing hot water for you to make tea. These are emptied and refilled every morning often quite early so if you don't want to be disturbed at say 7am, remember to put the 'Don't disturb' notice on your door. When you leave your room, you can put the thermos flask(s) outside your door so that they can be refilled before your return

Exercise 4 Make the following requests in Chinese using the pattern: **Néng bu néng gěi wǒ . . . ?**. If you want to be more polite, you can say **néng bu néng máfan nǐ(men) gěi wǒ . . . ?**. The measure word for each object is written in brackets after it.

a Can you send me up something to eat?
something to drink?
a cup of tea, with milk but no sugar?
two sandwiches, one cheese, and one ham?

tǎnzi (tiáo) **wèishēngzhǐ** (juǎn) **xiāngzào** (kuài) **nuǎnshuǐpíng** (gè)

b Can you give me a wake-up call?
give me a phone call?
buy me a bottle (**píng**) of wine?
give me another blanket/roll of toilet paper?
give me a bigger piece of soap?
give me a thermos flask (of hot water)?

◀》 **CD 2, TR 2, 05:25**

Exercise 5 Listen to the recording and fill in the following blanks. You need to remember the words **fúwù** (*service*) and **lǐmào** (*to be polite/courteous*). If you haven't got the recording, read the dialogue which comes after this exercise and then fill in the blanks.

a Frank now stays at _____ Hotel.
b The conditions in the hotel are _____ .
c The service there is _____ .
d The staff are _____ .
e He has changed his hotel _____ .

Lìli	Nǐ xiànzài zhù zài nǎr?
Frank	Dōngfāng Bīnguǎn.
Lìli	Tiáojiàn zěnmeyàng?
Frank	Tiáojiàn búcuò, kěshì fúwù bù zěnmeyàng.
Lìli	Fúwù zěnme bù hǎo?
Frank	Fúwùyuán bú tài lǐmào.
Lìli	Wèishénme bú huàn yí ge dìfang?
Frank	Wǒ yǐjing huàn le liǎng **cì**. Zhè shì dì-sān **cì** le.

Cì (*time*(s)) is like **tiān** (*day*) and **nián** (*year*) in that it acts as both a measure word and a noun. *Once* is **yí cì**, twice is **liǎng cì** (note that it is **liǎng** and not **èr**), *three times* is **sān cì**, and so on. To say the first time, the second time, and so on all you have to do is put the little word **dì** in front. Note, however, that the second time is **dì-èr cì** and not **dì liǎng cì**.

Exercise 6   The receptionist at a hotel is asking you a few questions. How would you respond?

	Fúwùyuán	Nǐ yùdìng le ma?
a	**You**	(*No. I hope* (**xīwàng**) *you've still got rooms.*)
	Fúwùyuán	Wǒmen hái yǒu jǐ jiān. Nǐ yào shénme fángjiān?
b	**You**	(*A double room and a single room.*)
	Fúwùyuán	Nǐmen dǎsuàn zhù jǐ tiān?
c	**You**	(*Three or four days. We'll tell you tomorrow when we'll be leaving. Is that OK?*)
	Fúwùyuán	Xíng. Jīntiān wǎnshang zài bīnguǎn chī wǎnfàn ma?
d	**You**	(*No thank you, we've already eaten.*)

Quick review

◀) CD 2, TR 2, 06:04

You are checking into a hotel. Ask the following questions in Chinese.

a Is breakfast included?
b When is lunch (**wǔfàn**)?
c Is there a television in the room?
d Have you got a bigger single room?
e How much is it per night?

Vocabulary

a 'Ānjìng' and 'chǎo' are opposite in meaning. What do they mean respectively?
b What is the Chinese for 'toilet'?
c Is 'shuāngrén fángjiān' a single room or a double room?
d 'Fúwù' means 'service'. What are 'fúwù-tái' and 'fúwù-yuán'?
e When you want to have milk to go with your coffee, do you ask for 'táng' or 'nǎi'?

13

....

Huǒchē、 piào hé chūzūchē
Trains, tickets and taxis

In this unit you will learn
- How to ask for and understand information about trains
- How to understand train announcements
- How to buy train tickets
- Many useful time expressions

Revise before you start

- yāo (*one*)   (3)
- numbers over 100   (7)
- measure words   (4)(7)
- use of **de**   (3)(5)
- making comparisons   (6)(7)
- tài . . . le   (7)
- noun + on   (5)

- **duō** + verb   (10)
- how long   (9)
- first . . . then . . .   (9)
- use of **háishi**   (6)
- use of **ba**   (3)
- when . . .   (10)

....

Insight

Trains in China

In China, trains are numbered but without indicating the destination. Most passenger trains are numbered by using a capital Chinese phonetic letter followed by numerals.

170

- C – Intercity train, Chéngjì Lièchē (城际列车) in Chinese
  They run between two nearby cities, such as the 120-kilometre Beijing–Tianjin Intercity Railway.

- D – Electric multiple units (EMU) train, Dòngchē (动车) in Chinese
  These trains are high-speed or bullet trains in China, widely used to provide fast and frequent transport between main cities, such as Beijing to Shanghai.

- G – High-speed train, Gāotiě (高铁) in Chinese
  These are the fastest long-distance trains running in China.

- K – Fast train, Kuàichē (快车) in Chinese
  The top speed of K trains is 120 km/h. They have more stops than T trains.

- L – Temporary train, Línshí Kèchē (临时客车) in Chinese
  This series of L trains is only in operation during peak travel times, such as Chinese Spring Festival and the National Holiday. These trains will not be listed in the official 'fixed' train timetables.

- T – Express train, Tèkuài (特快) in Chinese
  T trains have limited stops en route, mainly stopping in major cities. Almost every T series type of train is equipped with soft sleepers, soft seats, hard sleepers and hard seats.

- Y – Tourist train, Lǚyóu Lièchē (旅游列车) in Chinese
  Y trains are for the convenience of tourists and their destinations are the most popular tourist attractions. For example, there are Y trains from Beijing North Railway Station to the Great Wall.

- Z – Direct express train, Zhídá (直达) in Chinese
  Z-trains are generally non-stop or make very few stops en route.

Trains without a prefix letter are ordinary trains and usually have four digits in front of them.

In China, they don't have first-class tickets (**tóuděng piào**) and second-class tickets (**èrděng piào**). But they do have four types of tickets: **ruǎnwò**, **ruǎnzuò**, **yìngwò** and **yìngzuò**. **Ruǎnwò** is really a first-class sleeper. **Ruǎnzuò** is just first class. **Yìngwò** is second-class sleeper and **yìngzuò** is second class. As you may have noticed, these Chinese words involve different combinations of four characters: **ruǎn** meaning *soft*, **yìng** (*hard*), **wò** (*lying down*), and **zuò** (*seat*).

Note that train numbers use the word **cì** (see Unit 12) after the number:

train number 21 = **21 cì** (**èrshíyī cì**)
train number 161 = **161 cì** (**yìbǎi liùshíyī cì; yāo-liù-yāo cì**)

Train numbers of three digits can either be broken down into single digits or said as one number. **Yāo** is used instead of **yī** to avoid any confusion (see Unit 3).

When train announcements are made, the sequence is different from the one you are used to in English. The order is normally **kāi wǎng** (drive towards) + destination + number (of train). The time is not usually mentioned. Do note that your ticket is only valid for a particular time.

Kāi wǎng Tiāntán   *To Tiantan* (Temple of Heaven)

Exercise 1 What is the Chinese for these phrases?

a 'soft' sleeper
b 'hard' seat
c 'soft' seat
d 'hard' sleeper
e first class
f second class

What is the English for these Chinese words?

g kèchē
h tèkuài
i huǒchē
j kuàichē
k zhíkuài

cì	(number of trains)
dàgài	*approximately*
děi	*to need, must*
děng	*to wait*
hòutiān	*the day after tomorrow*
kāi	*to drive*
míngbai	*to understand* (colloquial)
něi zhǒng?	*which kind?*
rénmínbì	*Chinese currency*
shàng	*to board* (vehicle)
shuì	*to sleep*
suǒyǐ	*so, therefore*
ya	(end particle indicating surprise)
Yōnghé Gōng	*the Lama Temple* (in Beijing)
yǒu shénme . . . ?	*in what ways . . . ?* (lit. *has what*)
Yǒu shénme bù yíyàng?	*In what ways are they different?*
zhǎo (qián)	*to give change*

QUICK VOCAB

Travelling by train

èrděng	*second-class* (ticket)
ruǎnwò	*'soft' sleeper*
ruǎnzuò	*'soft' seat*
tèkuài	*special express*
tóuděng	*first-class* (ticket)
yìngwò	*'hard' sleeper*
yìngzuò	*'hard' seat*
zhíkuài	*express* (train)

Dialogues

Dialogue 1

◀) CD 2, TR 3

Frank is buying a train ticket from Běijīng to Shànghǎi. Listen to, or read, the dialogue and find out which trains go to Shànghǎi.

Frank	Wǒ xiǎng mǎi yì zhāng qù Shànghǎi de huǒchē piào.
Assistant	Něi tiān de?
Frank	Hòutiān de.
Assistant	Yào něi cì chē de?
Frank	Wǒ bù míngbai nǐde yìsi.
Assistant	Qù Shànghǎi de huǒchē yǒu shísān cì、 èrshíyī cì hé yāo-liù-yāo cì.
Frank	Tāmen yǒu shénme bù yíyàng?
Assistant	Shísān cì hé èrshíyī cì shì tèkuài, yìbǎi liùshíyī cì shì zhíkuài.
Frank	Shénme shì tèkuài hé zhíkuài?
Assistant	Tèkuài jiù shì fēicháng kuài de yìsi. Shísān cì tèkuài bǐ yāo-liù-yāo cì zhíkuài **kuài sì、 wǔ ge xiǎoshí.**
Frank	Shì bu shì tèkuài de piào yě bǐ zhíkuài de piào guì?
Assistant	Nà dāngrán le.

174

Note that if you want to say that train number 13 is four hours quicker than train number 161 you say:

    13 cì bǐ 161 cì **kuài** (*quick*) + *by how much*
    13 cì bǐ 161 cì **kuài sì ge xiǎoshí**

There is another example using **màn** *slow* in **Dialogue 2**. Look out for it!

This is the same pattern as you used in Unit 12, only here you are talking about a difference in time rather than money.

Shì bu shì can also be put at the beginning or in the middle of a sentence as well as at the end (see Unit 3). It conveys the idea that the speaker is confident that what she says is correct but wishes to soften the tone. You might have noticed that there is no tone on the second **shi** when it occurs at the end of a sentence.

Exercise 2   Answer the following questions based on the opening passage and **Dialogue 1**.

a Which trains go to Shanghai?
b Which train is faster, **zhíkuài** or **tèkuài**?
c Is it cheaper to buy a ticket for a **tèkuài** than for a **zhíkuài** train?
d What are the two ways of saying train number 351 in Chinese?
e Is train number 243 faster than train number 43?

Some useful time expressions

◀) **CD 2, TR 3, 01:25**

qiánnián	*the year before last*
qùnián	*last year*
jīnnián	*this year*
míngnián	*next year*
hòunián	*the year after next*

shàng shàng ge yuè	*the month before last*
shàng (ge) yuè	*last month*
zhè/zhèi (ge) yuè	*this month*
xià (ge) yuè	*next month*
xià xià ge yuè	*the month after next*
shàng shàng ge xīngqī	*the week before last*
shàng (ge) xīngqī	*last week*
zhè/zhèi (ge) xīngqī	*this week*
xià (ge) xīngqī	*next week*
xià xià ge xīngqī	*the week after next*
qiántiān	*the day before yesterday*
zuótiān	*yesterday*
jīntiān	*today*
míngtiān	*tomorrow*
hòutiān	*the day after tomorrow*

Dialogue 2

🔊 CD 2, TR 3, 02:12

Ann is now at the Beijing Railway Station ticket office. What type of ticket does she want to buy and what ticket does she buy in the end?

Ann	Qǐng wèn, hái yǒu shíbā hào èrshíyī cì de piào ma?
Assistant	Yǒu. Nín yào něi zhǒng piào?
Ann	Wǒ yào sān zhāng yìngwò.
Assistant	Duìbuqǐ, yìngwò zhǐ yǒu yì zhāng le. Wǒmen hái yǒu ruǎnwò hé yìngzuò.
Ann	Ruǎnwò bǐ yìngwò guì duōshao?
Assistant	Yìbǎi bāshí kuài.
Ann	Nàme shíbā hào yāo-liù-yāo cì hái yǒu yìngwò ma?
Assistant	Yǒu.
Ann	Tài hǎo le! Wǒ mǎi sān zhāng shíbā hào yāo-liù-yāo cì de yìngwò piào.
Assistant	Yāo-liù-yāo cì bǐ èrshíyī cì màn sì ge xiǎoshí.
Ann	Méi guānxi. Wǒmen kěyǐ zài huǒchē shàng duō shuì sì ge xiǎoshí.

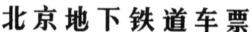

Ticket for the underground/subway

Train ticket

火车站 候车室

Huǒchēzhàn *Train station* **Hòuchēshì** *Waiting room*

Exercise 3 In Dialogue 2, there are two useful structures, or patterns, for buying tickets.

i **Qǐng wèn, hái yǒu X ma?** *Have you still got X?*
ii **Wǒmen mǎi X zhāng** *We would like to have*

(*time*) **de** (*type/event*) **piào**.   *X number of Y tickets for Z*
                                                   (where Y is the type
                                                   of ticket and Z is the time).

Now here's some practice: You want to know if the following kinds of tickets are still available.

Example: tickets for next Tuesday's football match
              You ask: **Qǐng wèn, hái yǒu xià ge xīngqī'èr de zúqiú piào ma?**

a tickets for tonight's film
b tickets for the flight (use **fēijī**) on 4th October
c tickets for train number 153
d tickets for trains going to Tianjin

If the answer to these questions is *yes*, you can simply say **Wǒ yào X zhāng**. If, however, you know the tickets you want to buy are available, you would use pattern **ii**.

Example: Two film tickets for 2 o'clock Sunday afternoon
              You say: **Wǒ mǎi liǎng zhāng xīngqī'èr xiàwǔ liǎng diǎn de diànyǐng piào.**

e three tickets for tonight's film
f four tickets for the flight on October 4th
g five tickets for train number 153
h six tickets for trains going to Tianjin

Exercise 4 Can you tell your Chinese friends something about British trains in Chinese?

a There are two types of tickets: first class and second class.
b First-class tickets are more expensive than second-class tickets.
c Trains in Britain are both fast and comfortable.

If you are from **Fǎguó, Měiguó, Déguó, Yìdàlì** or other countries, say something similar to the above sentences in Chinese.

Dialogue 3

🔊 CD 2, TR 3, 03:42

Chūzū qìchēzhàn *Taxi rank*

The following dialogue is between a taxi driver (**sījī**) and his customer (**chèngkè**). Before you read the dialogue, listen to the recording and answer the following two questions:

1 How many places did the man plan to visit?
2 How much did the taxi-driver charge him in the end?

Now read the dialogue and see if you answered the questions correctly.

Sījī	Nín qù nǎr?
Chèngkè	Wǒ xiǎng xiān qù Yōnghé Gōng, zài qù Tiāntán.
Sījī	Qǐng shàng chē ba.
Chèngkè	Nǐ néng bu néng xiān gàosù wǒ qù zhè liǎng ge dìfang dàgài děi duōshao qián?
Sījī	Qù Yōnghé Gōng sìshíwǔ kuài, zài qù Tiāntán yě shì sìshíwǔ kuài.
Chèngkè	Shì rénmínbì háishì měiyuán?
Sījī	Rénmínbì.
Chèngkè	Hǎo ba.
	(getting off at Tiāntán Park)
Chèngkè	Xièxie nǐ. Zhè shì yìbǎi kuài. Bié zhǎo (qián) le.
Sījī	Duìbuqǐ. Yígòng yìbǎi jiǔshí kuài.
Chèngkè	Zěnme shì yìbǎi jiǔshí kuài?
Sījī	Nǐ qù Yōnghé Gōng de shíhou, wǒ děng le nǐ liǎng ge xiǎoshí. Děng yí ge xiǎoshí wǔshí kuài. Suǒyǐ yígòng yìbǎi jiǔshí kuài.

| Chèngkè | Nǐ zěnme méi xiān gàosù wǒ? |
| Sījī | Nǐ méi wèn ya. |

Line 4 in **Dialogue 3** is a long sentence. **Bié zháojí** (*don't worry*)!
Try the following two exercises and you'll be able to say it fluently.

◀》 **CD 2, TR 3, 05:17**

Exercise 5   This exercise is called 'back chaining'. You practise long
sentences like these by reading them phrase by phrase (the whole
gradually increasing in length), starting with the end of the sentence first.

yìngwò piào
yāo-liù-yāo cì de yìngwò piào
shíbā hào yāo-liù-yāo cì de yìngwò piào
Wǒ mǎi sān zhāng shíbā hào yāo-liù-yāo cì de yìngwò piào

*I'll buy three second-class sleeper tickets for train number 161 on
the 18th.*
(*lit.* I buy three measure word eighteen number one six one time
hard sleeper ticket.)

duōshao qián?
dàgài děi duōshao qián?
qù zhèi liǎng ge dìfang dàgài děi duōshao qián?
xiān gàosu wǒ qù zhèi liǎng ge dìfang dàgài děi duōshao qián?
Nǐ néng bu néng xiān gàosu wǒ qù zhèi liǎng ge dìfang dàgài děi
duōshao qián?

*Can you first tell me roughly how much it costs to go to these
two places?*
(*lit.* you can not can first tell me go these two places roughly need
how much money?)

Exercise 6   The long sentence you have just practised has two parts.
The main part is:

Nǐ néng bu néng gàosu wǒ 'X'.   *Can you tell me 'X'?*

The second part can be an independent question such as *how old is he?* or *where does she live?*. In the dialogue the independent question is **qù zhè liǎng ge dìfang yào duōshao qián?** (*how much does it cost to get to these two places?*).

Now request the following information starting with **nǐ néng bu néng gàosu wǒ**:

Example: How old is he?
You ask: **Nǐ néng bu néng gàosu wǒ tā duō dà le?**

First try these independent questions and then combine each one with the main sentence.

a   Where does she live?
b   What is your telephone number?
c   How old is his daughter?
d   How long do they intend staying there?

Exercise 7   Put each group of phrases into the correct order to make complete questions in Chinese.

Example: How much, by train, go to Nanjing?
You ask: **Zuò huǒchē qù Nánjīng děi duōshao qián?**

a   How much/to go to Xī'ān/by train?
b   To fly/how long/from London to Shànghǎi?
c   To go to Hépíng Hotel/by taxi/how much?
d   By ship (**chuán**)/how long/to go from Japan to China?

Quick review

Can you match the Chinese words on the left with their English equivalents on the right? There will be one word in the left-hand column that you will not recognize. Which one is it? What must it mean? (Notice that all the Chinese words have the character **chē** in them.)

a	zìxíngchē	i	coach
b	huǒchē	ii	express (train)
c	chūzū (qì)chē	iii	bicycle
d	gōnggòng qìchē	iv	train
e	kuàichē	v	taxi
f	chángtú qìchē	vi	normal (passenger) train
g	pǔtōng kèchē	vii	bus

Chūzū qìchē

Now try and match these timewords:

a	hòutiān	i	the day before yesterday
b	qiántiān	ii	yesterday
c	míngtiān	iii	today
d	jīntiān	iv	tomorrow
e	zuótiān	v	the day after tomorrow

14

Yúlè huódòng
Free time and entertainment

In this unit you will learn
- How to say what you like doing in your free time
- How to ask somebody what they would like to do
- About sports and hobbies
- About making arrangements
- About summer and winter, indoor and outdoor activities

Revise before you start

- use of **de** after verb (8)
- **zuì** (*most*) (7)
- **gèng** (*even more*) (8)
- use of **háishi** (6)
- both . . . and . . . (9)

- to be in the middle of doing something (6)
- making comparisons (6)(7)
- A is the same as B (6)

A park in Chinese is actually a public garden. Do you remember Frank in Unit 6? If you go to China, try to get up early at least one morning, say at 6 o'clock, and go to a local park. You too will be fascinated by what some of the Chinese do there. The following passage tells us a little bit more about what people do in a park.

Qù gōngyuán   *Going to the park*

◀)) **CD 2, TR 4**

Hěn duō Zhōngguó-rén qǐ-de hěn zǎo. Tāmen rènwéi zǎo shuì zǎo qǐ duì shēntǐ hǎo. Zǎoshang tāmen zuò shénme? Bù shǎo rén qù gōngyuán.

Zài gōngyuán lǐ, tāmen dǎ tàijíquán、zuò qìgōng、chàng gē、tiào wǔ, děngděng. Yǒu de lǎo rén zài gōngyuán sàn lǐ bù、xià qí、dǎ pái、chàng jīngjù.

Hěn duō gōngyuán dōu yǒu hú. Zài běifāng xiàtiān kěyǐ zài hú lǐ yóuyǒng, dōngtiān kěyǐ zài hú shàng huá bīng.

běifāng	*the north*
chàng (gē)	*to sing (a song)*
chàng jīngjù	*to sing Peking opera*
dǎ pái	*to play cards*
děngděng	*etc.*
dōngtiān	*winter*
gōngyuán	*park*
hú	*lake*

QUICK VOCAB

184

huá bīng	*to skate*
lǎo	*old*
lǎo rén	*old person/people*
qǐ	*to get up*
rènwéi	*to think, to believe*
sàn bù	*to stroll*
shǎo	*few, less*
bù shǎo	*quite a lot*
tiào wǔ	*to dance*
xià qí	*to play chess*
xiàtiān	*summer*
yóuyǒng	*to swim*
zài (hú) lǐ/shàng	*in/on (the lake)*
zǎo	*early*
zǎo shuì	*early to bed*
zǎo qǐ	*early to rise*

QUICK VOCAB

Exercise 1 When you have the opportunity, ask a Chinese person these questions:

a Do the Chinese get up very early?
b Where do you go in the morning?
c What do old people do in the park?
d Do you swim in the lake?

Insight

There is a huge difference between the type of Chinese which is spoken and the type of Chinese which is written. Spoken Chinese is normally much more informal than written Chinese. Sometimes a different word is used in written Chinese to convey the same meaning as a simpler word in the spoken language. There is a good example of this in the passage above where **rènwéi** (*to be of the opinion that*) is used instead of **xiǎng** (*to think*).

This need not concern you very much on a practical level because you are concentrating on spoken Chinese. Unless, of course, you plan to get to grips with the Chinese writing system at some stage and therefore read material in Chinese

characters. Why not go on to *Complete Mandarin Chinese* once
you've finished this book or to *Read and write Chinese Script* if
you are especially interested in Chinese characters?

Àolínpǐkè	*Olympic*
bàn	*to handle*
bàng	*excellent* (colloquial)
biǎoyǎn	*show, performance; to act, perform*
dànyuànrúcǐ	*I hope so*
dào	*to arrive*
děng	*to wait*
fāngbiàn	*convenient*
gèng duō de	*more* (of something)
hǎo jiǔ bú jiàn	*long time no see*
hòu bàn (chǎng)	*second half* (of a show)
huódòng	*activity*
jīhuì	*opportunity*
juédìng	*to decide*
liànxí	*to practise, exercise*
lóushàng	*upstairs*
lǚxíng	*to travel; travel*
lǚxíngtuán	*tourist group*
niánqīng	*young*
pái	*row* (of seats)
X pái Y hào	*number Y in row X*
qiānzhèng	*visa*
qiūtiān	*autumn*
Shì nǐ ya!	*It's you!*
shòu	*thin*
shūfu	*comfortable*
tán	*to talk, chat*
tán liàn'ài	*to be in love, go steady* (lit. *talk love*)
tiào dísīkē	*to go disco dancing*
tǐng	*quite, fairly*
wèizi	*seat*
xué-hǎo	*to master* (see Unit 10)
yǎn	*to act*

yúlè	entertainment
yùndòng	sports, take exercises
yùndònghuì	sports meeting, games
zhǎo	to look for
zhěngtiān	all day
zìjǐ	oneself
zìyóu	freedom
zuìjìn	recent, recently

Dialogues

Nǐ xǐhuan shénme yùndòng?   *What's your favourite sport/game?*

dǎ	to play . . .	(tī) zúqiú	(play) football
dǎ pīngpāngqiú	. . . pingpong	qí mǎ	horse riding
dǎ lánqiú	. . . basketball		(lit. *to ride horse*)
dǎ yǔmáoqiú	. . . badminton	huá xuě	skiing (lit. *to slide snow*)
dǎ qūgùnqiú	. . . hockey		
dǎ wǎngqiú	. . . tennis	(dǎ) Taìjíjiàn	(do) *Tai Chi sword*

Dialogue 1

◀) CD 2, TR 4, 01:06

Edward and Xiǎo Fù are talking about their favourite sports. Listen to the recording and make a note of what sports they each like before you read the dialogue.

Edward	Nǐ xǐhuan shénme yùndòng?
Xiǎo Fù	Wǒ zuì xǐhuan **wǎngqiú** (i) hé **yóuyǒng** (ii).
Edward	Wǒ yě xǐhuan **wǎngqiú** (i), kěshì gèng xǐhuan **zúqiú** (iv).

Xiǎo Fù	Nǐ xǐhuan **tī** (iii) **zúqiú** (iv) háishì kàn **zúqiú** (iv)?
Edward	Dōu xǐhuān.
Xiǎo Fù	Wǒ zhǐ xǐhuan kàn, bù xǐhuan **tī** (iii).

Exercise 2 Use the groups of words below to substitute for the sports in **Dialogue 1**. a under column i substitutes for (i) in the dialogue, i.e. **pīngpāngqiú** substitutes for **wǎngqiú**; a under column ii substitutes for (ii) in the dialogue and so on. Do the same with b to e. Each time you have completed one row of substitution read out the dialogue using the new words.

	i	ii	iii	iv
a	pīngpāngqiú	huá bīng	dǎ	lánqiú
b	lánqiú	xià qí	dǎ	yǔmáoqiú
c	yǔmáoqiú	qí mǎ	dǎ	qūgùnqiú
d	qūgùnqiú	huá xuě	dǎ	tàijíquán
e	tàijíquán	taìjíjiàn	dǎ	pái

Exercise 3 What do you like and dislike?

You are given three activities each time. Use i to show an ascending order of preference. Use ii to rank your dislikes. We have given you sample answers in the **Key to the exercises**.

i   Wǒ xǐhuan A, gèng xǐhuan B, zuì xǐhuan C.
ii Wǒ bù xǐhuan A, gèng bù xǐhuan B, zuì bù xǐhuan C.

Example: diànyǐng, jīngjù, yīnyuèhuì
   i   Wǒ xǐhuan kàn jīngjù, gèng xǐhuan kàn diànyǐng, zuì xǐhuan tīng yīnyuèhuì.
   ii Wǒ bù xǐhuan tīng yīnyuèhuì, gèng bù xǐhuan kàn diànyǐng, zuì bù xǐhuan kàn jīngjù.

a   zuò fēijī, zuò chuán, zuò huǒchē
b   qí zìxíngchē, qí mǎ (*horse*), qí mótuōchē (*motorbike*)
c   zuò gōnggòng qìchē (*bus*), zuò dìtiě (*underground/subway*), zuò chūzū (qì)chē

188

d   kàn jīngjù, kàn diànshì, kàn diànyǐng
e   tīng gǔdiǎn (*classical*) yīnyuè, tīng xiàndài (*modern*) yīnyuè, tīng
     liúxíng (*pop*) yīnyuè

Dialogue 2

🔊 **CD 2, TR 4, 02:36**

Yáo Mínglì is asking Ann about her forthcoming holiday. Why has
Ann not yet made up her mind?

Mínglì	Tīngshuō jīnnián qiūtiān nǐ yào qù Zhōngguó lǚxíng.
Ann	Duì. Kěshì wǒ hái méi juédìng zěnme qù.
Mínglì	Zěnme qù? Dāngrán zuò fēijī qù. Zuò huǒchē yòu màn yòu bù shūfu.
Ann	Wǒ bú shì nèi ge yìsi. Wǒ hái méi juédìng gēn lǚxíngtuán qù háishì zìjǐ qù.
Mínglì	Gēn lǚxíngtuán qù hěn fāngbiàn, kěshì yòu guì yòu bú zìyóu.
Ann	Zìjǐ qù yòu piányi yòu zìyóu, kěshì zhēn bù fāngbiàn.
Mínglì	Zěnme bù fāngbiàn?
Ann	Wǒ yào zìjǐ qù bàn qiānzhèng、dìng fēijī piào、zhǎo lǚguǎn, děngděng.
Mínglì	Kěshì zìjǐ qù kěyǐ yǒu gèng duō de jīhuì liànxí Zhōngwén.
Ann	Duì, wǒ yídìng yào xué-hǎo Zhōngwén, èr-líng-líng-bā nián qù Běijīng kàn Àolínpǐkè Yùndònghuì.

Note that if you want to say that something still hasn't happened,
you put the word **hái** in front of **méi** (**yǒu**):

Kěshì wǒ **hái** méi juédìng zěnme qù.   *But I haven't yet decided*
                                            how to go.

Tā **hái** méi yǒu lái (ne).   *She still hasn't come.*

There is an optional **ne** at the end of such sentences.

Exercise 4   The following passage is based on **Dialogue 2**. Fill in the blanks (use one word per blank) according to the information given in the dialogue.

Ann jīnnián (**a**) dǎsuàn qù Zhōngguó (**b**). Kěshì tā (**c**) (**d**) juédìng gēn lǚxíngtuán qù (**e**) zìjǐ qù. Gēn lǚxíngtuán qù (**f**) guì (**g**) bú zìyóu. Zìjǐ qù yòu (**h**) yòu (**i**). Kěshì zìjǐ qù hěn (**j**) fāngbiàn. Tā yào zìjǐ qù (**k**) qiānzhèng, (**l**) fēijī piào, (**m**) lǚguǎn, děngděng.

Dialogue 3

Lǎo Qián and Xiǎo Zhào meet at the cinema entrance. Read the dialogue to find out what they have been doing lately.

diànyǐngyuàn   *cinema*

Xiǎo Zhào	Lǎo Qián, hǎo jiǔ bú jiàn.
Lǎo Qián	Xiǎo Zhào, shì nǐ ya!
Xiǎo Zhào	Nín xiànzài zài zuò shénme?
Lǎo Qián	Gēn yǐqián yíyàng. Měi tiān dǎda pái、xiàxia qí、dǎda tàijíquán, tǐng yǒu yìsi.
Xiǎo Zhào	Nín bǐ yǐqián niánqīng duōle.
Lǎo Qián	Nǎli, nǎli. Lǎo duōle. Xiǎo Zhào, nǐ zuìjìn zài zuò shénme?
Xiǎo Zhào	Wǒ zhèngzài tán liàn'ài. Zhěngtiān mǎi dōngxi、kàn diànyǐng、tiào dísīkē. Zhēn méi yìsi.
Lǎo Qián	Nǐ bǐ yǐqián shòu duōle.
Xiǎo Zhào	Tán liàn'ài yòu lèi yòu bú zìyóu.
Lǎo Qián	Nǐde nǚ péngyou ne?
Xiǎo Zhào	Tā hái méi lái ne. Wǒ zài děng tā.

Tán liàn'ài
To be in love

Gāng jié hūn
Just married

Sān nián yǐhòu
Three years later

◀) CD 2, TR 4, 04:03

Exercise 5   You are having a conversation with a Chinese friend. You begin:

a	**You**	(*Greet Xiǎo Wáng and say you haven't seen him for ages.*)
	Friend	Nǐ hǎo, Xiǎo Mǎ. Shì nǐ ya!
b	**You**	(*Ask him what he is up to these days.*)
	Friend	Gēn yǐqián yíyàng. Hái zài xuéxiào (*school*) gōngzuò.
c	**You**	(*Ask if he is married.*)
	Friend	Hái méi yǒu. Wǒmen míngnián jié hūn.
d	**You**	(*Ask him who he is waiting for.*)
	Friend	Wǒ zài děng wǒ nǚ péngyou. Nǐ qù nǎr?
e	**You**	(*Tell him that you are going swimming.*)
	Friend	Hǎo, zánmen yǐhòu zài tán.
f	**You**	(*Say goodbye to him.*)
	Friend	Zàijiàn!

Dialogue 4

Edward and Xiǎo Fù ran into each other during the interval of a show. Where are they sitting and what do they think of the performance tonight?

Edward	Nǐ zuò nǎr?	楼上
Xiǎo Fù	Wǔ pái sì hào.	
Edward	Nǐ de wèizi zhēn hǎo.	
Xiǎo Fù	Nǐ zài nǎr?	**Lóushàng**
Edward	Wǒ zài lóushàng shí pái sānshí hào.	*upstairs*
Xiǎo Fù	Nǐ juéde jīntiān de biǎoyǎn zěnmeyàng?	
Edward	Tāmen chàng-de tǐng hǎo. Nǐ juéde ne?	楼下
Xiǎo Fù	Wǒ juéde tāmen chàng-de hái bú cuò. Kěshì yǎn-de bù zěnmeyàng.	**Lóuxià** *downstairs*
Edward	Tīngshuō hòumiàn de biǎoyǎn hěn bàng.	
Xiǎo Fù	Dànyuànrúcǐ.	

Note that there are still a few traces of the classical Chinese language in use today. Classical Chinese was monosyllabic but it often put four characters together to express a particular idea. Many of these four-character phrases became set phrases and still appear in the language today. **Dànyuànrúcǐ** is an example of such a four-character phrase. Other examples are:

wànshìrúyì	(*lit*. 10,000 things like wish)	*your heart's desire*
yílùpíng'ān	(*lit*. all road peace)	*bon voyage*
yílùshùnfēng	(*lit*. all road following wind)	*bon voyage*

Such phrases are usually preceded by **zhù nǐ (men)** . . . (*wish you . . .*). This is sometimes omitted, especially in written Chinese.

Insight

Seating in Chinese cinemas and theatres: as you will see in **Exercise 6**, all the even seat numbers are grouped together on one side and all the uneven ones on the other. Only seat numbers 1 and 2 are next to each other sequentially. This means that when you go into a Chinese cinema you need to check whether your seat numbers are **shuānghào** (*even*) or **dānhào** (*odd*). If they are even, you will need to follow the sign for 双号 seats and if odd, the signs for 单号 seats. It is obviously important to understand the way the seating is organized if ever you are buying seats yourself.

Exercise 6 Three rows of seats are given in each section. Give the Chinese for the seat number ○ in each of the three sections A, B, and C.

双号   *Example*: Row 14, No. 19, upstairs   单号
      Lóushàng shísì pái shíjiǔ hào.

Shuānghào   **Dānhào**

A 1 30 28 26 24 ...... 8 6 4 2 1 3 5 7 ......21 23 ○ 27
   2 30 28 26 24 ...... 8 6 4 2 1 3 ○ 7 ......21 23 25 27
   3 30 28 ○ 24 ...... 8 6 4 2 1 3 5 7 ......21 23 25 27
B 24 30 28 26 ○ ...... 8 6 4 2 1 3 5 7 ......21 23 25 27
   25 30 28 26 24 ...... 8 6 ○ 2 1 3 5 7 ......21 23 25 27
   26 30 28 26 24 ...... 8 6 4 2 1 3 5 7 ......21 ○ 25 27
C [Lóushàng]
   11 30 28 26 24 ...... 8 ○ 4 2 1 3 5 7 ......21 23 25 27
   12 30 ○ 26 24 ...... 8 6 4 2 1 3 5 7 ......21 23 25 27
   13 30 28 26 24 ...... 8 6 4 2 1 3 5 7 ......○ 23 25 27

Exercise 7 Tell your Chinese guests where their seats are.

a	b	c	d
Row A No. 12	Row J No. 37	Row F No. 40 upstairs	Row K No. 2

Exercise 8 Your Chinese guests are planning a night out. Tell them in Chinese the options they have in their local area, which are shown in the advertisements overleaf.

bāléi	*ballet*	**gējù**	*opera*
huàjù	*play*	**tiān'é**	*swan*

You also need to know the word **bàng**. This time it means *pound in weight* (see Exercise 2, Unit 7, where it means *pound in money*). You should not now be surprised to learn that the Chinese character for **bàng** (*pound*) in money is different from the character for **bàng** (*pound*) in weight. Here they are:

bàng

The right-hand side is exactly the same for both, but a pound in money has metal or gold on the left-hand side and a pound in weight has stone or mineral.

bàng

Film: *Winter Time* 18.00, 20.00, 22.00 *Saturday, 25th October* *Tickets: £5, £6.50*	**Ballet:** *Swan Lake* Time: 19.30 *Sunday 26th October* *Tickets: £12, £18, £25*
Play: *When we were young* Time: 19.15 Saturday 25th October *Tickets: £10, £12.50*	**Opera:** *Carmen* Time: 20.00 Sunday 26th October *Tickets: £16, £24, £30*

Quick review

◀) CD 2, TR 4, 05:35

Yán Lóngfēng and his girlfriend Liú Língmǐn are discussing how they are going to spend the evening. Listen to, or read, the dialogue and answer the questions after it.

Yán	Zánmen qù kàn diànyǐng ba.
Liú	Yǒu shénme hǎo diànyǐng?
Yán	Tīngshuō «**Wǒmen niánqīng de shíhou**» búcuò.
Liú	Wǒ kàn-guo le. Méi yìsi.

Yán	Nàme wǒmen qù tīng yīnyuèhuì ba.
Liú	Yǒu shénme yīnyuèhuì?
Yán	Nǐ xiǎng tīng Zhōngguó yīnyuè háishì Xīfāng yīnyuè?
Liú	Dōu bù xiǎng tīng.
Yán	Nàme nǐ xiǎng zuò shénme?
Liú	Wǒ xiǎng qù tiào wǔ.

a What did Yán Lóngfēng first suggest that they did?
b Did Liú Língmǐn accept his suggestion? Why or why not?
c What types of concert did Yán Lóngfēng ask his girlfriend to choose from?
d Was Liú Língmǐn interested?
e What did Liú Língmǐn want to do?

Vocabulary

a What seasons are 'dōngtiān' and 'xiàtiān'?
b What activities are these: 'tiào wǔ', 'chàng gē', 'huá bīng' and 'yóuyǒng'?
c These two words: 'hùzhào' and 'qiānzhèng' are related. What do they mean?
d You have learnt two pairs of words: 'dānrén fángjiān'/'shuāngrén fángjiān' and 'dānhào'/'shuānghào'. Now what do 'dān' and 'shuāng' mean respectively?
e The word 'niánqīng-ren' is not in the vocabulary. Do you know what it means?

15

···

Zài yóujú hé huàn qián
At a post office and changing money

In this unit you will learn
- How to buy stamps
- How to send (and collect) a parcel
- How to make a long-distance call
- How to send a fax
- Numbers above 1000

Revise before you start

- from . . . to . . .   (9)
- measure words   (4)(7)
- money   (7)
- weights   (7)
- zuì (*most*)   (7)

- verb endings   (10)
- use of **háishi**   (6)
- use of **de**   (3)(5)
- **huì**   (9)
- foreign currency   (7)

The following passage tells you something about the **yóujú** (*post office*) in China. Are there things you can do in a Chinese **yóujú** that you don't normally do in a post office in Britain?

Yóujú *The post office*

post office

Zhōngguó de yóujú gēn Yīngguó de yóujú chàbuduō. Zài yóujú nǐ kěyǐ jì xìn、jì qián、jì bāoguǒ, yě kěyǐ mǎi yóupiào、xìnfēng hé míngxìnpiàn, hái kěyǐ zài yóujú cún qián、qǔ qián hé fù zhàng. Zài Zhōngguó de yóujú nǐ hái kěyǐ dǎ chángtú diànhuà hé guójì diànhuà.

Yóujú de kāi mén shíjiān chángcháng bù yíyàng. Yǒude shàngwǔ bā diǎn kāi mén, yǒude bā diǎn bàn kāi mén. Yǒude xiàwǔ wǔ diǎn bàn guān mén, yǒude wǎnshang qī diǎn guān mén. Xīngqīliù、xīngqītiān dōu kāi mén.

Shùnbiàn shuō yíxià, Zhōngguó de xìntǒng shì lǜsè de, Yīngguó de xìntǒng shì hóngsè de.

bāoguǒ	*parcel*
chàbuduō	*similar* (lit. *lacking not much*)
X gēn Y chàbuduō	*X is not much different to Y*
chángtú	*long distance*
dǎ chángtú diànhuà	*to make a long-distance/national call*
cún qián	*to deposit money*
fù zhàng	*to pay bills*
guójì	*international*
jì	*to post*
míngxìnpiàn	*postcard*
qǔ qián	*withdraw money*
shùnbiàn shuō yíxià	*by the way* (when speaking)
shùnbiàn wèn yíxià	*by the way* (when asking a question)
yǒude	*some*
yóujú	*post office*
yóupiào	*stamp*
xìn	*letter*
xìnfēng	*envelope*
xìntǒng	*postbox, mailbox*

QUICK VOCAB

Exercise 1 Now would you like to tell the Chinese something about post offices in Britain?

a You can deposit and withdraw money in a post office.
b Post offices in Britain do not usually open on Saturday afternoons and Sundays.
c Postboxes in Britain are red, not green.
d In Britain, you can't make long-distance calls in a post office.

Chinese stamps

chá	*to look up* (something)
chāo zhòng le	*to have exceeded the weight limit*
chèng	*scales*
chuánzhēn	*fax*
dào	*to go to; to*
diànzǐ yóujiàn or **yīmèi'ér**	*e-mail* (lit. *electronic mail*)
dìqū	*district*
fā	*to send* (a fax, e-mail, etc.)
fā-wán le	*have sent* (a fax) *through*
fàng	*to put*
fēng	(measure word for letters)
guāngpán	*compact disk* (CD)
hǎiyùn	(to post) *by sea*
hángkōng	(to post) *by air*
hǎokàn	*nice-looking*
jì dào	*to post to*
nèibiān	*over there*

shàng wǎng	*to use the internet* (lit. *on net*)
shōujù	*receipt*
shū	*book*
tào	*set* (stamps)
yè	*page*
yuànyì	*would like to, to be willing to*
zhàn xiàn	(line) *engaged*
zhèixiē/nèixiē	*these/those*
zhuǎn	*to change to* (extension)

Dialogues

Dialogue 1

◀) **CD 2, TR 5**

Ann is now at a post office in China. At the end of the dialogue she will have done three things. What are they?

Ann	Qǐng wèn, zhèi fēng xìn jì dào Yīngguó, duōshao qián?
Assistant	Qǐng fàng zài chèng shàng. . . . Chāo zhòng le. Sān kuài jiǔ.
Ann	Jǐ tiān néng dào?
Assistant	Bù yídìng. Yìbān wǔ、liù tiān. Zhè shì nínde yóupiào.
Ann	Zhèi zhāng yóupiào zhēn hǎokàn. Wǒ néng mǎi yí tào ma?
Assistant	Dāngrán kěyǐ. Yí tào liù kuài qī.
Ann	Wǒ hái xiǎng jì yí ge bāoguǒ.
Assistant	Shì shénme dōngxi?
Ann	Dōu shì shū hé guāngpán.
Assistant	Yě qǐng fàng zài chèng shàng. . . . Liǎng gōngjīn. Nín jì hángkōng háishi hǎiyùn?
Ann	Hángkōng.

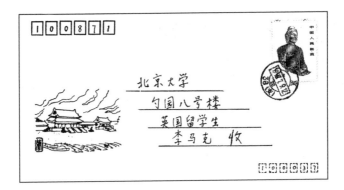

Insight

In China, only standardized envelopes with boxes for postcodes may be used (see envelope). The top left-hand corner is for the addressee's postcode and the bottom right-hand corner for the sender's.

◄) **CD 2, TR 5, 01:25**

Exercise 2   You are now in a post office talking to the assistant. You begin:

a	**You**	*(Say this parcel is for America.)*
	Assistant	Shì shénme dōngxi?
b	**You**	*(Say they are all books.)*
	Assistant	Qǐng fàng zài chèng shàng. . . . Yìbǎi wǔshísan kuài.
c	**You**	*(Ask how many days it takes (to get to America).)*
	Assistant	Bù yídìng. Yìbān sì、wǔ tiān.
d	**You**	*(Say you would like to buy postcards and ask how much it is for a set.)*
	Assistant	Zhèi tào dà de shíliù kuài. Nèi tào xiǎo de shísì kuài wǔ.
e	**You**	*(Say you'll have a set of the big ones, and two sets of the small ones.)*
	Assistant	Bāoguǒ yìbǎi wǔshísān kuài, yí tào dà de míngxìnpiàn shíliù kuài, liǎng tào xiǎo de èrshíjiǔ kuài, yígòng yìbǎi jiǔshíba kuài.

f	You	(Say here are 200 kuài.)
	Assistant	Zhǎo nín liǎng kuài.
g	You	(Say thank you and goodbye.)
	Assistant	Zàijiàn!

Dialogue 2

Colin zài **shāngwù zhōngxīn** fā chuánzhēn. (*Colin is sending a fax at a business centre.*)

Colin	Xiǎojie, qǐng wèn, kěyǐ zài zhèr fā **(yí) ge** chuánzhēn ma?
Assistant	Kěyǐ. Fā-dào nǎr?
Colin	Déguó.
Assistant	Yígòng jǐ yè?
Colin	Liǎng yè.
Assistant	Hǎo de. Qǐng gěi wǒ chuánzhēn hàomǎ.
Colin	Zhè shì chuánzhēn hàomǎ.
Assistant	Qǐng děngyiděng. . . . Fā-wán le. Zhè shì shōujù.
Colin	Duōshao qián?
Assistant	Sìshí kuài. Qǐng dào nèibiān fù qián.
Colin	Xièxie nǐ. Shùnbiàn wèn yíxià, kěyǐ zài zhèr shàng wǎng hé fā diànzǐ yóujiàn ma?
Assistant	Dāngrán kěyǐ.

商务中心

Shāngwù zhōngxīn
Business centre

Note that in spoken Chinese, when **yī** (*one*) occurs with a measure word the **yī** is often omitted.

🔊 **CD 2, TR 5, 03:34**

Exercise 3 You will find it useful to be able to ask and understand the following questions and instructions in Chinese. Look carefully at the example given in each section and then have a go at translating the English sentences which follow it into Chinese.

a Asking for services:

Example: **Qǐng wèn kěyǐ zài zhèr fā ge chuánzhēn mā?**

Can I make a phone call here?
Can I send a parcel here?
Can I send an e-mail here?

b Asking for items:

Example: **Qǐng gěi wǒ tāde chuánzhēn hào(mǎ).**

Can I have your telephone number?
Can I have their website address (**wǎngzhǐ**)?
Can I have your passport?
Can I have their address (**dìzhǐ**)?

c Giving instructions/directions:

Example: **Qǐng dào nèibiān fù qián.**

Please change money over there.
Please make the phone call outside (**wàibiān**).

Qǐng dào hòubiān pái duì (*Please queue at the back*) is another useful instruction you may wish to learn.

Dialogue 3

Xiè Qúnyì is making a long-distance call.

Operator	Nín hǎo. Nánfāng Dàxué.
Xiè	**Qǐng zhuǎn** sì-èr-qī fēnjī.
Operator	Duìbuqǐ, sì-èr-qī zhàn xiàn. Nín yuànyì děngyiděng háishì yìhuǐr zài dǎ **lái**?
Xiè	Wǒ zhè shì guójì diànhuà. Nín néng bu néng jiào sì-èr-qī de Wáng Bǎopíng gěi wǒ dǎ ge diànhuà?

Operator	Nínde hàomǎ shì duōshao?
Xiè	Yīngguó Lúndūn shì sì-sì-èr-líng-qī. Wǒde diànhuà shì èr-yāo-liù qī-qī-jiǔ-èr.
Operator	Nín guì xìng?
Xiè	Wǒ jiào Xiè Qúnyì.
Operator	Méi wèntí.
Xiè	Xièxie nín.

You learnt about straightforward telephone numbers in Unit 3. If, having got through to the main switchboard, you need to ask for an extension number, such as 473, you say:

Qǐng zhuǎn sì-qī-sān (fēnjī).   *Extension 473 please. (lit. invite transfer 4–7–3 branch machine)*

Note the little word **lái** at the end of the operator's second speech in **Dialogue 3:**

Nǐ yuànyì děngyiděng háishi yìhuǐr zài dǎ **lái?**   *Do you wish to wait or phone again in a little while? (lit. you wish wait a little while again hit [the electric speech] come?)*

This use of **lái** indicates direction towards the speaker (see also Unit 12).

Exercise 4   Read the dialogue and answer the following questions in English.

a   Where is the caller phoning?
b   Who does the caller want to speak to?
c   Why couldn't the operator connect the caller to the extension he gave her?
d   What seemed to be the mistake?

A telephone conversation

🔊 CD 2, TR 5, 04:48

Operator	Nín hǎo, Hépíng Bīnguǎn.
Mark	Qǐng zhuǎn wǔ-bā-sì fēnjī.
Operator	Duìbuqǐ, wǒmen méi yǒu wǔ-bā-sì fēnjī.
Mark	Shénme? Méi yǒu wǔ-bā-sì fēnjī?!
Operator	Nín yào zhǎo shéi?
Mark	Wǒ zhǎo cóng Měiguó lái de Bái Huá xiānsheng.
Operator	Tā zhù nǎ ge fángjiān?
Mark	Duìbuqǐ, wǒ bu zhīdào.
Operator	Qǐng děngyiděng. Wǒ chá yíxià. A, Bái Huá xiānsheng. Tā zhù wǔ-sì-bā fángjian. Tā de fēnjī yě shì wǔ-sì-bā.
Mark	Duìbuqǐ. Nàme qǐng gěi wǒ zhuǎn yíxià.

公用电话

Gōngyòng diànhuà
Public telephone

It is not difficult to change money in big cities, but it can be difficult in small cities and towns. The following passage tells us one of the reasons.

BANK OF CHINA
中国银行

Huàn qián *Changing money*

(Words in *italics* are explained in the Quick vocab box below the passage.)

Zài Zhōngguó huàn qián yì bān zhǐ néng zài dà yínháng de *fēnháng* huàn, *duìhuànlǜ* dōu chàbuduō. Yǒude dà fàndiàn hé dà shāngdiàn yě yǒu huàn qián de dìfang. Yínháng de kāi mén shíjiān gēn pǔtōng de shāngdiàn bù yíyàng, bǐ shāngdiàn kāi mén shíjiān wǎn yìdiǎn, guān mén shíjiān zǎo yìdiǎn. Kěshi, zài dà fàndiàn lǐ de huàn qián de dìfang kāi mén shíjiān bǐjiào *línghuó*, *kěnéng* huì kāi-dào hěn wǎn. *Jiānglái*, *qǔkuǎnjī* duō le, qǔ qián gèng fāngbiàn le, jiù bú yòng qù yínháng huàn qián le.

QUICK VOCAB

diǎn	*to count*
duìhuànlǜ	*exchange rate*
fēnháng	*branch* (of a bank)
jiānglái	*in the future*
kěnéng	*possible, possibly*
línghuó	*flexible*
qǔkuǎnjī	*ATM* (automatic teller machine)
zhènghǎo	*just right* (amount)

Exercise 5   Respond with **duì** or **bú duì** to the following statements about the passage above.

	duì	bú duì
a One can change money at any bank in China.	☐	☐
b You can change money in some big hotels.	☐	☐
c The opening hours of banks in China are different from those of ordinary shops.	☐	☐
d The opening hours of bureaux de change in big hotels are the same as at banks in the high street.	☐	☐

měiyuán	*US dollar*	**yīngbàng**	*UK pound*
rìyuán	*Japanese yen*	**gǎngbì**	*HK dollar*
ōuyuán	*euro*	**rénmínbì**	*Chinese yuan*

Numbers above 1000

1000	yìqiān	100,000	shíwàn (ten wàns)
10,000	yíwàn	480,000	sìshíbā wàn
20,000	èr/liǎng wàn	1,000,000	yìbǎi wàn
35,000	sānwàn wǔqiān		(100 wàns)

$9 \times 1000 = $ jiǔqiān
but $10 \times 1000 = $ yíwàn

There is no specific word for one million. It is *100 wàns*! Two million is therefore *200 wàns*, and so on.

Dialogue 4

◀) CD 2, TR 5, 06:06

The customer in the following dialogue wants to change some money. First he will have to fill out a **duìhuàndān** (*exchange memo*). Figures can be difficult to understand, so listen to the dialogue a few times and concentrate on the figures. What currency does the customer wish to exchange for **rénmínbì**? What is the exchange rate? How much does he want to change?

Customer	Qǐng wèn, jīntiān měiyuán hé rénmínbì de duìhuànlǜ shì duōshao?
Teller	Yī bǐ bā diǎnr jiǔ.
Customer	Yì měiyuán huàn bā kuài jiǔ, duì ma?
Teller	Duì.
Customer	Wǒ xiǎng huàn liǎngbǎi měiyuán de rénmínbì.
Teller	Qǐng xiān tián zhèi zhāng duìhuàndān.
Customer	. . . Tián-hǎo le. Zhè shì liǎngbǎi měiyuán.
Teller	Qǐng děngyiděng. . . . Zhè shì yìqiān qībǎi bāshí kuài. Qǐng diǎnyidiǎn.
Customer	Zhènghǎo. Xièxie nǐ.
Teller	Bú kèqi.

Exercise 6 How would you ask for the exchange rate of the following currency against **rénmínbì yuán**?

Example: (Jīntiān) rìyuán hé rénmínbì de duìhuànlǜ shì duōshao?

a £   c HK $
b US $ d € (euro)

Exercise 7 Now ask again for the exchange rates in **Exercise 6** and this time give the answer according to the table below. Try to use both expressions used in **Dialogue 4** for talking about the rates. (Leave out this exercise if you don't like working with figures.)

Example: 10,000 (Japanese) yen
            i Yíwàn (rìyuán) bǐ qībǎi bāshí'èr (kuài rénmínbì).
            ii Yíwàn rìyuán huàn qībǎi bāshí'èr kuài rénmínbì.

Foreign currencies		Rénmínbì (yuán)
US $	100.00	850.00
HK $	100.00	108.00
£	100.00	1320.00
euro €	100.00	910.00

Exercise 8 You want to change the following amount of currency into **RMB yuán**. What would you say?

Example: 75,000 rìyuán
            Wǒ xiǎng huàn qīwàn wǔqiān rìyuán de rénmínbì.

a £100   d 60,000 yen
b US $200   e €400
c HK $500

Quick review

How do you ask or say the following?

a How much is it to post this postcard to Britain?
b I want to buy a set of stamps.
c What's the exchange rate between sterling and RMB today?
d I want to change £150 for RMB.
e My extension is 2115.

Vocabulary

a What do these words mean: 'cún qián', 'qǔ qián', 'diǎn qián' and 'huàn qián'?
b Which word is the odd one out: 'xìn', 'míngxìnpiàn', 'yóupiào', 'chuánzhēn', and 'xìnfēng'?
c What verbs do you use for making a phone call, sending a fax and posting a letter respectively?
d When you ask for an ATM, what is the Chinese word you need to say?
e Which is quicker: 'hǎiyùn' or 'hángkōng'?

208

16

Zuò kè
Being a guest

In this unit you will learn
- How to make a toast
- How to make appropriate remarks and responses during a meal

---

Revise before you start

- when . . .   (10)
- cái   (7)
- measure words   (4)(7)
- polite talk   (4)(8)
- tài . . . le   (7)
- use of háishi   (6)
- verb endings   (10)

- duō + verb   (10)
- use of **de** after verb   (8)
- yǐjīng (*already*) + le (10)
- not any more   (10)
- gěi (*for*)   (6)
- verb + guo   (9)

No doubt you have eaten Chinese meals. But where? At a Chinese home or in a Chinese restaurant? Or both? Have you noticed some of the differences in the way westerners and Chinese eat their meals? Now read the following passage which sums up some of the differences in simple Chinese.

Chī Zhōngguó fàn *Eating Chinese food*

Zhōngguó-rén chángcháng wèi kèrén zuò hěn duō cài. Tāmen xīwàng kèrén duō hē jiǔ, duō chī cài.

Zhōngguó-rén hé Xīfang-rén chī fàn de xíguàn bù yíyàng. Zhōngguó-rén chī fàn yòng wǎn hé kuàizi; Xīfāng-rén chī fàn yòng pánzi hé dāochā. Dàbùfen Zhōngguó-rén yìbān xiān chī fàn, hòu hē tāng. Zài Xīfāng, rénmen yìbān xiān hē tāng, hòu chī fàn. Zhōngguó-rén chángcháng xiān hē jiǔ, chī liáng cài, ránhòu chī rè fàn、rè cài, zuìhòu chī shuǐguǒ. Xīfāng-rén xiān chī tóupán, ránhòu chī zhèngcān, zuìhòu chī tiánshí huò shuǐguǒ.

Zhōngguó-rén zài jiā lǐ chī fàn hé zài fànguǎn chī fàn chàbuduō, dàjiā yìqǐ chī suǒyǒude cài. Xīfāng-rén zài fànguǎn zìjǐ chī zìjǐ de cài. Zài jiā chī fàn de shíhou, bùtóng de cài xiān fàng zài zìjǐ de pánzi lǐ, ránhòu cái chī.

bùtóng de	*different*
chángcháng	*often*
dàbùfen	*majority*
dàjiā	*everyone*
dāochā (i.e. dāozi, chāzi)	*knife* (and) *fork*
hòu	*later*
huò(zhě)	*or* (used in statements)
jiǔ	*alcohol*
liáng	*cold, cool*
pān(zi)	*plate; tray*
rénmen	*people* (in general)
shuǐguǒ	*fruit*
suǒyǒude	*all*
tiánshí	*dessert*
tóupán	*starter*
wèi	*for* (formal)
Xīfāng	*west*
xíguàn	*habit, customs*
xīwàng	*to hope; hope*

QUICK VOCAB

zhèngcān	*main course*
zìjǐ chī zìjǐ de	*to eat one's own*
zuìhòu	*last*

We mentioned the enormous difference between spoken and written Chinese in Unit 14 and there are further examples of this in the passage about Chinese food. **Wèi** is used instead of **gěi** in the first sentence, **hòu** is used instead of **ránhòu** in the fourth sentence and **huò** is used instead of **huòzhě** in the seventh sentence. Using one-syllable words instead of two, or using a more 'ancient' word (**wèi** instead of **gěi**) gives a more formal feel to the language.

Note that **dōu** (*all*) can only be used in front of a verb. So, for example, when you want to say *all people* you have to use another word for *all* which is **suǒyǒude**:

Tā xǐhuan **suǒyǒude** rén. *She likes everybody
                          (lit. all people).*
Dàjiā yìqǐ chī **suǒyǒude** cài. *Everybody shares all the dishes
                          (lit. big family together eat all dish).*

Exercise 1   Choose the most appropriate words from the ones given in brackets to fill the blanks in the following sentences. You will be able to use all the words given in **a** and **b** but you will have to make a choice in **c**, **d** and **e**.

a Zhōngguó-rén yìbān xiān _____, ránhòu _____, zuìhòu _____.
   (hē tāng, chī rè fàn、 rè cài, hē jiǔ)
b Xīfāng-rén yìbān xiān _____, ránhòu _____, zuìhòu _____.
   (chī shuǐguǒ, hē tāng, chī zhèngcān)
c Zhōngguó-rén chī fàn yòng ____ hé ____.
   (dāozi, kuàizi, chāzi, pánzi, wǎn)
d Xīfāng-rén chī fàn yòng ____ gēn ____.
   (dāochā, kuàizi, pánzi, wǎn)
e ____ zài fànguǎnr chī fàn hé zài jiā lǐ chī fàn xíguàn yíyàng.
   (Zhōngguó-rén; Xīfāng-rén)

ài	*to love, to like very much; love*
báijiǔ	*strong alcohol*
chá	*tea*
chī-bu-xià le	*to be unable to eat any more*
chúfáng	*kitchen*
Gān bēi!	*Cheers!*
gān yì bēi	*to have a drink*
hǎochī (de)	*delicious* (food), *tasty*
hé	*box*
hē-bu-liǎo	*to be unable to drink*
hē-bu-xià le	*to be unable to drink any more*
huānyíng	*to welcome; welcome*
huí qù	*to go back*
jiācháng biànfàn	*simple home meal*
kètīng	*sitting room*
kètīng lǐ zuò ba	*come and sit in the sitting room*
màn zǒu	*take care* (as in goodbye; lit. *walk slowly*)
píjiǔ	*beer*
qiǎokèlì	*chocolates*
shìqing	*matter, thing*
shūshu	*uncle* (on father's side or someone of his generation)
tián (de)	*sweet*
wàiguó	*foreign country*
wàiguó-rén	*foreigner*
xiàndàihuà (de)	*modern*
xiāng	*fragrant*
zuò kè	*to be a guest*
zuǒshǒu	*left hand*
gōngzuò shùnlì	lit. *work smooth*
Lùshàng xiǎoxīn.	*Have a safe journey.* (lit. *on the road (be) careful*)
quánjiā xìngfú	lit. *whole family happy*
shēnghuó yúkuài	lit. *life pleasant*
wànshì rúyì	lit. *ten thousand things as you wish*
Gěi nǐ(men) tiān máfan le.	*Sorry to have troubled you.*

212

Nà jiù bù liú nǐ le.	*I won't keep you then.*
Nǐ tài kèqi le.	*You are being too polite.*
Wèi . . . gān bēi!	*To . . . (used as a toast).*
Wǒ chī/hē-bu-xià le.	*I can't eat/drink any more.*
Wǒ gāi huí qù le.	*I must be off now.*
Wǒ sòngsong nǐ.	*I'll see you out.*
Wǒ zìjǐ lái.	*I'll help myself.*

Dialogues

Dialogue 1

Mr White, who is called Lǎo Bái by his Chinese friends, is invited to dinner at the Yuáns' home. Read the dialogue and note how Mr White presents his gifts to the family.

Mr Yuán	Lǎo Bái, huānyíng, huānyíng.
Lǎo Bái	Lǎo Yuán, nǐ hǎo. Wǒ zhīdao nǐ ài hē jiǔ. Zhè shì gěi nǐde jiǔ.
Mr Yuán	Fǎguó pútáojiǔ! Nǐ tài kèqi le.
Lǎo Bái	Zhèi hé qiǎokèlì shì gěi nǐmen nǚ'ér de.
Mr Yuán	Zhēn Zhēn, kuài xièxie Bái shūshu.
Zhēn Zhēn	Xièxie Bái shūshu.
Lǎo Bái	Bú yòng xiè. . . . Zhēn xiāng a! Yuán tàitai, zuò shénme hǎochī de ne?
Mrs Yuán	Méi shénme hǎochī de. Dōu shì jiācháng biànfàn.
Lǎo Bái	Nǐmen de chúfáng tǐng xiàndàihuà de.
Mrs Yuán	Kěxī tài xiǎo le.
Mr Yuán	Lǎo Bái, kètīng lǐ zuò ba.
Lǎo Bái	Hǎo, hǎo. Nǐmen de kètīng zhēn piàoliang.
Mr Yuán	Nǎli, nǎli. Lǎo Bái, nǐ xiǎng hē diǎnr shénme?
Lǎo Bái	Hē diǎnr chá ba.

Note the various examples of **kèqi huà** (*polite talk*), which was referred to in Unit 8, and in **Dialogues 1, 2** and **3**.

Exercise 2 The two patterns below are often used when giving something to somebody. You will need a *measure word* (MW) in pattern **ii**:

i Zhè shì gěi nǐ de X.   *This is an X for you.*
ii Zhè MW X shì gěi nǐ de. *This MW X is for you.*

You have brought with you the following things as presents when invited to dinner with a Chinese family. How would you present them? Try to use both **i** and **ii** patterns.

Example: Zhè shì gěi nǐ de huà.
           Zhè fú huà shì gěi nǐ de.

  (hé)   (hé)   (běn)

  (píng)   (zhāng)   (fú)

Exercise 3 Now use the presents and the patterns in **Exercise 2**, but this time you've bought them for different people.

Example: my father, painting
              Zhè shì gěi wǒ bàba de huà.
              Zhè fú huà shì gěi wǒ bàba de.

a my elder sister, chocolates
b his wife, a tin of green tea
c her uncle, a book
d her boyfriend, a bottle of wine
e your (pl) friends, two film tickets
f their company (**gōngsī**), a painting

Chinese proverb: **Sì hǎi wéi jiā**
(*lit. Four seas like home*)

Dialogue 2

◀)) **CD 2, TR 6**

The following dialogue is between Mr White and his Chinese hosts, Mr and Mrs Yuán, during a meal. Listen out for the **kèqi huà**.

Mr Yuán	Lǎo Bái, zánmen xiān hē yì bēi.
Lǎo Bái	Hǎo a.
Mr Yuán	Nǐ hē píjiǔ, pútáojiǔ háishi lái diǎnr báijiǔ?
Lǎo Bái	Báijiǔ wǒ hē-bu-liǎo. Hē diǎnr pútáojiǔ ba.
Mr Yuán	Bái de háishi hóng de?
Lǎo Bái	Hóng de ba.
Mr Yuán	Zhèi zhǒng jiǔ bù tián. Wǒ zhīdao wàiguó-rén yìbān bù xǐhuān hē tián de jiǔ.
Lǎo Bái	Shì, wǒ bù xǐhuan hē tián de jiǔ.

Mr Yuán	Zánmen xiān gān yì bēi. Zhù nǐ gōngzuò shùnlì、shēnghuó yúkuài!
Lǎo Bái	Zhù nǐmen quánjiā xìngfú, wànshì rúyì!
Mr Yuán	Gān bēi!
Lǎo Bái	Gān bēi!
Mrs Yuán	Bié kèqi, duō chī diǎnr.
Lǎo Bái	Hǎo, hǎo, wǒ zìjǐ lái.
Lǎo Bái	Cài dōu fēicháng hǎochī.
Mr Yuán	Zài duō chī diǎnr.
Lǎo Bái	Wǒ yǐjīng chī-bǎo le.
Mrs Yuán	Nǐ chī-de tài shǎo le.
Lǎo Bái	Wǒ zhēnde chī-bu-xià le.
Mr Yuán	Nǐ tài kèqi le.
Lǎo Bái	Wǒ méi kèqi.

More examples of useful four-character phrases can be found in Unit 14).

Zhù nǐ(men)
- gōngzuò shùnlì! — *May your work go smoothly!*
- shēnghuó yúkuài! — *May your life be happy!*
- quánjiā xìngfú! — *May your whole family be blessed!*

Insight

Gān bēi (*Drain your glass*) does not have to be taken literally, particularly in the case of 70% proof **máotái** which is often used for toasts at banquets!

◀) CD 2, TR 6, 01:32

Exercise 4 The following are some useful expressions which might come in handy when you are having dinner with a Chinese family. Do you know how to say them in Chinese?

a Cheers!
b I really can't eat any more.
c It smells nice.

d I'll help myself.

e Wishing you every happiness.

Dialogue 3

◀) **CD 2, TR 6, 02:00**

Read the dialogue and note carefully the exchanges between the guest and his hosts.

Lǎo Bái	Wǒ kěyǐ yòng yíxià nǐmende cèsuǒ ma?
Mr Yuán	Zuǒshǒu dì-èr jiān jiù shì.
Lǎo Bái	O, yǐjing jiǔ diǎn duō le. Wǒ gāi huí qù le.
Mr Yuán	Hái zǎo ne. Zài zuò yìhuǐr ba.
Lǎo Bái	Bú zuò le. Míngtian zǎoshang wǒ hái yǒu shìqing.
Mr Yuán	Hǎo ba. Nà jiù bù liú nǐ le.
Lǎo Bái	Gěi nǐmen tiān máfan le.
Mr Yuán	Méi shénme. Huānyíng nǐ zài lái.
Lǎo Bái	Yídìng, yídìng.
Mr Yuán	Wǒ sòngsong nǐ.
Lǎo Bái	Bú yòng le. Qǐng huí qù ba.
Mr Yuán	Màn zǒu.
Mrs Yuán	Lùshàng xiǎoxīn.
Lǎo Bái	Méi wèntí. Zàijiàn!
Mr & Mrs Yuán	Zàijiàn!

Exercise 5   What do you say?

a What do you say when you think it's time to leave?

b How might your host respond if he/she doesn't want you to leave yet?

c How do you thank your host for all the trouble s/he has taken?

d What's your host's response to c?

e What do you say when your host suggests seeing you off?

f How do you tell somebody to take care driving or cycling?

g What's the common parting remark made by the host to his/her guest?

Dialogue 4

The following is a dialogue between a Chinese managing director, his wife and his foreign counterpart of a joint venture. They are at a banquet. Listen to the recording, and try to answer the following questions before you read the dialogue. Or read the dialogue and then answer the questions. This time the new words and expressions come after the dialogue, and we've given you the English translation of the questions.

Questions

a Bái xiānsheng kuàizi yòng-de zěnmeyàng?
   Does Mr White use chopsticks very well?
b Tā shuō tā Zhōngguó fàn zuò-de hǎo bu hǎo?
   How well does he say he cooks?
c Tā chángcháng qù nǎr chī Zhōngguó fàn?
   Where does he often go for Chinese meals?
d Duìhuà (*dialogue*) lǐ shuō Bái xiānsheng chī-guo/hē-guo shénme?
   i yànwō tāng
   ii Máotáijiǔ
   iii fèngzhǎo
   According to the dialogue which of the following has Mr White ever eaten/drunk?
   i *birds' nest soup*
   ii *Máotái*
   iii *chicken feet*

Dǒngshìzhǎng	Bái xiānsheng, nín kuàizi yòng-de zhēn hǎo.
Mr White	Wǒ chángcháng chī Zhōngguó fàn.
Fūren	Nín zìjǐ zuò fàn ma?
Mr White	Wǒ zuò-de bù hǎo. Wǒ cháng qù Zhōngguóchéng de fànguǎnr chī fàn.
Dǒngshìzhǎng	Lái, xiān hē yì bēi. Zhè shì Máotáijiǔ. Nín hē-guo ma?
Mr White	Hē-guo liǎng cì.
Dǒngshìzhǎng	Wèi wǒmen liǎng ge gōngsī de chénggōng hézuò gān bēi!

Mr White	Wèi Dǒngshìzhǎng hé Dǒngshìzhǎng fūren de jiànkāng gān bēi!
Fūren	Zhè shì yànwō tāng, fēicháng yǒu yíngyǎng.
Mr White	Wǒ tīngshuō-guo, kěshì méi hē-guo.
Dǒngshìzhǎng	Zhè shì fèngzhǎo, bù zhīdao nín chī-guo ma?
Mr White	Kàn-jiàn-guo, hái méi chī-guo.
Fūren	Zhènghǎo, qǐng chángchang ba.
Fūren	Duō chī diǎnr cài.
Dǒngshìzhǎng	Zài hē yì bēi.
Mr White	Wǒ chī-bu-xià le, yě hē-bu-xià le.
Dǒngshìzhǎng	Zài hē zuìhòu yì bēi. Wèi Zhōng-Yīng liǎng guó rénmín de yǒuyì gān bēi!
Mr White	Gān bēi! Xīwàng nǐmen yǒu jīhuì qù Yīngguó fǎngwèn.

QUICK VOCAB

cháng (chang)	*to taste*
chángcháng	*often*
chénggōng	*successful*
dǒngshìzhǎng	*managing director*
fǎngwèn	*visit* (formal)
fèngzhǎo	*chicken feet*
fūren	*wife* (formal), *madam*
gōngsī	*company*
hézuò	*co-operation, co-operate*
jiànkāng	*health, healthy*
jīhuì	*opportunity*
kàn-jiàn	*to see*
Máotái(jiǔ)	*Maotai* (a very strong Chinese spirit)
yànwō	*birds' nest*
yǒu yíngyǎng	*nutritious*
Zhōngguóchéng	*Chinatown*
Zhōng-Yīng liǎng guó rénmín de yǒuyì	*the friendship between the Chinese and British peoples*
liǎng guó	*two countries*
rénmín	*the people* (of a country)
yǒuyì	*friendship*
zuò (fàn)	*to cook*

Exercise 6   Look at the Chinese words in the left-hand column and pair each of them with one in the right-hand column.

a	fǎngwèn	i	co-operate, co-operation
b	hézuò	ii	madam
c	jīhuì	iii	to visit, visit (*formal*)
d	fūren	iv	success, successful
e	gōngsī	v	opportunity
f	chénggōng	vi	company

Exercise 7   The words in **Exercise 6** are some of the words you might need in formal business encounters.

Now cover up the Chinese and just look at the English. Can you remember how to say them in Chinese?

You met **zhè/zhèi** (*this*) and **nà/nèi** (*that*) in Unit 2 and **nǎ/něi** (*which?*) in Unit 7. They are normally followed by a measure word (see Unit 7). By putting the collective measure word **xiē** after **zhè/zhèi**, **nà/nèi** and **nǎ/něi** you have **zhèxiē/zhèixiē** (*these*), **nàxiē/nèixiē** (*those*) and **nǎxiē/něixiē** (*which?* plural):

zhèxiē (shū)	*these (books)*
nàxiē (cài)	*those (dishes)*
nǎxiē (jīhuì)	*which (opportunities)?*

Polite forms of address

The formal way of addressing a married woman in Chinese is **fūren** and not **tàitai**. Chinese speakers often translate **fūren** as *madam*:

Chén **fūren**   *Madam Chen*

When writing in English, a Chinese speaker may well address his or her letter to Madam Jones which seems rather strange to most English speakers. **Fūren** can also be put after titles which carry a certain status such as manager or headmaster and can refer to female postholders' or to male postholders' *wives*:

| Dǒngshìzhǎng **fūren** | *Madam Manager* (used in Mr White's toast) |
| Xiàozhǎng **fūren** | *Madam Headmaster* |

Quick review

🔊 **CD 2, TR 6, 05:38**

When you hear these toasts, do you know what they mean?

a   Zhù nǐ shēntǐ jiànkāng!
b   Zhù nǐ shēnghuó yúkuài!
c   Zhù nǐ wànshì rúyì!
d   Zhù nǐ gōngzuò shùnlì!
e   Zhù nǐ chénggōng!
f   Wèi wǒmen de yǒuyì gān bēi!
g   Wèi wǒmen de hézuò gān bēi!

17

Kàn yīshēng
Seeing a doctor

In this unit you will learn
- How to describe symptoms to the doctor or the pharmacist
- To understand the instructions on the medicine bottle
- About acupuncture, Chinese herbal medicine, tàijíquán and qìgōng

---

Revise before you start

- measure words   (4)(7)
- both . . . and . . .   (9)
- yǒu yìdiǎnr (*a bit*)   (8)
- sentences ending in le (4)
- verb + le   (9)
- shì bu shi   (3)
- use of háishi   (6)

- verb + guo   (9)
- use of ba   (3)
- on + noun   (5)
- when . . .   (10)
- bié (*don't*)   (10)
- gěi (*for*)   (6)

Zhōngguó de Yīliáo   *Medical care in China*

The Chinese medical system is not the same as in Britain. The following passage tells us a little about some of the differences. (Words in *italics* are explained in the **Quick vocab** box.)

Zài Zhōngguó, hěn duō *dānwèi* yǒu zìjǐ de *yīwùsuǒ*. Xiǎo de *yīwùsuǒ* zhǐ yǒu yí gè *yīshēng*, dà de kěyǐ yǒu *jǐ* ge yīshēng hé *hùshi*. Rúguǒ nǐ yǒu *bìng*, nǐ kěyǐ qù dānwèi de yīwùsuǒ, yě kěyǐ *zhíjiē* qù *yīyuàn*.

Zhōngguó de yīyuàn yìbān *fēnchéng* bùtóng de *kē*. *Yǒude* yīyuàn shì *zhuānkē* yīyuàn, zhǐ *kàn* yì、 liǎng *zhǒng bìng*. Dà de yīyuàn yìbān yòu yǒu *Zhōngyī*, yòu yǒu *Xīyī*. Nǐ kěyǐ kàn Zhōngyī, yě kěyǐ kàn Xīyī.

QUICK VOCAB

bìng	*illness*
bìngrén	*patient*
dānwèi	*work unit*
fēnchéng	*to divide/to be divided into*
hùshi	*nurse*
jǐ	*several, a few*
kàn bìng	*to see a doctor* (to have the illness looked at)
kē	*department* (in a hospital)
Xīyī	*western medical* (doctor); *western medicine*
yīliáo	*medical care*
yīshēng	*doctor*
yīwùsuǒ	*clinic* (attached to a work unit)
yīyuàn	*hospital*
zhíjiē	*direct*(ly)
zhǒng	*kind, sort* (measure word)
Zhōngyī	*Chinese medical* (doctor); *Chinese medicine*
zhuānkē	*specialized; speciality . . .*

Exercise 1   According to the passage, are the following statements duì or bú duì?

	duì	bú duì
a Yǒude dānwèi méi yǒu yīwùsuǒ.	☐	☐
b Zài dà de yīyuàn, Zhōngyī、 Xīyī dōu yǒu.	☐	☐
c Yǒude yīwùsuǒ méi yǒu hùshi.	☐	☐
d Bìngrén bù kěyǐ zhíjiē qù yīyuàn.	☐	☐

bú xiè	*not at all*
cānjiā	*to attend*
chī (yào)	*to take* (medicine)
dùzi	*stomach, tummy*
lā dùzi	*to have diarrhoea*
fàn hòu	*after meals*
fàn qián	*before meals*
fúyòng fāngfǎ	*instructions* (for taking medicine)
gǎnmào	*to have a cold*
Hànzì	*Chinese characters*
kāfēi	*coffee*
kāishuǐ	*boiled water*
késou	*cough*
kǔ	*bitter*
lì	*pill*; MW for pill-sized pieces, e.g. grain
ná	*to take, fetch*
piàn(r)	*tablet*; MW for small slices, e.g. snowflakes
píngzi	*bottle*
téng	*painful; pain*
tóuténg	*headache*
wán(r)	(Chinese medicine) *ball*
wēn	*warm*
Xīyào	*western medicine*
yànhuì	*banquet*
yào	*medicine*
yàofāng	*prescription*
yàofáng	*pharmacy*
yìxiē	*some*
yǒu shíhou	*sometimes*
yǒu xiào	*effective*
zhā	*to pierce, to put in a needle, to do acupuncture*
zhēnjiǔ	*acupuncture*
zhěnsuǒ	*clinic* (open to the general public)
zhèyàng/zhèiyàng	*like this, in this way*
Zhōngyào	*Chinese medicine*
Wǒ bù shūfu.	*I don't feel well.*
Wǒ . . . téng.	*My . . . hurts.*
Wǒde tiān a!	*Good heavens!* (lit. *my heaven*)

Dialogues

Dialogue 1

🔊 **CD 2, TR 7**

Mr White is not feeling at all well. He decides to go to the company's clinic. Listen to the dialogue and try to find out what's wrong with him. What does he think has caused the problem, and what does the doctor think the cause is? What medicine does the doctor prescribe?

Yīshēng	Nǐ nǎr bù shūfu?
Bái	Wǒ dùzi bù shūfu.
Yīshēng	Lā dùzi ma?
Bái	Yǒu yìdiǎnr.
Yīshēng	Nǐ zuótiān chī shénme le?
Bái	Wǒ cānjiā le yí ge yànhuì, chī le fèngzhǎo, hē le yànwō tāng.
Yīshēng	Nèixiē dōu shì hǎo dōngxi, duì nǐ shēntǐ hǎo.
Bái	Wǒ kěnéng chī-de tài duō le.
Yīshēng	Nǐ hē le hěn duō jiǔ, shì bu shi?
Bái	Bù duō, zhǐ hē le bā bēi.
Yīshēng	Wǒ míngbai le. Wǒ gěi nǐ yìxiē yào. Nǐ yuànyì shìshi Zhōngyào ma?
Bái	Wǒ méi chī-guo Zhōngyào. Tīngshuō Zhōngyào hěn kǔ, shì ma?
Yīshēng	Yǒude kǔ, yǒude bù kǔ. Wǒ gěi nǐ de yào bù kǔ.
Bái	Nà wǒ shìshi ba.
Yīshēng	Zhè shì yàofāng. Qǐng dào yàofáng qù ná yào.
Bái	Yīshēng, xièxie nín.
Yīshēng	Bú yòng xiè.

Shǒudū yīyuàn
Capital hospital

Jízhěnshì
Emergency room

Exercise 2 You have a cold, which is a common illness in China as well, and you're seeing a Chinese doctor. Complete the following dialogue.

	Yīshēng	Nǐ zěnme le?
a	**You**	(Tell her that you have a headache.)
	Yīshēng	Hái yǒu nǎr bù shūfu?
b	**You**	(Say you cough a bit.)
	Yīshēng	Wǒ xiǎng nǐ yǒu yìdiǎnr gǎnmào.
c	**You**	(Say you also feel it's a cold.)
	Yīshēng	Wǒ gěi nǐ diǎnr yào. Nǐ chī Zhōngyào ma?
d	**You**	(Say you've never taken it before and ask the doctor if Chinese medicine is effective.)
	Yīshēng	Yídìng yǒu xiào.
e	**You**	(Say it's OK and you will give it a try.)

Dialogue 2

Mr White is at the pharmacy.

Pharmacist	Zhè shì nínde yào.
Mr White	Zěnme chī ya?
Pharmacist	Píngzi shàng yǒu fúyòng fāngfǎ.
Mr White	Duìbuqǐ, wǒ hái bú rènshi Hànzì.
Pharmacist	O. Duìbuqǐ. Wǒ gàosù nǐ. Yì tiān chī sān cì, yí cì chī èrshí lì.
Mr White	Shénme? Yì tiān chī liùshí lì?!
Pharmacist	Duì.
Mr White	Wǒde tiān a!
Pharmacist	Chī yào de shíhou bú yào hē kāfēi、chá hé jiǔ. Yīnggāi hē wēn kāishuǐ.
Mr White	Wèishénme?
Pharmacist	Chī yào dōu yīnggāi zhèyàng.

药 房

Yàofáng Pharmacy

226

Mr White	Wǒde yào fàn qián chī háishì fàn hòu chī?
Pharmacist	Dōu kéyǐ.
Mr White	Xièxie nín.
Pharmacist	Bú xiè.

You have seen that 'time when' expressions such as *Tuesday, 9 o'clock*, come before the verb (Unit 1) and that 'time during which' expressions such as how long you do something for, come after the verb (Unit 9).

Time *within* which something happens comes *before* the verb:

Wǒ **yì tiān** chī liǎng cì.   *I eat twice (in) a day.*
Yì tiān yào chī liùshí lì.   *(You) have to take (lit. eat) 60 pills (in) a day.*

Fàn qián is a more formal way of saying **chī fàn yǐqián** (*before a meal – lit.* eat cooked rice before) and **fàn hòu** of saying **chī fàn yǐhòu** (*after a meal – lit.* eat cooked rice after). Note that (yǐ)qián and (yǐ)hòu go after the noun in Chinese, the reverse of the English word order.

Instructions for taking Chinese medicine are given in the reverse of the way they are usually given in English-speaking countries. The normal word order in Chinese is:

fàn qián/hòu	*meal before/after*
yì tiān	*per day*
jǐ cì	*how many times*
yí cì chī X lì/piàn/wán(r)	*every time eat X pills/tablets/balls*

Chinese medicine sometimes comes in the form of small balls, which you have to chew. This is not all unpleasant (they are often flavoured with liquorice), but this form of medicine is not so commonly found in Chinese herbal medicine shops in the west catering for westerners. The Chinese seem to believe that westerners prefer to take pills!

Exercise 3 Read the instructions about taking the following medicines. Indicate whether each medicine is to be taken before or after meals and fill in the gaps (two per line).

a before/after meal; _____ times a day; take _____ every time
b before/after meal; _____ times a day; take _____ every time
c before/after meal; _____ times a day; take _____ every time
d before/after meal; _____ times a day; take _____ every time

1 Zhèi zhǒng Zhōngyào fàn qián chī, yì tiān liǎng cì, yí cì yì wánr.
2 Zhèi ge yào fàn hòu chī, yì tiān chī sì cì, yí cì chī sān piànr.
3 Nèi ge yào bú yào fàn qián chī. Fàn hòu yí ge xiǎoshí zài chī. Yì tiān chī sān cì, yí cì hē yì sháo (*tablespoon*).
4 Zhè ge yào zǎoshang chī yí cì, wǎnshang chī yí cì. Yí cì chī liǎng、sān piàn.

服用方法

Fúyòng fāngfǎ
Instructions for taking (the) medicine

Dialogue 3

◀) CD 2, TR 7, 03:41

The following dialogue is between a westerner visiting a Chinese clinic and a Chinese doctor working at the clinic. Before reading the dialogue, listen to the recording and try **Exercise 4** first. You can then check your answers when you read it.

Visitor	Nǐmen zhěnsuǒ bìngrén duō ma?
Doctor	Bù shǎo.
Visitor	Nǐmen dōu kàn shénme bìng?
Doctor	Gèzhǒng gèyàng de bìng. Nǐ kàn, zhèi ge bìngrén chángcháng tóu téng. Tā kàn-guo Xīyī, chī-guo Xīyào, kěshì hái bù hǎo. Wǒmen gěi tā zhā le zhēnjiǔ, xiànzài tā hǎo duōle.

Visitor	Zhēnde? Wǒ yě yǒu shíhou tóu téng. Tā zhā le jǐ cì le?
Doctor	Sì cì le.
Visitor	Zhēnjiǔ shì bu shì hěn téng?
Doctor	Zhēnjiǔ shì bù shūfu, kěshì chángcháng hěn yǒu xiào.
Visitor	Zhēnde ma?
Doctor	Nǐ yǒu shénme bìng? Wǒ kěyǐ gěi nǐ zhā.
Visitor	Bú yòng、bú yòng, wǒ méi bìng. Wǒde shēntǐ hěn hǎo. Xièxie nín.

Exercise 4   Select the correct answer to complete the statements which are based on **Dialogue 3.**

a There are ____ patients visiting the clinic. (*a lot, quite a few, few*)

b The clinic treats ____ illnesses. (*all sorts of, some, one or two kinds of*)

c The patient being treated in the clinic often has ____ . (*diarrhoea, headaches, stomach ache*)

d The visitor declined the offer of acupuncture because he ____ . (*was scared, had no illness, did not have the time*)

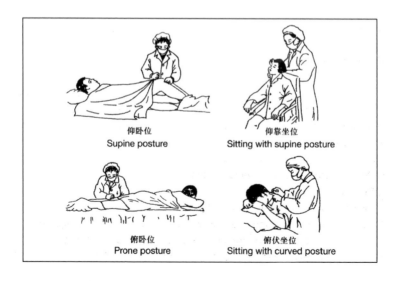

仰卧位
Supine posture

仰靠坐位
Sitting with supine posture

俯卧位
Prone posture

俯伏坐位
Sitting with curved posture

When two 'le's occur in the same sentence, as in the visitor's 3rd line in **Dialogue 3**, one after the verb and one at the end of the sentence, they convey the idea that the action of the verb is still going on:

(Nǐ gěi) tā zhā **le** jǐ cì (zhēnjiǔ) **le**?   *How many times have you given her acupuncture (so far)?*

Tā zài Lúndūn zhù **le** sān nián **le**.   *He's been living in London for three years (and still is).*

By putting **shì** in front of a verb or adjective you emphasize it:

Zhēnjiǔ **shì** bu shūfu.   *Acupuncture is uncomfortable.*

Xiě Hànzì **shì** hěn nán.   *Writing Chinese characters is difficult.*

Insight

To the Chinese way of thinking, each individual (and on a much larger scale the universe) is made up of **yīn** (*the female or passive/negative principle*) and **yáng** (*the male or active/positive principle*). To enjoy good health your **yīn** and **yáng** must be in balance. Chinese medicine seeks to redress any imbalance that exists.

Exercise 5 When a part of your body aches, you say **Wǒ(de) ____ téng.**

If you feel uncomfortable somewhere, you may say **Wǒ(de) ____ bù shūfu.**

If you don't know the Chinese word for the part of body you want to refer to, you can simply point at the place and say **Wǒ zhèr** (*here*) **téng**, or **Wǒ zhèr bù shūfu.**

230

Now practise these two patterns using the different parts of the body in turn (the Chinese for them is given in the drawing). You are answering the doctor's question **Nǐ nǎr bù shūfu?** So for the back you would say:

Wǒ yāo téng, *or*
Wǒ yāo bù shūfu.

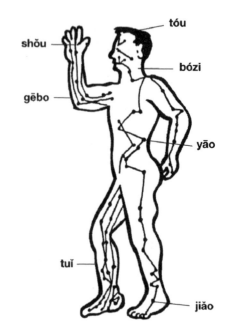

tóu
shǒu
bózi
gēbo
yāo
tuǐ
jiǎo

....

Insight

Acupuncture is an ancient Chinese method of treating diseases. It is based on the theory that the human body has a whole series of meridians up and down it through which your **qì** (sometimes written **ch'i** in the west) (*vital energy*) flows.

Having made his/her diagnosis, the acupuncturist inserts fine needles at various points (which all have different names) in your meridians to clear any blockages to your **qì**.

Some conditions seem to respond particularly well to acupuncture – rheumatoid-arthritis, gynaecological problems and the after-effects of a stroke to mention just a few.

Why not be brave and try acupuncture treatment yourself if you suffer from a long-standing condition that has not improved with conventional methods? But be sure to go to a reputable acupuncturist who is accredited or better still ask your GP or enquire at your local health shop to see if they can recommend someone.

....

Exercise 6 Find the Chinese equivalents in Section B to match the English sentences in Section A. Then put the Chinese sentences in the same order as the English sentences and you'll see a short passage about **qìgōng** in Chinese.

Section A:
a There are all kinds of qigong.
b Many people believe that qigong can cure all sorts of illness.
c Qigong is very popular nowadays in China.
d It's good for your health to do qigong very often.
e Both Tai Chi and qigong are slow forms of exercise.
f Some forms (of qigong) are not difficult (to practise); some are not easy.

Section B:
 i Xiànzài zài Zhōngguó, zuò qìgōng hěn liúxíng.
 ii Yǒude qìgōng bù nán, yǒude hěn bù róngyì.
 iii Chángcháng zuò qìgōng duì shēntǐ hǎo.
 iv Qìgōng yǒu gèzhǒng gèyàng de.
 v Hěn duō rén rènwéi qìgōng kěyǐ zhì gèzhǒng gèyàng de bìng.
 vi Qìgōng gēn tàijíquǎn dōu shì hěn màn de yùndòng.

Quick review

◀) CD 2, TR 7, 04:41

a You see your Chinese friend looking unwell. Ask what's wrong with her (*lit.* where she is not comfortable).
b Say you want to try acupuncture.
c Say you think you have a cold.
d Tell the doctor that you have never taken Chinese medicine.
e Tell the doctor that you sometimes have a headache.

18

Duìfu wèntí
Coping with problems

In this unit you will learn
- How to ask for help
- Some key expressions to describe your problems
- Some expressions required in an emergency
- The basic Highway Code in China

Revise before you start

- **gēn . . . yíyàng** (6)
- **zuì** (*most*) (7)
- noun + on (5)
- **yòu . . . yòu** (9)
- helping verbs (6)
- measure words (4)(7)
- use of **háishi** (6)

- how long (9)
- reduplicated verbs (6)
- **méi yǒu** (*not to have*) (2)
- **gěi** (*for*) (6)
- verb endings (10)
- **yǒu (yì)diǎnr** (8)
- sentences ending in **le** (4)

Zhōngguó de *Jiāotōng*   *Transport in China*

What do you know about transport in China? A lot of bikes? That's right. But read the passage below and find out something more about it. (Words in *italics* are explained in the **Quick vocab** box.)

Zài Zhōngguó, kāi chē hé qí zìxíngchē dōu *zǒu lù de yòubiān*. Zhè gēn zài Měiguó hé Ōuzhōu dàlù yíyàng, gēn zài Yīngguó bù yíyàng.

Zhōngguó shì *shìjiè shàng* zìxíngchē zuì duō de *guójiā*. Zài dà *chéngshì* yǒu hěn duō *zìxíngchē dào*. Xiànzài zài Zhōngguó *zū* qìchē hái hěn nán, kěshì zū zìxíngchē bǐjiào fāngbiàn. Qí zìxíngchē yòu piányi yòu yǒu yìsi.

Zài Zhōngguó yǒu *dìtiě* de chéngshì hěn shǎo. Bù shǎo chéngshì yǒu *diànchē*.

Yīnwei Zhōngguó-rén tài duō, suǒyǐ *lù shàng zǒngshì* hěn jǐ, chángcháng *dǔ chē*. Gōnggòng qìchē yě fēicháng jǐ. Dāngrán nǐ kěyǐ zuò chūzū (qì)chē. Chūzū (qì)chē bù jǐ, kěshì bù piányi.

Yàoshi nǐ cóng yí gè chéngshì qù *lìng yí gè* chéngshì, nǐ kěyǐ zuò fēijī、 huǒchē, yě kěyǐ zuò *chángtú qìchē*. Chángtú qìchē yǒu shíhou bú tài shūfu.

chángtú qìchē	*coach* (lit. *long-distance vehicle*)
chéngshì	*city*
diànchē	*tram* (lit. *electric vehicle*)
dìtiě	*underground/subway*
dǔ chē	(to be in a) *traffic jam*
duìfu	*to cope with*
gōnggòng qìchē	*bus* (lit. *public together steam vehicle*)
guójiā	*country*
jiāotōng	*transport, traffic*
lìng yí gè	*another; another one*
lù shàng	*on the road*
Ōuzhōu (dàlù)	*(continental) Europe*
shìjiè (shàng)	*(in the) world*
yàoshi	*if*
yīnwei/yīnwéi	*because*
yòu	*right*
yòubiān	*right side*

QUICK VOCAB

QUICK VOCAB

zǒu lù de yòubiān	*to drive/cycle on the right*
zìxíngchē dào	*bicycle lane*
zǒngshì	*always*
zū	*to hire, rent*
zuǒ	*left* (opposite of right)

Exercise 1   How do you say the following in Chinese about traffic in the west?

At first sight, the sentences may seem to be difficult. But if you model them on the sentences in the passage you should find them quite manageable.

a In Britain, driving and cycling are on the left-hand side of the road.

b This is the same as in Japan and Ireland but not the same as on the continent.

c America is the country that has the most cars in the world.

d In the west, it's not difficult to hire a car.

QUICK VOCAB

bāo	*bag*
qiánbāo	*purse/wallet*
bié rén	*other/another person*
chēdài	*tyre*
bǔ chēdài	*to mend a tyre*
chéng lǐ	*in the city, in urban areas*
cuò	*fault, mistake*
dàshǐguǎn	*embassy*
dēng	*lights*
diū	*to lose*
duō yuǎn?	*how far?*
Hái yǒu duō yuǎn?	*How far is it still to . . . ?*
gāoxìng	*happy*
guǎi	*to turn*
hǎoxiàng	*to seem*

hòulái	*later*
huài	*broken, not working; bad*
jǐngchá	*police officer*
jǐn(yi)jǐn	*to tighten*
lǐ	*inside*
liàng	(measure word for vehicles including bicycles)
líng	(for brakes) *to work well*
mǎshàng	*at once*
shāndìchē	*mountain bike*
shéide?	*whose?*
shēnfènzhèng	*identity card*
shīfu	title used when addressing a skilled worker (lit. *master*)
shǒu	*hand*
shuāi le yì jiāo	*to have had a fall*
tōngzhī	*to inform*
xiāoxi	*news, information*
yī . . . jiù	*no sooner . . . than . . . , as soon as*
yòng-bu-zháo	*not necessary*
zěnme huí shì?	*what's the matter?*
zhá	*brakes*
zhàoxiàngjī	*camera*
zhuàng	*to collide*
zhuàng-huài (le)	*damage(d)* (lit. *collide broken*)
Zhēn dǎoméi!	*How unfortunate! Bad luck!*

Placewords such as **lǐ** (*inside*) as in **chéng lǐ** can also have a longer form, so you will sometimes see **lǐmiàn(r)** (*lit.* in surface) or **lǐbiān(r)** (*lit.* in side) instead of just **lǐ**. There is no difference in meaning, however. This also applies to words like **shàng** (*on* or *on top of*), **xià** (*underneath*) and **wài** (*outside*).

Note that **shìjiè shàng** does not mean *on top of the world* but *in the world*. **Lǐ** is only used when you can actually get inside something, such as a shop, or when referring to money *in* a purse.

236

Dialogues

Dialogue 1

◀) **CD 2, TR 8**

When visiting a Chinese city, it is worth hiring a bicycle to explore the local area. It's economical too! This is what Ann and her friend are trying to do when they visit Nanjing. Listen to, or read, the dialogue and find out what kind of bicycle is available and how much they cost.

Ann	Wǒ xiǎng zū liǎng liàng zìxíngchē.
Shopkeeper	Yǒu shēnfènzhèng ma?
Ann	Yǒu. Zhè shì wǒde hùzhào.
Shopkeeper	Hǎo. Nín zū něi zhǒng chē?
Ann	Wǒ yào yí liàng xiǎo de. Wǒde péngyou yào yí liàng dà de.
Shopkeeper	Nǐmen zū jǐ tiān?
Ann	Yì tiān.
Shopkeeper	Nèi liǎng liàng shāndìchē búcuò. Nǐmen shìshi ba.
Ann and her friend try the bikes.	
Ann	Zhèi liàng chē de zhá hǎoxiàng bú tài líng.
Shopkeeper	Shì ma? Wǒ gěi nǐ jǐnyijǐn.
Ann	Zhèi xiē chē zěnme dōu méi yǒu dēng?
Shopkeeper	Zài chéng lǐ yòng-bu-zháo dēng.
Ann	Hǎo ba. Wǒ zū zhèi liǎng liàng. Duōshǎo qián?
Shopkeeper	Zhèi liàng dà de yì tiān shíbā kuài. Nà liàng xiǎo de yì tiān shíwǔ kuài. Yígòng sānshísān kuài.
Ann	Gěi nín sìshí kuài.
Shopkeeper	Zhǎo nín qī kuài.

Insight

Bicycle parking lots (**Cúnchēchù**) abound in Chinese cities. For a very modest charge you can leave your bicycle there. It will be much safer.

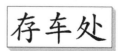

Cúnchēchù

Bicycles in China are not required by law to have lights. It is worth bearing this in mind as a cyclist or a motorist: as a cyclist it means you are difficult to be seen, as a motorist it means you have to be extra alert when driving in the dark.

◀) **CD 2, TR 8, 01:32**

Exercise 2   Now you are visiting Taiwan and you want to hire a car. Complete the dialogue that follows. **Dialogue 1** should help you.

a	**You**	(*Say you would like to hire a car.*)
	Clerk	Nín yǒu jiàzhào (*driving licence*) ma?
b	**You**	(*Say yes and yours is a British one.*)
	Clerk	Nín yào něi zhǒng chē?
c	**You**	(*Say you'd like to have a small one.*)
	Clerk	Zhèi liàng kěyǐ ma?
d	**You**	(*Say it's fine.*)
	Clerk	Nín zū jǐ tiān?
e	**You**	(*Say two days.*)
	Clerk	Qǐng dào nèibiān fù qián.
f	**You**	(*Ask if they take credit cards.*)
	Clerk	Shōu.

Dialogue 2

Unfortunately, Ann has got a flat tyre on her bike. She sees a bike repair man by the side of the road and walks over for help.

Ann	Shīfu, wǒde chēdài huài le, nín néng bāng wǒ xiūxiu ma?
Shīfu	Méi wèntí.
Ann	Děi duō cháng shíjiān?
Shīfu	Yìhuǐr jiù xíng.
Ann	Shīfu, chōu zhī yān ba.
Shīfu	Hǎo、hǎo. Xièxie、xièxie.
Ann	Shīfu, qù Xiāngshān hái yǒu duō yuǎn?
Shīfu	Wǎng běi qí èrshí fēnzhōng, zài wǎng xī guǎi jiù dào le.

*   *   *

Shīfu	Xiū-hǎo le.
Ann	Zhēn kuài. Xièxie nín. Zhèi liàng chē de zhá bú tài líng, nín néng kànkan ma?
Shīfu	Kěyǐ. Wǒ gěi nín jǐnjin. . . . Xíng le.
Ann	Xièxie nín. Yígòng duōshao qián?
Shīfu	Bǔ chēdài liǎng kuài wǔ. Jǐn zhá jiù bù shōu nǐ qián le.
Ann	Xièxie shīfu. Nín zài chōu zhī yān ba.

雪中送碳

Chinese proverb: **Xuě zhōng sòng tàn**
Send charcoal in snowy weather – provide timely help

Exercise 3 In **Dialogue 2**, you saw several noun phrases consisting of a verb and an object, such as: **bǔ chēdài**, **jǐn zhá** and **qù Xiāngshān**.

These phrases can be used at the beginning of a sentence as a kind of topic – the opposite of the word order in English. You can see this clearly from the example:

> **Kāi chē shàng bān** děi duō   *How long does it take **to drive***
> cháng shíjiān?   ***to work?***

Now try the same thing with the sentences below when you put them into Chinese.

a It takes an hour *to drive to work.*
b How much does it cost *to have the tyre mended*?
c How do I *get to the Fragrant Hills* (Xiāngshān) *by bus*?
d It costs 30 yuan *to hire a bike.*

Dialogue 3

◀) **CD 2, TR 8, 03:02**

Ānyīn notices that her friend Ben is looking rather unhappy. Listen to, or read, the dialogue and find out what happened to Ben.

Ānyīn	Nǐ hǎoxiàng yǒu diǎnr bù gāoxìng.
Ben	Méi shénme.
Ānyīn	Nǐde shǒu zěnme le?
Ben	O, wǒ shuāi le yì jiāo.
Ānyīn	Zěnme huí shì?
Ben	Zhēn dǎoméi! Wǒ gēn bié rén zhuàng chē le.
Ānyīn	Shì shéide cuò?
Ben	Wǒ shuō shì tāde cuò, tā shuō shì wǒde cuò.
Ānyīn	Chē zhuàng-huài le ma?
Ben	Zhuàng-huài le.
Ānyīn	Nǐmen zhǎo jǐngchá le ma?
Ben	Zhǎo le. Jǐngchá shuō wǒmen dōu yǒu cuò.
Ānyīn	Hòulái ne?
Ben	Hòulái, wǒmen dōu qù xiū zìjǐ de chē le.

Insight

In many cities in China, you may turn right at a red light (**hóng dēng**) so be very alert when you see a red traffic light whether you are driving a car or riding a bicycle. **Hónglǜdēng** means *traffic lights* (*lit.* red green light).

◄) CD 2, TR 8, 04:04

Exercise 4   Say whether the following statements are **duì** or **bú duì** (true or false).

		duì	bú duì
a	Ānyīn hěn bù gāoxìng.	☐	☐
b	Ben gēn bié rén zhuàng chē le.	☐	☐
c	Nà ge rén shuō shì Ben de cuò.	☐	☐
d	Zhuàng chē yǐhòu, Ben zhǎo le jǐngchá.	☐	☐
e	Ben de chē zhuàng-huài le.	☐	☐
f	Jǐngchá shuō shì Ben de cuò.	☐	☐
g	Ben qù xiū Ānyīn de chē le.	☐	☐

Dialogue 4

◀) CD 2, TR 8, 05:06

Ben is now at a local police station. He really has had bad luck. Read the dialogue, and find out what his problem is and what he is advised to do.

Jǐngchá	Nín yǒu shénme shì?
Ben	Wǒde bāo diū le.
Jǐngchá	Bāo lǐmiàn yǒu shénme?
Ben	Yǒu wǒde hùzhào hé qiánbāo. Qiánbāo lǐ yǒu wǒde xìnyòng kǎ, sìbǎi duō rénmínbì hé liǎngbǎi měiyuán. O, hái yǒu yí ge xiǎo zhàoxiàngjī.
Jǐngchá	Nín diū le hùzhào, yīnggāi tōngzhī nǐmen guójiā de dàshǐguǎn.
Ben	Wǒ gěi dàshǐguǎn dǎ diànhuà le.
	(The policewoman takes down the details of the incident.)
Jǐngchá	Nín xiànzài zhù zài nǎr?
Ben	Yùlóng Fàndiàn sān-líng-yāo fángjiān.
Jǐngchá	Qǐng nín xiān huí qù. Wǒmen **yī** yǒu xiāoxi **jiù** mǎshàng tōngzhī nín.

Linking words (also known as *conjunctions*) often come in pairs in Chinese so it is good to memorize them as such. There are two examples in this unit.

yīnwei . . . suǒyǐ . . .	because . . . therefore . . .
. . . yī + verb¹ jiù + verb²	as soon as verb¹ happens, then verb² will happen (**Dialogue 4**)

Exercise 5 Now you have listened to, or read, **Dialogue 4** answer the following questions.

a What was Ben's problem?
b What was in the bag?
c How much money had he taken with him?
d Where was Ben staying?

e What was he advised to do about the loss of the passport?
f What did the police say they would do?

Exercise 6 Make at least one statement about the problems in the following pictures.

Nǐ zuò-cuò chē le. *You've taken the wrong bus.*

Quick review

◀) CD 2, TR 8, 06:08

You happen to have run into a problem:

a How would you say 'What bad luck!'?
b Say that it's not your fault.
c Say that you think they should go to the police.
d Say that you've lost your credit card.
e Something has gone wrong with your bike (or anything), ask if someone can have a look at it.

19

Xuéxí Zhōngwén
Learning Chinese

In this unit you will learn
- The basic vocabulary to describe the characteristics of a language
- How to talk about your future plans
- How to respond to compliments or forthright remarks

Revise before you start

- use of **háishi** (6)
- **gēn . . . yíyàng** (6)
- use of **de** after verbs (8)
- **tài . . . le** (7)
- helping verbs (6)

- be in the middle of doing something (6)
- **gèng** (*even more*) (8)
- verb endings (10)
- **zuì** (*most*) (7)
- **duō** + verb (10)

Zhōngwén háishi Hànyǔ? *The Chinese for 'Chinese'!*

Which Chinese word describes the language you have been learning in this book? Is it **Hànyǔ**, **Zhōngwén**, **Pǔtōnghuà**, **Guóyǔ** or **Huáyǔ**? Read the passage and find out.

Zhōngwén yìbān zhǐ Hànyǔ. *Zhōng*wén de *zhōng* shì **Zhōngguó** de *zhōng*. **Wén** shì *writing* huòzhě *language* de yìsi. **Hànyǔ** de *hàn* shì

Hànzú de hàn. Yǔ shi yǔyán de yǔ, yě shì *language* de yìsi. Hànyǔ jiù shì Hànzú-rén de yǔyán. Zhōngguó de hěn duō shǎoshù mínzú dōu yǒu zìjǐ de yǔyán.

Hànyǔ yǒu hěn duō zhǒng fāngyán. Shànghǎihuà shì yì zhǒng fāngyán. Shànghǎi-rén shuō Shànghǎihuà. Guǎngdōnghuà yě shì yì zhǒng fāngyán. Guǎngdōng-rén hé Xiānggǎng-rén shuō Guǎngdōnghuà.

Wǒmen xuéxí de Zhōngwén shì Pǔtōnghuà. Pǔtōnghuà bú shì fāngyán, shì guānfāng yǔyán. Táiwān-rén jiào tā Guóyǔ, Dōngnányà de Huá-rén jiào tā Huáyǔ. Guóyǔ hé Huáyǔ jiù shì Pǔtōnghuà. Pǔtōnghuà bú shì Běijīnghuà. Běijīnghuà hé Pǔtōnghuà chàbuduō. Hěn duō Běijīng-rén shuō de Pǔtōnghuà yǒu Běijīng kǒuyīn.

Dōngnányà	*Southeast Asia*
fāngyán	*dialect*
guānfāng	*official*
Guóyǔ	*national language*
Hànzú	*Han nationality*
Hànzú-rén	*the Han people*
Huá	another word for *China*
Huá-rén	*overseas Chinese people*
kǒuyīn	*accent*
Pǔtōnghuà	*Chinese (Mandarin)* (lit. *common language*)
shǎoshù mínzú	*national minority*
wén	*language, writing*
yǔ (yán)	*language*
zhǐ	*to refer to*

QUICK VOCAB

Exercise 1 There are several language terms in the passage above. You will find them very useful. Without referring to the vocabulary list, can you match the words with their correct meanings?

a Pǔtōnghuà   i   Cantonese
b Guóyǔ   ii   Chinese (spoken by overseas Chinese)

c	Guǎngdōnghuà	iii	Chinese language
d	fāngyán	iv	Chinese (spoken in Mainland China)
e	Zhōngwén	v	accent
f	kǒuyīn	vi	Chinese (spoken in Taiwan)
g	Huáyǔ	vii	dialect

Exercise 2 Fill in the blanks with suitable words. You will find it useful to go back to the passage on the previous page.

a Dàbùfen Zhōngguó-rén shì _____ rén. Tāmen shuō _____.

b Sìchuānhuà bú shì Pǔtōnghuà, shì yì zhǒng _____. Yǒude Sìchuān-rén shuō de Pǔtōnghuà yǒu Sìchuān _____.

c Pǔtōnghuà zài Táiwān jiào _____, zài Dōngnányà jiào _____.

d Zài Zhōngguó, hěn duō shǎoshù mínzú de rén huì shuō tāmen zìjǐ de _____, yě huì shuō _____.

bù xíng	*not that good*
cōngming	*clever*
dàjiā	*everyone*
duì . . . yǒu/gǎn xìngqu	*to be interested in*
duō tīng/shuō/dú/xiě	*to listen/speak/read/write more*
Éguó-rén	*Russian (person)*
èrhú	*a two-stringed musical instrument*
fāngfǎ	*method*
fānyì	*interpreter, translator; to translate*
guòjiǎng	*to exaggerate, to flatter*
Hánguó-rén	*Korean (person)*
jiǎndān	*simple*
jièshào	*to introduce; introduction*
jīngjì	*economy*
jìzhě	*journalist*
Kǒngzǐ	*Confucius*
Lǎozǐ	*an ancient philosopher*
Lǐ Bái	*an ancient poet*
lìshǐ	*history*
liúlì	*fluent*

QUICK VOCAB

pípa	*a musical instrument*
qiānxū	*modest*
shēng	*tone (e.g.* **dì-yī/èr shēng** = the 1st/2nd tone)
shēngdiào	*tones*
wénxué	*literature*
xiānsheng	*husband*
xiě	*to write*
xìngqu	*interest*
xuésheng	*student*
yánjiū	*to study, to research*
yǔfǎ	*grammar*
yǔyīn	*pronunciation*
zhéxué	*philosophy*
zhǐyào … jiù …	*so long as … then …*
Zhuāngzǐ	*an ancient philosopher*

Dialogues

Dialogue 1

◄) CD 2, TR 9

Lányīn, a student of Chinese, is talking to Huáyàn, a Chinese student of English, about learning foreign languages. Listen to, or read, the dialogue and find out the secret of Lányīn's success in learning Chinese.

Huáyàn	Nǐde Zhōngwén zhēn bàng, shuō-de zhēn liúlì.
Lányīn	Nǎli, nǎli, shuō-de bù hǎo.
Huáyàn	Nǐde yǔyīn、shēngdiào dōu fēicháng hǎo.
Lányīn	Bù xíng, bù xíng, hái chà-de hěn yuǎn.
Huáyàn	Nǐ xué le jǐ nián le?
Lányīn	Sān nián le.
Huáyàn	Shénme? Zhǐ yǒu sān nián?! Nǐ tài cōngming le.
Lányīn	Nǐ guòjiǎng le.

Huáyàn	Wǒ xué le liù nián Yīngyǔ le, kěshì shuō-de hái hěn chà.
Lányīn	Nǐ zhēn qiānxū.
Huáyàn	Nǐ yídìng yào gàosù wǒ nǐde xuéxí fāngfǎ.
Lányīn	Hěn jiǎndān. Wǒ xiānsheng shì Zhōngguó-rén.

Exercise 3 Answer the following questions in English, based on Dialogue 1.

a In what aspects is Lányīn's Chinese good?
b How long has Lányīn been learning Chinese?
c How good is Huáyàn's English?
d How long has Huáyàn been learning English?
e What does Huáyàn want to know from Lányīn?
f Who does Lányīn think she owes her success to?

The following table lists the degrees of goodness you have met in descending order.

QUICK VOCAB

zuì hǎo	*the best*
fēicháng hǎo	*extremely good/well*
búcuò	*pretty good/well*
(hěn) hǎo	*(very) good/well*
bú tài hǎo	*not very good/well*
bù hǎo	*not good/well*
hěn bù hǎo/hěn chà	*very poor/badly*

Note that **hǎo** translates as *good* or *well* depending on whether it is being used as an adjective/verb, when it means *good*, or as an adverb, when it means *well*.

Tā shuǒ-de hěn **hǎo**.	*He speaks very well.*
Tāde Yīngwén hěn **hǎo**.	*Her English is very good.*

Dialogue 2

On the first day of a Chinese summer course, the students introduce themselves and talk about their reasons for studying Chinese. Read the dialogue to find out where they are from and why they want to learn Chinese.

Lǎoshī	Nǐmen hǎo. Wǒ xìng Táng, shì nǐmen de lǎoshī. Nǐmen kěyǐ jiào wǒ Táng lǎoshī. Wǒ hái bú rènshi nǐmen. Xiān qǐng dàjiā jièshào yíxiàr zìjǐ.
Wèimín	Wǒ shì Éguó-rén. Wǒ jiào Bái Wèimín. Bái shì Lǐ Bái de Bái. Wǒ hěn xǐhuan Zhōngguó wénxué. Jiānglái wǒ xiǎng dāng fānyì.
Ānfāng	Wǒ xìng Cuī, jiào Cuī Ānfāng. Wǒ shì Hánguó-rén. Wǒ duì Zhōngguó yīnyuè hěn yǒu xìngqu. Wǒ xiànzài zài xuéxí èrhú hé pípa.
Wénzhé	Wǒ shì Měiguó-rén. Wǒ de Zhōngwén míngzi jiào Shǐ Wénzhé. Shǐ shì lìshǐ de shǐ, wén shì wénxué de wén, zhé shì zhéxué de zhé. Wǒ yě xǐhuan Zhōngguó wénxué. Wǒ gèng xǐhuan Zhōngguó zhéxué. Wǒ yào yánjiū Kǒngzǐ、Lǎozǐ hé Zhuāngzǐ.
Lányīn	Wǒ shì Yīngguó-rén. Wǒ duì Zhōngguó de shǎoshù mínzú hěn yǒu xìngqu. Wǒ jiānglái xiǎng yánjiū tāmen de lìshǐ hé yǔyán.
Lǎoshī	Nǐ jiào shénme míngzi?
Lányīn	O, duìbuqǐ. Wǒ jiào Lányīn. Wǒ hái bù zhīdao jiānglái zuò shénme, kěnéng dāng jìzhě.
Shānběn	Wǒ jiào Shānběn, shì Rìběn-rén. Wǒ xiànzài zài yánjiū Zhōngguó jīngjì.
Lǎoshī	Xièxie dàjiā de jièshào.

Exercise 4 Refer to **Dialogue 2** and fill in the blanks in the sentences saying who is who and who is doing what.

a ____ xuésheng Cuī Ānfāng zài xuéxí ____ hé ____.
b Lányīn shì ____ -rén. Tā xiǎng yánjiū ____ de yǔyán hé lìshǐ.
c Nà ge ____ xuésheng jiào Shānběn. Tā duì ____ yǒu xìngqu.
d Bái Wèimín xiǎng dāng ____. Lányīn xiǎng dāng ____.

e Wénzhé de wén shì _____ de wén, zhé shì _____ de zhé. Tā shuō tā duì _____ yǒu xìngqu, duì _____ gèng yǒu xìngqu.

Exercise 5 Imagine that you are one of the students in the class (in **Dialogue 2**) and try to introduce your teacher and fellow students in Chinese. You could use some of the sentences in **Exercise 4**.

Dialogue 3

CD 2, TR 9, 02:29

Is Chinese difficult? Let's hear what the students in **Dialogue 2** have to say.

Lǎoshī	Nǐmen juéde Zhōngwén nán bu nán?
Shānběn	Hànzì bù nán, yǔyīn hěn nán.
Lányīn	Yīnwei nǐ shì Rìběn-rén, huì xiě Hànzì, suǒyǐ nǐ juéde Hànzì bù nán. Wǒ juéde Hànzì tài nán le.
Wénzhé	Hànzì bù róngyì, kěshì yǔfǎ gèng nán. Wǒ zǒngshì bù zhīdao shénme shíhou yòng **le**, shénme shíhou bú yòng **le**.
Wèimín	Hànyǔ yǔfǎ bú tài nán, shēngdiào zhēn bù róngyì. Wǒ chángcháng shuō-bu-hǎo dì-èr shēng hé dì-sì shēng.
Ānfāng	Wǒ juéde dì-sān shēng zuì nán.
Lǎoshī	Zhōngwén bù róngyì, kěshì **zhǐyào** wǒmen duō tīng、 duō shuō、 duō dú、 duō xiě, wǒmen **jiù** yídìng kěyǐ xué-hǎo.

This is a good time to go back over the **Pronunciation guide** and to practise your tones. If you have the recording, go right back to the beginning again and repeat all the sounds and tones. Hopefully this will now seem very easy!

Here's another pair of linking words to add to the ones you met in Unit 18.

Zhǐyào . . . jiù . . .   *if only/as long as . . . then . . .*

He can read when it suits him!

请勿 随地吐痰	请勿吸烟	请勿照相	小心触电
No spitting	No smoking	No photography	Danger: electric shock

Exercise 6 Do you speak other languages? What would you say about them in terms of pronunciation and grammar? How well do you speak them? Do you speak them with an accent or not? Try to use some of the sentences in **Dialogue 3**. (We have provided sample answers in the **Key to the exercises**.)

Here are some phrases you might find useful:

bàng	fēicháng hǎo	hěn hǎo/liúlì
búcuò	tǐng hǎo	hái kěyǐ
bú* (tài) hǎo/liúlì	hěn bù hǎo/liúlì	hěn chà

*bù is 4th tone if 'tài' is omitted.

a Wǒ huì shuō _____ (hé _____).
b Wǒde _____ búcuò. *or* Wǒde _____ shuō-de _____.
c Wǒ huì shuō yìdiǎnr _____.
d Wǒ shuō_____ shuō-de yǒu (yìdiǎnr) _____ kǒuyīn.
e _____ (a language) de yǔyīn _____.

Quick review

◀) CD 2, TR 9, 03:42

How do you say/ask the following in Chinese?

a Do you find English pronunciation difficult?
b I can only write a few Chinese characters.
c I speak a little Chinese but I find tones difficult.
d You are modest.
e I find it difficult to understand her accent.
f Your English/French/German is pretty good.
g You are flattering me.

20

···

Lǚxíng hé tiānqi
Travel and weather

In this unit you will learn
- How to get to somewhere
- About Chinese festivals
- About regional differences
- How to talk about the weather

―――――――――――――――――――――

Revise before you start

―――――――――――――――――――――

Qìhòu hé tiānqi   *Climate and weather*

◄» **CD 2, TR 10**

This passage, together with the dialogues in this unit, will help you talk in Chinese about the weather, a topic for all seasons! Can you work out from this passage which seasons Chinese people prefer and why?

Zhōngguó hěn dà, dōng、xī、nán、běi de *qìhòu* chángcháng hěn bù yíyàng. *Yìbānláishuō, nánfāng* de xiàtiān bǐ běifāng de rè, běifāng de dōngtiān bǐ nánfāng de *lěng*.

Zài Zhōngguó, dàbùfen dìfang yǒu sì ge *jìjié*: chūn、xià、qiū、dōng. *Chūntiān* cóng sānyuè dào wǔyuè. Liùyuè、qīyuè、bāyuè shì xiàtiān. *Qiūtiān* shì jiǔ、shí hé shíyīyuè. Shí'èryuè dào èryuè shì dōngtiān. Yìbān qī、bāyuè zuì rè; yī、èryuè zuì lěng.

Zhōngguó-rén *bǐjiào xǐhuan* chūntiān hé qiūtiān, yīnwéi chūntiān hé qiūtiān bù lěng yě bú rè.

bǐjiào xǐhuan	*to prefer*
chūn(tiān)	*spring*
jìjié	*seasons*
lěng	*cold*
nánfāng	*the south*
qìhòu	*climate*
qiū(tiān)	*autumn*
yìbānláishuō	*generally speaking*

QUICK VOCAB

Exercise 1 Follow the sentences in paragraph two in the passage and talk about the seasons in your part of the world or a country or region that you know well. We have given sample answers for Europe in the **Key to the exercises**.

a Chūntiān cóng _____ dào _____.
b _____、_____、_____ shì xiàtiān.
c Qiūtiān shì _____、_____、_____.
d _____ dào _____ shì dōngtiān.

Exercise 2 How would you answer these questions that a Chinese person might ask you?

a Nǐmen guójiā yǒu jǐ ge jìjié?
b Nǎ ge yuè zuì rè? Nǎ ge yuè zuì lěng?
c Nǐ bǐjiào xǐhuan nǎ ge jìjié?
d Zài nǐmen guójiā běifāng shì bu shì bǐ nánfāng lěng?

QUICK VOCAB

ānpái	*arrangement; to arrange*
Wǒ lái ānpái ba.	*I'll make the arrangements.*
cónglái	*ever*
dàibiǎotuán	*delegation*
dāng	*to be; to work/act as*
dù	*degree (°C)*
fādá	*developed*
fēngjǐng	*scenery*
gōngzuò	*work; to work*
hěn shǎo	*seldom; (very) few*
huí guó	*return to one's own country*
huí lái	*to come back*
jiàn miàn	*to meet*
kāi xué	*start of term*
měi	*beautiful*
qìwēn	*(weather) temperature*
tè	*extremely*
Wǔtái Shān	*Mount Wutai*
	(in Shānxī Province)
xiǎng	*to miss, long for*
(tiānqi) yùbào	*(weather) forecast*
yúkuài	*happy, pleasant*

fēng	*wind*	**guā fēng**	*windy (lit. blow wind)*
yǔ	*rain*	**xià yǔ**	*to rain (lit. descend rain)*
xuě	*snow*	**xià xuě**	*to snow (lit. descend snow)*
nuǎn(huo)	*warm*	**liáng(kuai)**	*cool*

Dialogues

Dialogue 1

🔊 **CD 2, TR 10, 01:13**

Colin, who is studying in Tiānjīn, is ringing his Chinese friend, Sūlán, in Kūnmíng, Yúnnán Province to arrange a meeting between them during the winter vacation.

Colin	Zhè jǐ tiān Tiānjīn tè lěng, kěshì fēngjǐng zhēn měi. Zuótiān xià xuě le.
Sūlán	Xuě dà ma?
Colin	Bù xiǎo. Tiānqi yùbào shuō, míngtiān hái yào xià xuě.
Sūlán	Kūnmíng cónglái bú xià xuě. Wǒ zhēn xiǎng qù Tiānjīn kàn xuě.
Colin	Nǐ nàr tiānqi zěnmeyàng?
Sūlán	Bù nuǎnhuo. Jīntiān de qìwēn shì shíwǔ dù.
Colin	Shénme? Shíwǔ dù? Gēn Tiānjīn de chūntiān yíyàng nuǎnhuo.
Sūlán	Kěshì wǒ juéde lěng. Jīntiān shàngwǔ xià le xiǎo yǔ.
Colin	Wǒ zuì xǐhuan xiǎo yǔ. Kěshì Tiānjīn dōngtiān hěn shǎo xià yǔ.
Sūlán	Nǐ lái Kūnmíng kàn yǔ, wǒ qù Tiānjīn kàn xuě, zěnmeyàng?
Colin	Zhēn shì ge hǎo zhǔyì! Wǒ lái ānpái ba.
Sūlán	Děngyiděng! Nàme wǒmen zài nǎr jiàn miàn ne?

Exercise 3 Are these statements about **Dialogue 1 duì** or **bú duì**?

	duì	bú duì
a Tiānjīn zuótiān xià le xiǎo xuě.	☐	☐
b Kūnmíng jīntiān xià le xiǎo yǔ.	☐	☐
c Sūlán bù xǐhuan kàn xuě.	☐	☐
d Kūnmíng tiānqi bù lěng, kěshì Sūlán juéde leng.	☐	☐
e Colin rènwéi tāmen yīnggāi zài Kūnmíng jiàn miàn.	☐	☐

Exercise 4 Zhèi liǎng tiān tiānqi zěnmeyàng? *What's the weather been like the last two days?*

Read the following statements, and decide whether each is true. If not, negate it.

Example: Zuótiān xià yǔ le.
* Duì. (*i.e.* Zuótiān xià yǔ le.)
* Bú duì. Zuótiān méi xià yǔ.

a Jīntiān tiānqi hěn nuǎnhuo.
b Jīntiān zǎoshang guā fēng le.
c Jīntiān wǎnshang yǒu dà yǔ.
d Jīntiān èrshí dù.
e Zuótiān tiānqi tè rè.
f Zuótiān shàngwǔ xià le xiǎo xuě.
g Zuótiān xiàwǔ fēng bú dà.

Dialogue 2

◄) **CD , TR 10, 03:02**

The students from Unit 19 are discussing where they plan to go during the holiday.

Lǎoshī	Jiàqī nǐmen dǎsuàn qù nǎr?
Shānběn	Wǒ xǐhuan dà chéngshì. Wǒ xiān qù Shànghǎi, ránhòu qù Guǎngzhōu. Shànghǎi hé Guǎngzhōu de jīngjì zuì fādá.
Lányīn	Wǒ bù xǐhuan dà chéngshì. Wǒ yào qù Yúnnán hé Guìzhōu. Nàr yǒu hěn duō shǎoshù mínzú.
Wénzhé	Yúnnán hé Guìzhōu dōu zài Zhōngguó de nánfāng, xiàtiān yídìng hěn rè. Wǒ qù Shānxī de Wǔtái Shān. Nàr yídìng hěn liángkuai.
Wèimín	Zhè ge jiàqī wǒ yǒu gōngzuò. Wǒ qù Tiānjīn gěi yí ge dàibiǎotuán dāng fānyì.
Lǎoshī	Ānfāng, nǐ ne?
Ānfāng	Wǒ zhēn xiànmu nǐmen. Kěshì wǒ yào huí Hánguó. Wǒ tài xiǎng wǒ bàba、māma le. Kāi xué de shíhou wǒ zài huí lái.

星期日	星期一	星期二	星期三	星期四	星期五	星期六
	1 ⁷ 元旦	2 ⁸ 初八	3 ⁹ 初九	4 ¹⁰ 初十	5 ¹¹ 小寒	6 ¹² 十二
7 ¹³ 十三	8 ¹⁴ 十四	9 ¹⁵ 十五	10 ¹⁶ 十六	11 ¹⁷ 十七	12 ¹⁸ 十八	13 ¹⁹ 十九
14 ²⁰ 二十	15 ²¹ 廿一	16 ²² 廿二	17 ²³ 廿三	18 ²⁴ 廿四	19 ²⁵ 廿五	20 ²⁶ 大寒
21 ²⁷ 廿七	22 ²⁸ 廿八	23 ²⁹ 廿九	24 ¹ᐟ¹ 正月	25 ² 初二	26 ³ 初三	27 ⁴ 初四
28 ⁵ 初五	29 ⁶ 初六	30 ⁷ 初七	31 ⁸ 初八			

The Chinese New Year starts on 24 January in this particular year.

Insight
Major Chinese festivals

The most important Chinese festival is **Chūnjié** the *Spring Festival* or the *Chinese Lunar New Year*, which falls on the first day of the first lunar month. The Lunar New Year itself may occur as early as 21 January and as late as 21 February. It is the major festival in China (rather like Christmas in the west) and most people try to get home to celebrate it with their families even if it means travelling long distances.

Firecrackers are set off on New Year's Eve and New Year's Day to ward off evil spirits even though many Chinese have probably forgotten the origin of this custom.

Other major festivals are the *Lantern Festival*, the *Pure Brightness* or *Grave Sweeping Festival*, the *Dragon Boat Festival* and the *Mid-Autumn Festival*, which was originally to pay homage to the full moon.

You could visit your local library to find out more about these festivals: what their origins are, when they occur and how they are celebrated. Most overseas Chinese communities observe these festivals too. You could learn a lot about Chinese traditions. It would also give you an insight into the traditional Chinese way of life which has helped to shape their language.

Exercise 5 Match the sentences in Column A with their English equivalents in Column B.

Column A
a Nàr xiàtiān yídìng hěn liángkuai.
b Dà chéngshì de jīngjì hěn fādá.
c Nàr yǒu hěn duō shǎoshù mínzú.
d Jiàqī wǒ dǎsuàn qù lǚxíng.
e Kāi xué de shíhou wǒ zài huí lái.

Column B
i During the holidays I plan to travel.
ii There are many minorities there.
iii I will come back again when term starts.
iv The economy in big cities is developed.
v It must be cool there in the summer.

Exercise 6 Now cover up Column B in **Exercise 5** and say what the sentences in Column A mean in English. Once you have done that, cover up Column A and say what the sentences in Column B mean in Chinese.

Dialogue 3

🔊 **CD 2, TR 10, 05:01**

Listen to the dialogue and find out how these students plan to travel to the places they are going to visit during the holiday. Go straight to **Exercise 7** *without reading the dialogue*! If you haven't got the recording, read the dialogue, and then do **Exercise 7**.

Lǎoshī	Nǐmen zěnme qù?
Wèimín	Tiānjīn bù yuǎn. Wǒ zuò huǒchē qù. Liǎng、sān ge xiǎoshí jiù dào le.
Lányīn	Yúnnán lí Běijīng hěn yuǎn. Wǒ kěyǐ zuò huǒchē, yě kěyǐ zuò fēijī. Wǒ hái méi yǒu juédìng.
Lǎoshī	Fēijī bǐ huǒchē kuài duōle, kěshì yě guì duōle.
Wénzhé	Wǔtái Shān bù yuǎn yě bú jìn. Wǒ xiǎng xiān zuò huǒchē, zài zuò chángtú qìchē.
Lǎoshī	Shānběn, nǐ yào qù liǎng ge dìfang. Nǐ zěnme qù?
Shānběn	Wǒ xiǎng xiān zuò fēijī dào Shànghǎi, zài zuò huǒchē qù Guǎngzhōu.
Ānfāng	Wǒ bù xǐhuan zuò fēijī, kěshì wǒ zhǐ néng zuò fēijī huí guó.
Lǎoshī	Hǎo. Zhù dàjiā jiàqī yúkuài.

走马看花

Chinese proverb: **Zǒu mǎ kàn huā**
*Look at flowers while riding on horseback –
gain a superficial understanding*

Exercise 7 How will the students in **Dialogue 3** get to their destinations?

a Wèimín zuò _____ qù Tiānjīn.
b Lányīn zuò _____ huòzhě _____ qù Yúnnán.
c Wénzhé zuò _____ hé _____ qù Wǔtái Shān.
d Shānběn zuò _____ qù Shànghǎi, zuò _____ qù Guǎngzhōu.
e Ānfāng zuò _____ huí Hánguó.

Exercise 8 Make complete sentences with the words or phrases given. You will have to supply a missing word in each case. Pay attention to the word order.

Example: Lúndūn/fēijī/lái/tā/bù
          Tā bú zuò fēijī lái Lúndūn.

a tā/qù/Shànghǎi/huǒchē/míngtiān
b lái/wǒde péngyou/wǒ jiā/gōnggòng qìchē
c qù gōngyuán/zìxíngchē/bù/wǒ
d mǎi dōngxi/chē/tāmen/chángcháng/qù
e dìtiě/huí jiā/xiànzài/wǒ

◀ゥ **CD 2, TR 10, 06:15**

Exercise 9 Your Chinese friend, Yànmíng, is asking you about the holiday you plan to take.

Yànmíng		Nǐ dǎsuàn qù shénme dìfang?
a	**You**	(*Say you want to go to Hong Kong and Macao.*)
	Yànmíng	Nǐ zěnme qù?
b	**You**	(*Say you will fly to Hong Kong and then go to Macao by boat.*)
	Yànmíng	Nàr de tiānqi zěnmeyàng?
c	**You**	(*Say it's hot there in August.*)
	Yànmíng	Xià bu xià yǔ?
d	**You**	(*Say sometimes it rains.*)
	Yànmíng	Nǐ qù jǐ tiān?
e	**You**	(*Say you haven't decided yet.*)

Exercise 10   Listen to the following passage and then answer the questions about it.

Běijīng de Jìjié

Běijīng de dōngtiān yòu *cháng* yòu lěng; xiàtiān yòu cháng yòu rè. Běijīng de chūntiān hěn duǎn yě hěn nuǎnhuo, kěshì chángcháng guā fēng.

Běijīng zuì hǎo de jìjié shì qiūtiān. Qiūtiān bù lěng yě bú rè. *Báitiān* hěn nuǎnhuo, zǎoshang hé wǎnshang hěn liángkuai. Qiūtiān *qíngtiān* duō, *yīntiān* shǎo. Bù chángcháng guā fēng, yě hěn shǎo xià yǔ.

cháng	*long*	**qíngtiān**	*sunny (day)*
báitiān	*daytime*	**yīntiān**	*cloudy (day)*

a Běijīng de xiàtiān hěn duǎn, shì bu shi?
b Běijīng de dōngtiān shì bu shì hěn lěng?
c Běijīng de chūntiān zěnmeyàng?
d Běijīng de chūntiān shì zuì hǎo de jìjié ma?
e Wèishénme Běijīng-rén hěn xǐhuan qiūtiān?

Quick review

The following pictures show what the weather was, is and will be like. Make two statements about each of them in relation to what time it is now. It's 10am Friday.

Example: Jīntiān zǎoshang xià dà yǔ le.
(Jīntiān zǎoshang) qìwēn (shì) qī dù.

a xīngqīsì shàngwǔ

b xīngqīsì wǎnshang

c xīngqīwǔ shàngwǔ

d xīngqīwǔ xiàwǔ

e xīngqīliù

f xià xīngqīyī

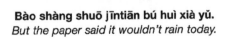

Bào shàng shuō jīntiān bú huì xià yǔ.
But the paper said it wouldn't rain today.

21

Tán gǎnxiǎng
Experiences, feelings and reflections

In this unit you will learn
- How to talk about things that happened in the past
- How to ask people about their impressions
- How to express regret
- How to express satisfaction
- How to write a thank you note

Revise before you start

- measure words   (4)(7)
- numbers from 100
  to 1000   (7)
- verb + **guo**   (9)
- helping verbs   (6)
- **gèng** (*even more*) (8)
- verb + **de**   (8)
- reduplicated verbs   (5)

- **zuì** (*most*)   (7)
- verb endings   (10)
- . . . **de shíhou**   (10)
- new situation **le**   (5)
- **shì bu shì**   (3)
- **tài . . . le**   (7)
- sentence **le**   (4)
- **gěi** (*for*)   (6)

Qù Zhōngguó xuéxí、*lǚyóu* hé gōngzuò

Go to China to study, travel and work

With China opening up more and more, it attracts more and more visitors: students, tourists and businesspeople. What do the students study? What are the tourists interested in? Why are businesspeople going to China? Read the passage that follows to find out.

Měi nián yǒu hěn duō wàiguó-rén qù Zhōngguó xuéxí. Tāmen xuéxí Zhōngguó de yǔyán、wénxué、*wénhuà*、lìshǐ、*zōngjiào*, děngděng. Zài Zhōngguó de *jǐ bǎi duō suǒ dàxué* lǐ, yǒu jǐ *wàn* ge wàiguó *liúxuéshēng*.

Qù Zhōngguó lǚyóu de wàiguó-rén *yuè lái yuè* duō. *Tāmen hěn duō rén* duì Zhōngguó de wénhuà hé lìshǐ gǎn xìngqu. Hěn duō rén qù-guo Zhōngguó hěn duō cì.

Zhè jǐ nián qù Zhōngguó gōngzuò de wàiguó-rén yě yuè lái yuè duō. Zài Zhōngguó de *wàizī qǐyè* hé *hézī qǐyè* yě yuè lái yuè duō. Hěn duō gōngsī dōu xiǎng zài Zhōngguó kuòdà *shēngyi*.

dàxué	*university*
hézī qǐyè	*joint venture*
jǐ bǎi duō	*more than several hundred* (lit. *several hundred more*)
kuòdà	*to expand*
liúxuéshēng	*overseas student*
lǚyóu	*to travel*
shēngyi	*business*
suǒ	(measure word for schools, and so on)
tāmen hěn duō rén	*many of them* (lit. *they many people*)
yuè lái yuè . . .	*more and more . . .*
wàizī qǐyè	*foreign enterprise*
wàn	*ten thousand*
wénhuà	*culture*
zōngjiào	*religion*

QUICK VOCAB

Here's another pair of linking words to add to your list: **yuè lái . . . yuè . . .**

yuè lái yuè duō	*more and more*
yuè lái yuè hǎo	*better and better*
yuè lái yuè kuài	*quicker and quicker*

If you replace **lái** with another adjective/verb, you get:

yuè **kuài** yuè **hǎo**	*the quicker the better*
yuè **duō** yuè **hǎo**	*the more the better*

Exercise 1   How would you say the following?

a   More and more Chinese come to Britain to study.
b   Many of them are interested in the history and culture of Britain.
c   Every year many foreign students come to Britain to study English.
d   More and more European companies want to expand their business in China.

bāo	*to wrap; to make* (**jiǎozi**)
chángshòu (miàn)	*long life* (noodles)
chī-de-guàn	*to be used to the food*
chī-bu-guàn	*to be not used to the food*
dǒng	*to understand*
duì X yǒu shénme yìnxiàng?	*what is your impression of X?*
duì shénme (zuì) mǎnyì?	*(most) satisfied with what?*
fāzhǎn	*to develop*
jiàoxué	*teaching*
jiǎozi	*(Chinese) dumplings*
jiùshi	*it's just that*
kuàilè	*happy*
mǎnyì	*satisfied*
měi(-jíle)	*(extremely) beautiful*
nàli/nàr	*there*
nánshuō	*difficult to say*
qìngzhù	*to celebrate*
shān qū	*mountain(ous) area*

tán(yi)tán	*to talk (a bit) about*
tèsè	*feature, characteristics*
tīng-bu-dǒng	*to be unable to understand*
	(verbal speech)
tóngshì (men)	*colleague(s)*
tóngxué (men)	*fellow student(s)*
xià ge	*next*
xuéxiào	*school*
yìnxiàng	*impression*
yíqiè	*everything*
yìzhí	*all the time*
yǒuhǎo	*friendly*

Dialogues

Dialogue 1

◀) CD 2, TR 11

The group of students you met in Units 19 and 20 are now all safely back in college. What do they think of the places they have just visited? Let's find out.

Lǎoshī	Tóngxuémen, nǐmen jiàqī guò-de hǎo ma?
Xuésheng	Hěn hǎo.
(chorus)	Bú tài hǎo.
	Fēicháng hǎo.
	Hái kěyǐ.
Lǎoshī	Qǐng měi ge rén dōu tányitán, hǎo ma?
Wénzhé	Wǒ qù le Wǔtái Shān. Nàli yíqiè dōu hǎo, jiùshi fàn bù hǎo.
Lǎoshī	Fàn zěnme bù hǎo?
Wénzhé	Tāmen bù chī ròu. Kěshì wǒ zuì ài chī ròu, suǒyǐ wǒ chángcháng juéde è.
Wèimín	Nǐ yīnggāi gēn wǒ yìqǐ qù Tiānjīn. Wǒmen de dàibiǎotuán měi tiān dōu yǒu yànhuì.

Lǎoshī	Lányīn, shǎoshù mínzú de fàn nǐ chī-de-guàn ma?
Lányīn	Kāishǐ de shíhou chī-bu-guàn, hòulái jiù chī-de-guàn le. Nàxiē shǎoshù mínzú de rén zhēn yǒuhǎo.
Lǎoshī	Nàr shì bu shì hěn rè?
Lányīn	Wǒ qù de dìfang shì shān qū, suǒyǐ bú tài rè. Nàr de fēngjǐng měi-jíle.
Lǎoshī	Shānběn, nǐ duì Shànghǎi hé Guǎngzhōu yǒu shénme yìnxiàng?
Shānběn	Zhè liǎng ge chéngshì de jīngjì dōu fāzhǎn-de hěn kuài. Kěxī wǒ tīng-bu-dǒng Shànghǎihuà hé Guǎngdōnghuà.
Lǎoshī	Zhè liǎng zhǒng fāngyán dōu bù róngyì dǒng. Ānfāng, nǐ bàba、 māma dōu hǎo ma?
Ānfāng	Tāmen dōu hěn hǎo, xièxie nín. Wǒ bàba、 māma shuō xià ge jiàqī tāmen yào lái Zhōngguó. Wǒmen yìqǐ zài Zhōngguó lǚyóu.
Dàjiā	Nà tài hǎo le!

Learning tip

Keep reading all the dialogues in the book whenever you have a spare moment: better still listen to the recording whenever you can. Practise covering up the English words in the **Quick vocab** boxes and see how many of the Chinese words you know, then do the reverse. You can go back to the beginning of the book and do this right the way through for useful revision.

Exercise 2 Where did you go on your last holiday? Here are some questions a Chinese person might ask you:

a Nǐ de jiàqī guò-de hǎo bu hǎo?
b Nǐ qù le duō cháng shíjiān?
c Nàli de tiānqi zěnmeyàng?
d Nàli de fàn nǐ chī-de-guàn ma?
e Nàli de fēngjǐng měi bu měi?

Exercise 3 Nǐ duì shénme gǎn/yǒu xìngqu? *What are you interested in?*

State whether you are interested in the following things.

Example: Zhōngguó lìshǐ
     i Wǒ duì Zhōngguó lìshǐ gǎn/yǒu xìngqu.
     ii Wǒ duì Zhōngguó lìshǐ bù gǎn xìngqu *or*
     iii Wǒ duì Zhōngguó lìshǐ méi (yǒu) xìngqu.

a liúxíng (*popular*) yīnyuè   b Yìdàlì fàn
c dísīkē   d shōují (*collect*) yóupiào
e Déguó diànyǐng

Exercise 4   Are you used to the following food or drinks?

If you are, say **Wǒ chī/hē-de-guàn X**. If you are not, say **Wǒ chī/hē-bu-guàn Y**. Remember, you can also put the noun (the sort of thing) at the beginning of the sentence for emphasis.

    tángcù yú   *sweet and sour fish*

i **Wǒ chī-de-guàn** tángcù yú.
ii Tángcù yú wǒ **chī-bu-guàn**.

    suānlà tang   *hot and sour soup*

i Suānlà tāng wǒ **hē-de-guàn**.
ii Wǒ **hē-bu-guàn** suānlà tāng.

Start with **tángcù yú** and **suānlà tāng**. And then:

a Yìndù (*Indian*) fàn?
b tián pútáojiǔ?
c dòufu (*tofu*)?
d Kěkǒukělè?
e mángguǒ (*mango*)?
f kāfēi?

Dialogue 2

◀) CD 2, TR 11, 02:06

Mr Ford has lived and worked in China for nearly 12 years. He is interviewed by a Chinese journalist on his 60th birthday. What is he most satisfied and dissatisfied with?

Jìzhě	Fútè xiānsheng, zhù nín shēngrì kuàilè!
Ford	Xièxie, xièxie.
Jìzhě	Nín zài Zhōngguó jǐ nián le?
Ford	Chàbuduō shí'èr nián le.
Jìzhě	Nín yìzhí zài dàxué gōngzuò ma?
Ford	Duì. Wǒ fēicháng xǐhuan dāng lǎoshī.
Jìzhě	Zài Zhōngguó nín duì shénme zuì mǎnyì?
Ford	Dāngrán shì wǒde gōngzuò. Wǒmen xuéxiào de jiàoxué yuè lái yuè hǎo.
Jìzhě	Nàme nín duì shénme zuì bù mǎnyì?
Ford	Wǒ duì hěn duō shìqing bù mǎnyì. Kěshì hěn nánshuō duì shénme zuì bù mǎnyì.
Jìzhě	Nín dǎsuàn zěnme qìngzhù nínde shēngrì?
Ford	Zǎoshang wǒ tàitai gěi wǒ zuò le Zhōngguó de chángshòu miàn. Wǎnshang tóngshìmen lái wǒ jiā bāo jiǎozi.
Jìzhě	Nínde shēngrì guò-de zhēn yǒu Zhōngguó tèsè.
Ford	Wǒ xiànzài yǐjīng shì bàn ge Zhōngguó-rén le.

Do you remember meeting two phrases using **duì** in Unit 10?

A **duì** shēntǐ (bu) hǎo.   *A is (not) good **for the health/body**.*
Y **duì** X (bù) hǎo.   *Y is/(not) good **to X**.*

Here are some more useful phrases with **duì**:

Nǐ **duì** X yǒu shénme yìnxiàng?   *What impression have you of X?*

Wǒ **duì** X de yìnxiàng hěn hǎo.   *I have a very good impression of X.*

Nǐ **duì** shénme (zuì) bù mǎnyì?   *What are you (most) dissatisfied with?*

A **duì** B bù mǎnyì.   *A is not satisfied with B.*

A **duì** B **zuì** bù mǎnyì.   *A is **most** dissatisfied with B.*

Insight

It is very common for elderly people (the Chinese tend to regard people of 60 and over as elderly!) to eat 'long-life noodles' (**chángshòu miàn**) on their birthdays!

Miàntiáo
Noodles

Jiǎozi
Dumplings

On special occasions such as birthdays and the Chinese New Year the family (plus close friends or colleagues) might make Chinese dumplings (**bāo jiǎozi**) together. It is a very companionable activity which also requires some skill. Beginners can usually spot which **jiǎozi** are theirs when it comes to eating them as they tend to be the unsightly ones or the ones which have burst!

Exercise 5 Your Chinese friend is asking you about your visit to China. This passage is a brief account of your visit.

You visited China on a package tour for two weeks. You visited Beijing, Shanghai and Guilin. You liked all three places, but for different reasons. There were many parks in Beijing which you liked a lot. Shanghai was developing very fast, which impressed you. But there were too many people there and it was very crowded. The scenery at Guilin was extremely beautiful.

Now answer your friend's questions:

	Friend	Nǐ zài Zhōngguó duōshao tiān?
a	**You**	_____
	Friend	Nǐ qù le shénme dìfang?
b	**You**	_____

	Friend	Nǐ duì Shànghǎi yǒu shénme yìnxiàng?
c	You	_____
	Friend	Nàme Běijīng ne?
d	You	_____
	Friend	Nǐ duì Guìlín de yìnxiàng zěnmeyàng?
e	You	_____

◄» CD 2, TR 11, 03:39

Exercise 6 Listen to the thank-you message on Lányīn's answerphone. Then decide whether the statements below are **duì** or **bú duì**. Read the new words before you listen to the message.

bāngzhù	*help*	gǎnxiè	*to thank* (formal)
tèbié	*especially*	wèn XX hǎo	*say hello to XX*
dāngmiàn	*face to face*		

a Xiǎo Qīng jīntiān shàngwǔ qù Lányīn de xuéxiào le.
b Xiǎo Qīng dāngmiàn gēn Lányīn shuō le zàijiàn.
c Xiǎo Qīng qù-guo Lányīn de jiā.
d Xiǎo Qīng méi jiàn-guo Lányīn de bàba hé māma.

Lányīn,

Nǐ hǎo! Wǒ shì Xiǎo Qīng. Jīntiān xiàwǔ wǒ qù nǐde xuéxiào zhǎo nǐ, kěshì nǐ bú zài. Zhēn kěxī, wǒ bù néng dāngmiàn gēn nǐ shuō 'zàijiàn'.

Zhè cì lái Yīngguó fǎngwèn, wǒ guó-de zhēn yúkuài. Nǐ gěi le wǒ hěn duō bāngzhù. Wǒ fēicháng gǎnxiè nǐ. Tèbié gǎnxiè nǐ qǐng wǒ qù nǐde jiā chī fàn. Wǒ gěi nǐ hé nǐ bàba、màma tiān le hěn duō máfan.

Xīwàng nǐ jiānglái yǒu jīhuì yě qù Zhōngguó fǎngwèn. Zhù nǐ shēntǐ jiànkāng、shēnghuó yúkuài、gōngzuò shùnlì、wànshì rúyì!

Wèn nǐ bàba、māma hǎo! Zàijiàn!

Final review

1 Do you remember the opposites of these words? What is the opposite of:

a lěng   e piányi   i zǎo   m xià

b niánqīng   f ānquán   j yìng   n zuǒ

c shòu   g yuǎn   k hòu   o běi

d ānjìng   h liáng(kuai)   l yǐqián   p dōngnán

2 Can you find the Chinese equivalents in Section B to match the English sentences in Section A?

Section A

a Excuse me, is this seat taken?

b Could you please speak more slowly?

c Please come a little earlier tomorrow.

d Please tell the teacher I am not well today.

e Could you please say it again?

Section B

i Qǐng gàosu lǎoshī wǒ jīntiān bù shūfu.

ii Qǐng nǐ zài shuō yí biàn.

iii Qǐng nǐ shuō màn yìdiǎn.

iv Qǐng wèn, zhè ge wèizi yǒu rén zuò ma?

v Qǐng míngtiān zǎo yìdiǎnr lái.

3 We have given you the literal translations of some Chinese words in this book. Here are some new words with their literal translations. See if you can guess what they mean.

a shǒujī (*lit.* hand machine)

b diànnǎo (*lit.* electronic brain)

c guǎnggào (*lit.* extensive telling)

d lùxiàngjī (*lit.* record image machine)

e tiěfànwǎn (*lit.* iron rice bowl)

f nuǎnshuǐpíng (*lit.* warm water bottle)

g tiānxiàn (*lit.* sky thread)

4 Numbers are important. This listening exercise will give you some more practice. Listen to the message on the answerphone and fill in the missing information. The only new word is **shǒujī** (*mobile phone*) which you've just met in the previous exercise. If you have not got the recording, the passage is included in the **Key to the exercises**.

a Time of arrival in Guangzhou is _____

b His room number is _____

c The hotel's number is _____

d His mobile number is _____

e Length of his stay in Guangzhou is _____

f Date of his departure is _____

g Time of the train is _____

h Stay in Shenzhen for _____ days.

i Date and time of flight back to the UK is _____

5 How do you say to or ask a Chinese person the following?

a Say you are not used to eating hot/spicy dishes.

b Ask her if she is interested in pop (**liúxíng**) music or classical (**gǔdiǎn**) music.

c Say there are more and more people going abroad for holidays.

d Ask her what is her impression of Britain (the US etc.).

e Ask her what she is (most) satisfied and/or not satisfied with.

f Wish her happy birthday!

有志者，事竟成

Chinese proverb: **Yǒu zhì zhě, shì jìng chéng**
Where there's a will, there's a way

Zhùhè nǐ! *Congratulations!*

You have completed *Get started in Mandarin Chinese* and are now a competent speaker of basic Chinese. You should be able to handle most everyday situations on a visit to China and to communicate with Chinese people sufficiently to make friends. Should you wish to comment on any aspect of this book, you can contact us c/o Hodder & Stoughton Educational, 338 Euston Road, London NW1 3BH.

Taking it further

If you would like to extend your ability so that you can develop your confidence, fluency and scope in the language, whether for social or business purposes, why not take your Chinese a step further with *Complete Mandarin Chinese?*

You could see if there are any Chinese language classes taking place in your area. Many big universities have Chinese departments or language centres which run courses in a number of foreign languages including Chinese. Large cities often have an annual publication listing all the courses taking place that year and where they are held.

You can also go online and look at the following websites, but do remember these are constantly changing and new ones are being added all the time.

Pinyin practice: http://www.ctcfl.ox.ac.uk/Pinyin_Notes.htm – Everything you need to know about *pinyin*.

http://www.newconceptmandarin.com/support/Intro_Pinyin.asp – *pinyin* with the indication of tones.

For beginners: http://www.bbc.co.uk/languages/chinese/ and http://www.bbc.co.uk/languages/chinese/real_chinese/ – a good starting point.

More comprehensive websites: http://www.learningchineseonline.net – a comprehensive website with English and Chinese (in simplified and traditional scripts). http://www.zhongwen.com/ – English and Chinese (full-form characters). Brief introduction to Chinese language, writing, *pinyin*, etc. Texts in Chinese (classical texts, and some modern texts).

http://www.mandarintools.com/ – another site which has many links to China-related websites.

All the instructions are in English. English and Chinese (simplified characters). Online English–Chinese and Chinese–English dictionary. Illustration of stroke order.

(You can get a Chinese name by typing in your English name.)

Chūkǒu *Exit*

Key to the exercises

Unit 1

1 a Nǐ hǎo! **b** Xièxie. **c** Bú yòng xiè.
2 a Nǐ hǎo! **b** Bú yòng xiè. **c** Xièxie. **d** Zàijiàn!
3 a Nǐ hǎo! **b** Lǐ tàitai hǎo ma? **c** Lǐ xiānsheng zài ma?
d Xièxie (nǐ).
4 a Xièxie. **b** Bú yòng xiè. **c** Zàijiàn. **d** Míngtiān jiàn.
e Qǐng jìn. **f** Qǐng zuò. **g** Wǒ/Tā hěn hǎo. **h** Nǐ/Tā hǎo ma?
5 a = iv, **b** = iii, **c** = ii, **d** = i.

Quick review

a Lǐ xiānsheng, nǐ hǎo! *or* Nǐ hǎo, Lǐ xiānsheng!
b Nǐ tàitai hǎo ma? **c** Duìbuqǐ. **d** Xièxie nǐ.
e Bú yòng xiè. **f** Zàijiàn.

Vocabulary and pronunciation

a 3rd	**b** lǎoshī
c míngtiān	**d** jiàn

Unit 2

Let's try

a Qǐng jìn. **b** Nǐ hǎo. **c** Qǐng zuò. **d** Míngtiān jiàn.

1 a shénme; jiào. **b** huì; shuō. **c** shì; rènshi.
2 a Tāmen shì Lǐ xiānsheng、Yīng tàitai. **b** Tā jiào Lǐ Jīnshēng.
c Duì. Tā xìng Yīng. **d** Bù. Tā xìng Lǐ. **e** Wǒ (bú) rènshi tāmen.

3 a Wáng. b Lányīng. c A little bit. d Chinese teacher. e No, she doesn't. f She's beautiful. g Yes.

4 a Tā jiào Zhào Huá. Tā shì jǐngchá. b Zhè shì Liú Guāng. Tā shì sījī. c Nà shì Guō Jié. Tā shì dàifu. d Tā jiào Lǐ Mínglì. Tā shì lǎoshī. e Zhè shì Zhōu Jiābǎo. Tā shì xuésheng. f Nà shì Wú Zébì. Tā shì chúshī.

5 a bú duì, b bú duì, c bú duì, d bú duì, e bú duì, f duì.

6 a Nǐ huì shuō Yīngwén ma? Nǐ huì bu huì shuō Yīngwén? b Nǐmen shì lǎoshī ma? Nǐmen shì bu shì lǎoshī? c Xiǎo Zhèng zài ma? Xiǎo Zhèng zài bu zài? d Lǐ xiānsheng jīntiān lái ma? Lǐ xiānsheng jīntiān lái bu lái? e Wáng Fāng yǒu Yīngwén míngzi ma? Wáng Fāng yǒu mei yǒu Yīngwén míngzi? f Lín lǎoshī jiào Lín Péng ma? Lín lǎoshī jiào bu jiào Lín Péng?

Quick review

a Nín guì xìng? Nǐ xìng shénme? **b** Wǒ jiào xxx.
c Wǒ méi yǒu Zhōngwén míngzi. **d** Wǒ bú rènshi tā.
e Méi guānxi. **f** Wǒde péngyou bú shì lǎoshī.

Vocabulary and pronunciation

a dāngrán **b** shuō
c shéi **d** wén

Unit 3

Let's try

a Nǐ hǎo. Wǒ jiào X. Nǐ jiào shénme? *or* Nín guì xìng?

b Nǐ/Nín yǒu háizi ma? Nǐ/Nín yǒu mei yǒu háizi?

1 a shì/bú shì, b shì/bú shì, c shì/bú shì, d shì/bú shì, e shì/bù zhīdào, f shì/bù zhīdào.

2 *Speaker 1*: Nǐ hǎo! Wǒ jiào Chén Lìmǐn. Wǒ shì Xiānggǎng-rén. Wǒ zhù zài Xiānggǎng Lì Yè Lù 8 hào. Wǒde diànhuà hàomǎ shì 507 1293.

Speaker 2: Nǐ hǎo! Wǒ jiào Wú Yìfēi. Wǒ shì Shànghǎi-rén. Wǒde diànhuà hàomǎ shì 874 3659. Wǒ zhù zài Shànghǎi Nánjīng Lù 9 hào.

Speaker 3: Wǒ jiào Guō Wànjí. Wǒ shì Fǎguó-rén. Wǒ zhù zài Běijīng Hépíng Lù 6 hào. Wǒde diànhuà hàomǎ shì 724 6274.

4 a Běijīng Cháoyáng Lù èr hào, Lǐ Mínglì lǎoshī. b Sūzhōu Lónghǎi Lù jiǔ hào, Dōngfāng Fàndiàn sān-bā-sì fángjiān, Zhào Huá xiānsheng. c Nánjīng Xīchéng Qū Hépíng Lù wǔ hào, Zhào Jiābǎo xiǎojie.

5 a iii, b vii, c i, d v, e ii, f iv, g vi.

Quick review

a Tā shì shéi?　　　　　b Nǐ zhù (zài) nǎr?
c Wǒ bú zhù (zài) Lúndūn.　d Nǐde diànhuà hàomǎ shì duōshao?
e Diànhuà shì shénme yìsi?　f Zhè shì wǒde fēijī piào.

Vocabulary and pronunciation

a hào
b Lúndūn
c guó
d meaning

Unit 4

Let's try

a Nǐ zhù zài shénme fàndiàn? (Nǐ zhù zài) jǐ hào fángjiān?
b Zhè shì wǒde míngpiàn.

1 a èrshíjiǔ, b qīshíyī, c sānshí'èr.
2 a èrshíyī, b qīshí, c liùshíliù, d sìshíjiǔ e sānshí, f liùshí, g shíwǔ, h sānshísān.
3 Dīng Fèng is married. She's got two children, a son and a daughter. Her son is called Dīng Míng and is 12 this year. Her daughter's name is Dīng Yīng. She is 14 years old.

4 a Méi yǒu. b Méi yǒu. c Bú shì (Tā bú shì lǎoshī.) d Wǒ méi
yǒu háizi. e Wǒ méi yǒu dìdi.

5 a Are you married? = iv b How old is she? = iii c What's Mr
Wang, the teacher, called? = i d Have you any children? = v
e Has Mrs Li a daughter? = ii

6 Wǒ jiào Mǎlì, jīnnián shíqī suì. Wǒ méi yǒu jiějie, méi yǒu mèimei.
Wǒ yǒu yí ge gēge、yí ge dìdi. Wǒ gēge jiào Hēnglì. Tā èrshí suì.
Wǒ dìdi jiào Bǐdé. Tā shíwǔ suì. Wǒmen dōu shì xuésheng.

Quick review

a Nǐ hǎo! b Nǐ jiào shénme? c Nǐ jǐ suì?
d Nǐ yǒu xiōngdì、jiěmèi ma? e Xièxie (nǐ). f Zàijiàn!

Vocabulary and pronunciation

a liǎng   b xiǎo
c gēge   d hé

Unit 5

Let's try

a Chén xiānsheng, nǐ hǎo ma? Nǐ jiào shénme míngzi? Nǐ huì bu
huì shuō Yīngwén? Nǐ zhù zài nǎr? Nǐ jié hūn le ma? Nǐ yǒu háizi
ma? Nǐ(de) háizi jǐ suì/duō dà? Nǐde diànhuà hàomǎ shì duōshao/
shénme? Nǐ rènshi bu rènshi X? Nǐ shì Běijīng-/Shànghǎi-/
Guǎngdōng-rén ma? Nǐ bàba\māma dōu zài (Běijīng) ma?

b liùshísì, èrshíjiǔ, wǔshíqī, sānshíbā, shí'èr, jiǔshíwǔ, sìshí, èr,
qīshísān, shí.

1 a yīyuè yī hào, b shí'èr yuè èrshíwǔ hào, c sānyuè bā hào,
d shíyuè yī hào.

3 a September 9th b Sunday morning, c Thursday, November
28th, d 10.45am Saturday, e 3.30pm Friday, July 6th, f 11am
Monday, December 31st.

4 a Wǔ diǎn yí kè; wǔ diǎn shíwǔ fēn. **b** Chà wǔ fēn wǔ diǎn; sì diǎn wǔshíwǔ fēn. **c** (Hái yǒu) sìshí fēnzhōng. **d** Zǎoshang wǔ diǎn líng wǔ fēn. **e** Wǔ diǎn líng qī fēn.

Quick review

a Sānyuè sānshí hào. **b** Xīngqīsì. **c** Sì diǎn èrshíqī fēn. **d** Sì diǎn sān kè *or* chà yí kè wǔ diǎn. Dì-sān zhàntái. **e** Sì diǎn wǔshí fēn *or* Wǔ diǎn chà shí fēn. Dì-yī zhàntái.

Vocabulary and pronunciation

a dōu **b** shàngwǔ **c** three weeks
d 'sānyuè' is March while 'sān ge yuè' means 'three months'
e 'zhīdāo' means 'to know'

Unit 6

Let's try

1 Wǒ yào xīngqīsì shàngwǔ jiǔ diǎn bàn de huǒchē piào.
2 a yī-jiǔ-jiǔ-qī nián yīyuè liù hào **b** èr-líng-líng-líng nián sānyuè èrshíyī hào **c** yī-jiǔ-sì-sān nián bāyuè shíwǔ hào.

1 a Tā zài mǎi dōngxi. **b** Tāmen zài kàn zájì. **c** Tā zài huàn qián. **d** Tā zài dǎ tàijíquán. **e** Tāmen zài kàn diànyǐng. **f** Tā zài tīng yīnyuè.
3 a bù yíyàng (gāo), **b** yíyàng (dà), **c** bù yíyàng (zhòng), **d** bù yíyàng (gāo), **e** yíyàng (zhòng), **f** bù yíyàng (dà).
4 a Bú duì. Xǔ bǐ Hú gāo. **b** Bú duì. Hú bǐ Qū zhòng. **c** Bú duì. Tāmen yíyàng dà. **d** Duì. **e** Duì.
5 a Xīngqītiān, **b** xīngqīsì xiàwǔ, **c** xīngqīsān wǎnshang, **d** shàngwǔ, **e** xīngqīliù.

Quick review

a Nǐ míngtiān xiǎng zuò shénme?
b Xiǎo Mǎ gēn tā jiějie yíyàng gāo.

c Wǒ juéde zájì bǐ jīngjù yǒu yìsi.

d Xiǎo Zhào, jīntiān wǎnshang nǐ xiǎng qù nǎr?

e Lǐ xiǎojie, nǐ xiǎng qù kàn diànyǐng háishi tīng yīnyuèhuì?

Vocabulary and pronunciation

a gēn   **b** in question forms
c yǒu wèntí   **d** nán
e yīnyuè

Unit 7

Let's try

a Nǐmen xiǎng tīng yīnyuèhuì háishi kàn xì?

b Nǐmen xǐhuan (tīng) Xīfāng yīnyuè ma? Nǐmen xǐhuan bu xǐhuan (tīng) Xīfāng yīnyuè? **c** Zài Xīfāng dāngrán tīng Xīfāng yīnyuè.

1 **a** wǔ máo èr (fēn), **b** liǎng/èr kuài liǎng/èr máo wǔ, **c** shí'èr kuài qī máo liù, **d** jiǔshíjiǔ kuài jiǔ máo jiǔ, **e** èr/liǎngbǎi líng wǔ kuài wǔ máo sì. **f** bā kuài líng qī (fēn).

2 **a** Píngguǒ jiǔshí biànshì yì jīn. **b** Pútao yí bàng sì-jiǔ yì jīn. **c** Cǎoméi yí bàng qī-wǔ yì hé. **d** Xiāngjiāo wǔshíbā biànshì yì jīn.

3 **a** **Xīhóngshì** zěnme mài? **b** Báicài yì jīn **duōshao** qián? **c** **Tǔdòu duōshao** qián yì jīn?

4 **Recording:** **a** Yú zěnme mài? Qī kuài líng jiǔ yì jīn. **b** Cǎoméi duōshao qián yì hé? Qī kuài sì yì hé. **c** Báicài yì jīn duōshao qián? Yí kuài èr yì jīn. **d** Pútao guì bu guì? Bú guì. Yí kuài jiǔ yì jīn. **e** Wǒ mǎi liǎng jīn tǔdòu. Sān kuài èr.

5 **a** Tài dà le! **b** Tài rè le! **c** Tāde qián tài duōle! **d** (Piào) tài guì le! **e** Fǎwén tài nán le!

6 **a** Pútao bǐ píngguǒ guì (yìdiǎnr). **b** Xiǎo Wáng bǐ Lǎo Lǐ gāo yìdiǎnr. **c** Běijīng bǐ Lúndūn rè duōle. **d** Bái xiānsheng bǐ Bái tàitai dà deduō.

7 **a** jiù, **b** jiù, **c** cái, **d** jiù, **e** cái.

Quick review

a Zhǐ yào wǔ fēnzhōng jiù dào.
b Yào/děi wǔshí fēnzhōng cái dào.
c Zài wǒ jiǎ wǒ bàba zuì dà.
d Diànyǐngyuàn lí wǒ jiā bù yuǎn.
e Xiāngjiāo sìshíjiǔ biànshì yí bàng.

Vocabulary and pronunciation

a jīn: half a kilogram; jìn: near, close
b mǎi: to buy; mài: to sell
c jiàn (as for a sweater)
d bǎi
e shìshi

Unit 8

Let's try

1 No, she didn't. One was too big, one was too small, and one was too expensive.
2 He said his apples were a little bigger, his grapes were much sweeter, his strawberries were a lot fresher, and his things were the best.

1 a v, b vi, c iv, d i, e ii, f vii, g iii.
2 a yí jiàn bái chènyī, b yí jiàn huáng dàyī, c yí tào lán xīfú, d yì tiáo lǜ qúnzi, e yì shuāng hēi xié, f yì tiáo hóng kùzi.
3 Xiǎo Cài is wearing a white shirt, a blue skirt, and a pair of red leather shoes. Xiǎo Zhào is wearing a blue silk shirt, black trousers, and green cloth shoes. Lǎo Fāng is wearing a black suit, a white shirt, and a pair of black leather shoes.
4 a Lǎo Mǎ chuān yì shuāng hēi píxié、yí jiàn lán chènyī. b Xiǎo Qián chuān yí jiàn hóng chènyī、(yì tiáo) hēi kùzi、yì shuāng bùxié. c Liú xiānsheng chuān yí tào huī xīfú、huáng chènyī、zōng píxié.

5 **a** Lǐ xiānsheng Déwén (*German*) shuō-de fēicháng hǎo. **b** Zhāng tàitai jiàqī guò-de bú tài hǎo. **c** Cháo xiǎojie Yīngwén xué-de kuài-jíle. **d** Mǎlì yòng kuàizi yòng-de bù zěnmeyàng. **e** Hēnglì shuō Rìyǔ shuō-de hěn qīngchu.
6 **a** Mǎ Fēng méi yǒu Zhāng Tóng gāo. Zhāng Tóng méi yǒu Mǎ Fēng dà, yě méi yǒu tā zhòng. **b** Zhāng Tóng de diànshì méi yǒu Mǎ Fēng de diànshì guì, yě méi yǒu Mǎ Fēng de diànshì dà. **c** Mǎ Fēng de zì méi yǒu Zhāng Tóng de zì qīngchu.

Quick review

a Nǐde Yīngwén shuō-de zhēn hǎo.
b Zhè jiàn chènyī tài xiǎo le.
c Nǐde jiàqī guò-de zěnmeyàng?
d Yīnggélán bǐ Ài'ěrlán dà.
e Déguó méi yǒu Fǎguó dà.

Vocabulary and pronunciation

a dà: big; xiǎo: small **b** guì **c** màn **d** yǔ **e** yǐhòu

---

Unit 9

Let's try

1 **a** Yìbǎi wǔshí kuài. **b** Sān zhāng zúqiú piào.
2 **a** Fǎguó de dōngxi bǐ Yīngguó de (dōngxi) guì. Fǎguó de dōngxi méi yǒu Yīngguó de (dōngxi) guì. Fǎguó de dōngxi gēn Yīngguó de (dōngxi) yíyàng guì. **b** Nǎli, nǎli, shuō-de bù hǎo. (*or* Xièxie.)

2 **Recording:** First walk southwards. When you get to East Sea Road, take an eastbound bus for two stops and you will find the cinema on the south side of the road opposite the shop. The answer is F.
3 Wǎng xī zǒu, guò liǎng ge lùkǒu, wǎng běi guǎi. Fàndiàn jiù zài lù de dōngbianr.

4 B = school; C = shop; D = Donghai Park; E = Bank of China.
8 **a** Fǎguó hé Yìdàlì. **b** Sì tiān. **c** Gēn tāde Fǎguó péngyou.
Tāmen kāi chē qù. **d** Yí ge xīngqī. **e** Zuò fēijī. **f** Kāi chē.
Recording: Mr White is going on holiday soon. He is going to
two places. He'll first go from London to Paris by train. He
plans to stay in Paris for four days. After that he and his French
friend will drive to Italy. They will stay in Italy for a week.
Lastly he will fly back to London from Italy. His friend will
drive back to France.

Quick review

a Qù Zhōngguó Yínháng zěnme zǒu?
b Zuò shí lù (gōnggòng) qìchē. **c** Zuò wǔ zhàn.
d Wǒde péngyou méi (yǒu) qù-guo Zhōngguó.
e Kuài (yào) xià yǔ le.

Vocabulary and pronunciation

a Xiānggǎng   **b** nàr
c Macao   **d** from
e Yes. It's 'huàn'.

Unit 10

Let's try

1 **a** Wǒ xiān zuò fēijī qù Xiānggǎng. Zài nàr zhù liǎng tiān.
b Ránhòu (cóng Xiānggǎng) zuò huǒchē qù Shànghǎi. **c** Wǒ
dǎsuàn bāyuè shí hào (cóng Shànghǎi) zuò fēijī qù Běijīng.
2 Nǐ qù-guo Shànghǎi ma? Nǐ qù-guo Shànghǎi méi you?

1 **Recording:** Mr. Jones ordered **yúxiāng ròusī** (fish flavoured
shredded meat), **zhàcài tāng** (preserved vegetable soup) and
Wǔxīng píjiǔ (Fivestar beer).
2 **a** yì wǎn chǎomiàn, **b** sì píng pútáojiǔ, **c** wǔ tīng kěkǒukělè,
d liù zhī yān, **e** liǎng wǎn tāng, **f** sān zhāng piào.

4 a Fúwùyuán, qǐng jié zhàng. **b** Chī-hǎo le. Xièxie. **c** Nǐ suàn-cuò le ba. **d** Méi guānxi.
5 a bù, **b** méi, **c** méi, **d** bù.

Halfway review

1 1066, 1462, 1798, 1914, 1945, 2000, 2008.
2 a Tāmen shì bu shì jiěmèi? Tāmen shì jiěmèi ma? **b** Tāde chǎomiàn hǎochī bu hǎochī? Tāde chǎomiàn hǎochī ma? **c** Míngtiān tā tàitai qù bu qù mǎi dōngxi? Míngtiān tā tàitai qù mǎi dōngxi ma? **d** Nǐ rènshi bu rènshi tā? Nǐ bú rènshi tā ma? **e** Xiǎo Lǐ yǒu mei yǒu yì tiáo hóng kùzi? Xiǎo Lǐ yǒu yì tiáo hóng kùzi ma?
3 a Y, **b** X, **c** Y, **d** X.
4 a = v, **b** = i, **c** = ii, **d** = vi, **e** = iii, **f** = iv
5 a Méi qù-guo. **b** Qù Měiguó le. **c** Huì shuō. **d** Qù-guo. **e** Bù chōu le. **f** Chī-guo. **g** Qù Zhōngguó hé Rìběn.

Unit 11

1 a 2, **b** 6, **c** 10, **d** 5, **e** 11, **f** 24, **g** 83, **h** 69, **i** 57, **j** 36.
2 a 三 **b** 八 **c** 十 **d** 十五 **e** 四十二 **f** 九十八 **g** 六十七
3 a 天 **b** 三 **c** 六 **d** 四
4 a 天／日, **b** 期 **c** 期 **d** 星 **e** 星
5 a 3 November, **b** 16 June **c** 11 July **d** 14 October **e** 29 August
6 a 十二月二十五日 **b** 三月八日
7 a 2008, **b** 1937 **c** 1949 **d** 1885 **e** 1642
8 a 9:15, **b** 12:25, **c** 6:30 **d** 3:50, **e** 7:45
9 a 六点二十分, **b** 差一刻十二点，（十一点三刻，十二点差一刻）**c** 十点十分, **d** 四点四十八分, **e** 七点半.

Unit 12

1 a lǚguǎn, lǚdiàn, fàndiàn, bīnguǎn. **b** Lǚ means *travel*. Diàn and **guǎn** both mean *house*. Fàn means *food*. Bīn means *guest.* c No. d It says there are all kinds of reasons. e Chinese people can stay in any hotel.

2 a Bú duì. b Bú duì. c Duì. d Duì (UK); Bú duì (USA). e Duì.

3 a Wǒ shì sān-líng-yāo fángjiān de (*your name*). Wǒde fángjiān tài xiǎo le. Néng bu néng huàn yì jiān dà yìdiǎn de? b Shuāngrén fángjiān duōshao qián yì tiān? c Tài guì le. Hái yǒu, wǒde fángjiān lǐ zěnme méi yǒu diànshì? d Zúqiú sài bàn ge xiǎoshí yǐhòu jiù kāishǐ le!

4 a Nǐ néng bu néng gěi wǒ sòng lái yìdiǎnr chī de/yìdiǎnr hē de/ yì bēi chá, jiā nǎi, bù jiā táng/liǎng ge sānmíngzhì, yí ge nǎilào de, yí ge huǒtuǐ de? b Nǐ néng bu néng dǎ diànhuà jiàoxǐng wǒ/gěi wǒ dǎ diànhuà/gěi wǒ mǎi yì píng jiǔ/zài gěi wǒ yì tiáo tǎnzi/yì juǎn wèishēngzhǐ/yí kuài dà yìdiǎnr de xiāngzào/yí ge nuǎnshuǐpíng?

5 a Dōngfāng, b pretty good, c not at all good, d not polite, e three times.

6 a Wǒ xīwàng nǐmen hái yǒu fángjiān. b Yì jiān shuāngrén fángjiān, yì jiān dānrén fángjiān. c Sān、 sì tiān. Wǒ míngtiān gàosu nǐ wǒmen shénme shíhou zǒu, kěyǐ ma? d Bù, wǒmen yǐjīng chī le.

Quick review

a Bāo zǎocān ma?
b Wǔfàn shì jǐ diǎn? Wǔfàn shì shénme shíhou?
c Fángjiān lǐ yǒu diànshì ma?
d Nǐmen yǒu méi yǒu (yì jiān) dà yìdiǎnr de dānrén fángjiān?
e Yì tiān/wǎnshang duōshao qián?

Vocabulary

a 'Ānjìng' means 'quiet' and 'chǎo' means 'noisy'
b cèsuǒ
c a double room
d 'Fúwù-tái' is 'reception' or 'service desk' and 'fúwù-yuán' is 'attendant' or 'serving person'
e nǎi

Unit 13

1   **a** ruǎnwò, **b** yìngzuò, **c** ruǎnzuò, **d** yìngwò, **e** tóuděng, **f** èrděng, **g** passenger train, **h** special express, **i** train, **j** express, **k** express.

2   **a** trains no. 13, no. 21 and no. 161. **b** tèkuài, **c** No. **d** sānbǎi wǔshíyī cì, *or* sān-wǔ-yāo cì, **e** No.

3   **Qǐng wèn, hái yǒu:** **a** jīntiān wǎnshang de diànyǐng piào, **b** shíyuè sì hào de fēijī piào, **c** yāo-wǔ-sān cì de huǒchē piào, **d** qù Tiānjīn de huǒchē piào. **Wǒ mǎi:** **e** sān zhāng jīntiān wǎnshang de diànyǐng piào, **f** sì zhāng shíyuè sì hào de fēijī piào, **g** wǔ zhāng yāo-wǔ-sān cì de huǒchē piào, **h** liù zhāng qù Tiānjīn de huǒchē piào.

4   **a** Yǒu liǎng zhǒng (huǒchē) piào: tóuděng hé èrděng. **b** Tóuděng piào bǐ èrděng piào guì. **c** Zài Yīngguó huǒchē yòu kuài yòu shūfu. *or* Yīngguó de huǒchē yòu kuài yòu shūfu.

6   **a** Nǐ néng bu néng gàosu wǒ tā zhù zài nǎr? **b** Nǐ néng bu néng gàosu wǒ nǐde diànhuà hàomǎ? **c** Nǐ néng bu néng gàosu wǒ tā nǚ'ér duō dà le? **d** Nǐ néng bu néng gàosu wǒ tāmen yào zhù duō cháng shíjiān?

7   **a** Zuò huǒchē qù Xī'ān duōshao qián? **b** Cóng Lúndūn dào Shànghǎi zuò fēijī děi duō cháng shíjiān? **c** Zuò chūzūchē qù Hépíng Bīnguǎn děi duōshao qián? **d** Cóng Rìběn dào Zhōngguó zuò chuán yào/děi duō cháng shíjiān?

Quick review

a = iii, **b** = iv, **c** = v, **d** = vii, **e** = ii, **f** = i, **g** = vi.
The new word is **chángtú qìchē** (*coach*).
Timewords

a/v	b/i	c/iv	d/iii	e/ii

Unit 14

1   **a** Zhōngguó-rén qǐ-de hěn zǎo ma? **b** Zǎoshang nǐ qù nǎr? **c** Lǎo rén zài gōngyuán zuò shénme? **d** Nǐ(men) zài hú lǐ yóuyǒng ma?

3 **a** Wǒ xǐhuan zuò huǒchē, gèng xǐhuan zuò fēijī, zuì xǐhuan zuò chuán. **b** Wǒ bù xǐhuan qí mǎ, gèng bù xǐhuan qí zìxíngchē, zuì bu xǐhuan qí mótuóchē. **c** Wǒ bù xǐhuan zuò chūzūchē, gèng bù xǐhuan zuò dìtiě, zuì bù xǐhuan zuò gōnggòng qìchē. **d** Wǒ xǐhuan kàn jīngjù, gèng xǐhuan kàn diànshì, zuì xǐhuan kàn diànyǐng. **e** Wǒ xǐhuan tīng liúxíng yīnyuè, gèng xǐhuan tīng xiàndài yīnyuè, zuì xǐhuan tīng gǔdiǎn yīnyuè.

4 **a** qiūtiān **b** lǚxíng **c** hái **d** méi **e** háishi **f** yòu **g** piányi **i** zìyóu **j** bù **k** bàn **l** dìng/mǎi **m** zhǎo/dìng.

5 **a** Xiǎo Wáng, hǎo jiǔ bú jiàn. **b** Nǐ zuìjìn zài zuò shénme? **c** Nǐ jié hūn le ma? **d** Nǐ zài děng shéi? **e** Wǒ qù yóuyǒng. **f** Zàijiàn!

6 **a** yì pái èrshíwǔ hào; èr pái wǔ hào; sān pái èrshíliù hào. **b** èrshísì pái èrshísì hào; èrshíwǔ pái sì hào; èrshíliù pái èrshísān hào. **c** Lóushàng shíyī pái liù hào; lóushàng shí'èr pái èrshíbā hào; lóushàng shísān pái èrshíyī hào.

7 **a** A pái shí'èr hào, **b** J pái sānshíqī hào, **c** lóushàng F pái sìshí hào, **d** K pái èr hào.

8 **a** Shíyuè èrshíwǔ hào xīngqīliù wǎnshang liù diǎn、bā diǎn hé shí diǎn. Diànyǐng jiào (is called) 《Dōngtiān》. Diànyǐng piào wǔ bàng、liù bàng wǔ yì zhāng. **b** Shíyuè èrshíwǔ hào xīngqīliù wǎnshang qī diǎn yí kè. Huàjù jiào 《Wǒmen niánqīng de shíhou》. Huàjù piào yì zhāng shí bàng、shí'èr bàng wǔ. **c** Shíyuè èrshíliù hào xīngqītiān wǎnshang qī diǎn bàn. Bāléi 《Tiān'é Hú》. Piào yì zhāng shí'èr bàng、shíbā bàng hé èrshíwǔ bàng. **d** Shíyuè èrshíliù hào xīngqīrì wǎnshang bā diǎn. Gējù 《Kǎmén》. Yì zhāng piào shíliù bàng、èrshísì bàng hé sānshí bàng.

Quick review

a Go to see a film. **b** No, because she had already seen it. **c** Chinese music or western music. **d** No. **e** To go dancing.

Vocabulary

a 'Dōngtiān' is 'winter' and 'xiàtiān' is 'summer'
b 'tiào wǔ' is 'dancing'; 'chàng gē' is 'singing'; 'huá bīng' is 'skating'; and 'yóuyǒng' is 'swimming'

c 'hùzhào' means 'passport', 'qiānzhèng' means 'visa'
d 'dān' means 'single', 'shuāng' means 'two or double'
e young person/people

Unit 15

1 a Nǐ kěyǐ zài yóujú cún qián、qǔ qián. b Yīngguó de yóujú xīngqīliù xiàwǔ hé xīngqītiān yìbān bù kāi mén. c Zài Yīngguó xìntǒng shì hóngsè de, bú shì lǜsè de. d Zài Yīngguó bù kěyǐ zài yóujú dǎ chángtú diànhuà.

2 a Zhè ge bāoguǒ jì dào Měiguó. b Dōu shì shū. c Yào duōshao/jǐ tiān? d Wǒ xiǎng mǎi míngxìnpiàn. Duōshao qián yí tào? e Wǒ yào yí tào dà de, liǎng tào xiǎo de. f Gěi nín liǎng/èr bǎi kuài. g Xièxie. Zàijiàn.

3 a Qǐng wèn, kěyǐ zài zhèr dǎ (ge) diànhuà ma? Qǐng wèn, kěyǐ zài zhèr jì (ge) bāoguǒ ma? Qǐng wèn, kěyǐ zài zhèr fā (ge) e-mail (diànzǐ yóujiàn) ma? b Qǐng gěi wǒ nǐde diànhuà hàomǎ. Qǐng gěi wǒ tāmende wǎngzhǐ. Qǐng gěi wǒ nǐde hùzhào. Qǐng gěi wǒ tāmende dìzhǐ. c Qǐng dào nèibiān huàn qián. Qǐng dào wàibiān dǎ diànhuà.

4 a Hépíng Bīnguǎn. b Bái Huá xiānsheng. c There is no such extension number. d The caller had got the number wrong.

5 a Bú duì. b Duì. c Duì. d Bú duì.

6 a Qǐng wèn, jīntiān yīngbàng hé rénmínbì de duìhuànlǜ shì duōshao? b Qǐng wèn, jīntiān měiyuán hé rénmínbì de duìhuànlǜ shì duōshao? c Qǐng wèn, jīntiān gǎngbì hé rénmínbì de duìhuànlǜ shì duōshao? d Qǐng wèn, jīntiān ōuyuán hé rénmínbì de duìhuànlǜ shì duōshao?

7 a yìbǎi bǐ bābǎi wǔshí; yìbǎi měiyuán huàn bābǎi wǔshí yuán. b yìbǎi bǐ yìbǎi líng bā; yìbǎi gǎngbì huàn yìbǎi líng bā yuán. c yìbǎi bǐ yìqiān sānbǎi èrshí; yìbǎi yīngbàng huàn yìqiān sānbǎi èrshí yuán. d yìbǎi bǐ jiǔbǎi yīshí; yìbǎi ōuyuán huàn jiǔbǎi yīshí yuán.

8 a Wǒ xiǎng huàn yìbǎi yīngbàng de rénmínbì. b Wǒ xiǎng huàn èrbǎi měiyuán de rénmínbì. c Wǒ xiǎng huàn wǔbǎi gǎngbì de rénmínbì. d Wǒ xiǎng huàn liùwàn rìyuán de rénmínbì. e Wǒ xiǎng huàn sìbǎi ōuyuán de rénmínbì.

Quick review

a Zhèi zhāng míngxìnpiàn jì dào Yīngguó duōshao qián?
b Wǒ xiǎng mǎi yí tào yóupiào.
c Jīntiān yīngbàng hé rénmínbì de duìhuànlǜ shì duōshao?
d Wǒ xiǎng huàn yìbǎi wǔshí yīngbàng de rénmínbì.
e Wǒde fēnjī shì èr-yāo-yāo-wǔ.

Vocabulary

a 'cún qián' 'to deposit money'; 'qǔ qián' 'to withdraw money';
  'diǎn qián' 'to count money'; and 'huàn qián' 'to change money'
b chuánzhēn
c dǎ (diànhuà), fā (chuánzhēn) and jì (xìn)
d qǔkuǎnjī
e hángkōng

Unit 16

1 a hē jiǔ, chī rè fàn、 rè cài, hē tāng, b hē tāng, chī zhèngcān, chī shuǐguǒ, c wǎn/kuàizi, d dāochā/pánzi, e Zhōngguó-rén.

2 a Zhè shì gěi nǐ de (yì hé) qiǎokèlì. Zhè hé qiǎokèlì shì gěi nǐ de. b Zhè shì gěi nǐ de (yì píng) jiǔ. Zhè píng jiǔ shì gěi nǐ de. c Zhè shì gěi nǐ de (liǎng zhāng) diànyǐng piào. Zhè liǎng zhāng diànyǐng piào shì gěi nǐ de. d Zhè shì gěi nǐ de (yì hé) lǜ chá. Zhè hé lǜ chá shì gěi nǐ de. e Zhè shì gěi nǐ de (yì běn) shū. Zhè běn shū shì gěi nǐ de.

3 a Zhè shì gěi wǒ jiějie de (yì hé) qiǎokèlì. Zhè hé qiǎokèlì shì gěi wǒ jiějie de. b Zhè shì gěi tā tàitai de (yì hé) lǜ chá. Zhè hé lǜ chá shì gěi tā tàitai de. c Zhè shì gěi tā shūshu de (yì běn) shū. Zhè běn shū shì gěi tā shūshu de. d Zhè shì gěi tā nán péngyou de (yì píng) jiǔ. Zhè píng jiǔ shì gěi tā nán péngyou de. e Zhè shì gěi nǐmende péngyou de (liǎng zhāng) diànyǐng piào. Zhè liǎng zhāng diànyǐng piào shì gěi nǐmende péngyou de. f Zhè shì gěi tāmen gōngsī de (yì fú) huà. Zhè fú huà shì gěi tāmen gōngsī de.

4 **a** Gān bēi! **b** Wǒ chī-bu-xià le. **c** Zhēn xiāng a! **d** Wǒ zìjǐ lái. **e** Zhù nǐ wànshìrúyì!

5 **a** Wǒ gāi zǒu le. **b** Hái zǎo ne. Zài zuò yìhuǐr ba. **c** Gěi nǐmen tiān máfan le. **d** Méi shénme (máfan). **e** Bú yòng le. Qǐng huí qù ba. **f** Lùshàng xiǎoxīn. **g** Màn zǒu. Màn zǒu.

6 **a** = iii, **b** = i, **c** = v, **d** = ii, **e** = vi, **f** = iv.

Quick review

a Wishing you good health! To your good health!
b Wishing you a happy life!
c Wishing you every happiness!
d May your work go smoothly/well!
e Wishing you success! To your success!
f To our friendship!
g To our co-operation!

Unit 17

1 **a** Duì. **b** Duì. **c** Duì. **d** Bú duì.

2 **a** Wǒ tóu téng. **b** Wǒ yǒu (yì) diǎnr késou. **c** Wǒ yě juéde shì gǎnmào. **d** Wǒ méi chī-guo Zhōngyào. Zhōngyào yǒu xiào ma? **e** Hǎo ba. (Xíng.) Wǒ shìshi ba.

3 **a** before/twice/one ball, **b** after/4 times/3 tablets, **c** one hour after meal/3 times/one spoonful, **d** twice (early morning and evening)/2–3 tablets.

4 **a** quite a few, **b** all sorts of, **c** headaches, **d** was scared.

6 **a** = iv, **b** = v, **c** = i, **d** = iii, **e** = vi, **f** = ii.

Quick review

a Nín nǎr bù shūfu?   **b** Wǒ xiǎng shìshi zhēnjiǔ.
c Wǒ juéde wǒ gǎnmào le.   **d** Wǒ méi chī-guo Zhōngyào.
e Wǒ yǒu shíhou tóu téng.

Unit 18

1 a Zài Yīngguó kāi chē hé qí zìxíngchē dōu zǒu lù de zuǒbiān. **b** Zhè gēn zài Rìběn hé Ài'ěrlán yíyàng, gēn zài Ōuzhōu dàlù bù yíyàng. **c** Měiguó shì shìjiè shàng qìchē zuì duō de guójiā. **d** Zài Xīfāng zū qìchē bù nán.

2 a Wǒ xiǎng zū yí liàng chē. **b** Yǒu. Shì Yīngguó de (jiàzhào). **c** Wǒ xiǎng zū yí liàng xiǎo de (*or*) xiǎo chē. **d** Kěyǐ. **e** Liǎng tiān. **f** Nǐmen shōu bu shōu xìnyòng kǎ?

3 a Kāi chē shàng bān yào/děi yí ge xiǎoshí. **b** Bǔ chēdài yào/děi duōshao qián? **c** Zuò gōnggòng qìchē dào Xiāngshān zěnme qù? **d** Zū yí liàng zìxíngchē yào/děi sānshí kuài.

4 a Bú duì. **b** Duì. **c** Duì. **d** Duì. **e** Duì. **f** Bú duì. **g** Bú duì.

5 a He'd lost his bag. **b** His passport, wallet, credit card, some money, and a small camera. **c** More than 400 yuan and 200 US dollars. **d** Yulong Hotel. **e** Report its loss to his Embassy. **f** Inform him once they'd got any news.

6 a Tāde chēdài huài le. **b** Tāde chē huài le. **c** Tāde bāo diū le. **d** Tāmen zhuàng chē le. **e** Tā tóu téng. **f** Tāde chē dēng huài le.

Quick review

a Zhēn dǎoméi!

b Bú shì wǒde cuò.

c Wǒ xiǎng tāmen yīnggai qù zhǎo jǐngchá.

d Wǒde xìnyòng kǎ diū le.

e Wǒde zìxíngchē huài le. Nín néng bu néng bāng wǒ kàn(yi) kan?

Unit 19

1 a = iv, **b** = vi, **c** = i, **d** = vii, **e** = iii, **f** = v, **g** = ii.

2 a Hànzú, Hànyǔ; **b** fāngyán, kǒuyīn; **c** Guóyǔ, Huáyǔ; **d** yǔyán, Hànyǔ.

3 a Fluent with good pronunciation and tones. **b** Three years. **c** Not good (according to himself). **d** Six years. **e** Her learning method(s). **f** Her husband.

4 a Hánguó, pípa, èrhú; **b** Yīngguó, shǎoshù mínzú; **c** Rìběn, Zhōngguó jīngjì; **d** fānyì, jìzhě; **e** wénxué, zhéxué, wénxué, zhéxué.

6 a Wǒ huì shuō **Déwén** (hé **Fǎwen**). **b** Wǒde **Rìyǔ** búcuò or Wǒde **Yìdàlìyǔ** shuō-de bú tài **liúlì**. **c** Wǒ huì shuō yìdiǎnr **Éyǔ**. **d** Wǒ shuō **Zhōngwén** shuō-de yǒu (yìdiǎnr) Měiguó kǒuyīn. **e** **Fǎyǔ** de yǔyīn hěn nán.

Quick review

a Nǐ juéde Yīngwén (de) yǔyīn nán ma?
b Wǒ zhǐ huì xiě jǐ ge/yìxiē Hànzì.
c Wǒ huì shuō yìdiǎnr Zhōngwén, kěshì wǒ juéde shēngdiào hěn nán.
d Nǐ hěn qiānxū. (Nǐ tài qiānxū le.)
e Wǒ juéde tāde kǒuyīn hěn nán dǒng.
f Nǐde Yīngyǔ/Fǎyǔ/Déyǔ búcuò.
g Nǐ guòjiǎng le.

Unit 20

1 a sānyuè, wǔyuè **b** liùyuè、qīyuè、bāyuè **c** jiǔyuè、shíyuè、shíyīyuè **d** shí'èryuè, èryuè.
3 a Bú duì. **b** Duì. **c** Bú duì. **d** Duì. **e** Bú duì.
5 a = v, **b** = iv, **c** = ii, **d** = i, **e** = iii.
7 a huǒchē; **b** huǒchē, fēijī; **c** huǒchē, chángtú qìchē; **d** fēijī, huǒchē; **e** fēijī.
8 a Tā míngtiān zuò huǒchē qù Shànghǎi. **b** Wǒde péngyou zuò gōnggòng qìchē lái wǒ jiā. **c** Wǒ bù qí zìxíngchē qù gōngyuán. **d** Tāmen chángcháng kāi/zuò chē qù mǎi dōngxi. **e** Wǒ xiànzài zuò dìtiě huí jiā.
9 a Wǒ xiǎng qù Xiānggǎng hé Àomén. **b** Wǒ (xiān) zuò fēijī qù Xiānggǎng, zài zuò chuán qù Àomén. **c** Nàr/nàli bāyuè hěn rè. **d** Yǒu shíhou xià yǔ. **e** Wǒ hái méi juédìng(ne).

294

10 a Shì. b Shì. c Hěn duǎn yě hěn nuǎnhuo, kěshì chángcháng guā fēng. d Bú shì. e Qiūtiān bù lěng yě bú rè. Qíngtiān duō, yīntiān shǎo. Bù cháng guā fēng, yě hěn shǎo xià yǔ.

Quick review

a Zuótiān shàngwǔ xià yǔ le, qìwēn èrshí dù.
b Zuótiān wǎnshang guā fēng le, qìwēn wǔ dù.
c Jīntiān shàngwǔ shì qíngtiān, qìwēn shí'èr dù.
d Jīntiān xiàwǔ yǒu xiǎo yǔ, qìwēn shíbā dù.
e Míngtiān yīntiān, qìwēn sān dù.
f Xià xīngqīyī yǒu/xià xuě, qìwēn líng dù.

Unit 21

1 a Yuè lái yuè duō de Zhōngguó-rén lái Yīngguó xuéxí. b Tāmen hěn duō rén duì Yīngguó de lìshǐ hé wénhuà yǒu xìngqu. c Měi nián hěn duō wàiguó xuésheng lái Yīngguó xuéxí Yīngwén. d Yuè lái yuè duō de Ōuzhōu gōngsī xiǎng zài Zhōngguó kuòdà shēngyi.

5 a Liǎng ge xīngqī. b Wǒ qù le Běijīng、Shànghǎi hé Guìlín. c Shànghǎi fāzhǎn-de hěn kuài. d Běijīng yǒu hěn duō gōngyuán. Wǒ hěn xǐhuan tāmen. e Guìlín de fēngjǐng měi-jíle.

6 a Bú duì. b Bú duì. c Duì. d Bú duì.

Final review

1 a rè b lǎo c pàng d chǎo e guì f wēixiǎn g jìn h nuǎn(huo) i wǎn j ruǎn k qián l yǐhòu m shàng n yòu o nán p xīběi.
2 a = iv, b = iii, c = v, d = i, e = ii.
3 a mobile, b computer, c advertise/advertisement, d video recorder, e job guaranteed for life, f thermos flask, g aerial, antenna.
4 a 8:30pm the day before yesterday b 1147 c 9764 3772 d 2437 8910 e About a week f Next Thursday g 12:15pm h two i 7:10am on the 17th.

Recording: Ānní, wǒ shì Cài Míng. Wǒ yǐjing dào le Guǎngzhōu. Wǒ shì qiántiān wǎnshang bā diǎn bàn dào de. Wǒ xiànzài zhù zài Báiyún Bīnguǎn. Wǒ de fángjiān shì yāo-yāo-sì-qī. Qǐng nǐ gěi wǒ dǎ ge diànhuà. Bīnguǎn de diànhuà shì jiǔ-qī-liù-sì sān-qī-qī-èr. Yàoshi wǒ bú zài fángjiān lǐ, qǐng nǐ dǎ wǒ de shǒujī. Wǒ de shǒujī hàomǎ shì èr-sì-sān-qī bā-jiǔ-yāo-líng. Wǒ huì zài Guǎngzhōu zhù chàbuduō yí ge xīngqī. Xià xīngqīsì zhōngwǔ shí'èr diǎn yí kè zuò huǒchē qù Shēnzhèn. Wǒ zài Shēnzhèn zhù liǎng tiān, ránhòu qù Xiānggǎng, shíqī hào zǎoshang qī diǎn shí fēn zuò fēijī huí Lúndūn.

5 a Wǒ chī-bu-guàn là de cài. b Nǐ duì gǔdiǎn yīnyuè háishi duì liúxíng yīnyuè yǒu/gǎn xìngqu? c Yuè lái yuè duō de rén qù wàiguó dù jià. d Nǐ duì Yīngguó de yìnxiàng zěnmeyàng? e Nǐ duì shènme (zuì) mǎnyì, shénme (zuì) bù mǎnyì? f Zhù nǐ shēngrì kuàilè!

Chinese–English vocabulary

The number after each vocabulary item indicates the unit in which it first appears.

ài *love; to love, to like very much* 16
Ài'ěrlán *Ireland* 3
àiren (sometimes used in the People's Republic) *husband/wife* 10
ānjìng *quiet* 12
ānpái *arrangement, to arrange* 20
ānquán *safe* 9
Àolínpǐkè *Olympic* 14
Àolínpǐkè Yùndònghuì *Olympic Games* 14
Àomén *Macao* 9

ba (particle indicating suggestion) 3
bàba *dad, father* 4
bǎi *hundred* 7
báijiǔ *strong alcohol* 16
bái(sè) (de) *white* 7
báitiān *daytime* 20
bàn *half* 5
bàn *to handle* 14
bāng *to help* 5
bàng *excellent* 14
bāo *bag* 18
bāo *to include; to make* (jiǎozi) 21
bāoguǒ *parcel* 15

bēi *a cup of; cup* 10
běi *north* 9
běifāng *the north* 14
bǐ *compared to* 6
biān *side* 9
biǎo *form* 12
biǎoyǎn *show, performance; to act/to perform* 14
bié *don't* 9
bié rén *other/another person* 18
biéde *other* 12
bǐjiào *relatively* 12
bǐjiào xǐhuan *to prefer* 20
bìng *illness* 17
bīngqílín *ice-cream* 10
bìngrén *patient* 17
bù *not* 1
bǔ chēdài *to mend a tyre* 18
bú kèqi *you are welcome* 4
bú xiàng *not look it* 4
bú xiè *not at all* 17
bù xíng *not that good* 19
bú yòng xiè *not at all* (lit. *no need thank*) 1
bù zěnmeyàng *not so good* 8
búcuò *pretty good, not bad* 7
búguò *but, however* 12
bùtóng de *different* 16

cái *not . . . until, only then* 7

cài *dish* 10

càidān *menu* 10

cānjiā *to attend* 17

cāntīng *restaurant, canteen* 12

cǎoméi *strawberry* 7

cèsuǒ *toilet* 12

chá *to look up (something)* 15

chá *tea* 16

chà *lacking, short of* 5

chàbuduō *similar* (lit. *different not much*) 15

cháng *long* 20

chàng (gē) *to sing (a song)* 14

chàng jīngjù *to sing Peking opera* 14

cháng(chang) *to taste* 16

chángcháng *often* 16

Chángchéng *the Great Wall* 10

chángshòu (miàn) *long life (noodles)* 21

chángtú *long distance* 15

chángtú qìchē *coach* 18

chǎo *noisy* 12

chǎomiàn *stir-fried noodles* 10

chāozhòng le *exceeded the weight limit* 15

chē *vehicle (bus, bike, car)* 6

chēdài *tyre* 18

chèng *scales* 15

chéng lǐ *in the city, in urban areas* 18

chénggōng *success, successful* 16

chéngshì *city* 18

chēzhàn *bus/train stop or station* 9

chī *to eat* 10

chī (yào) *to take (medicine)* 17

chī-bǎo le *to eat one's fill* 10

chī de *something to eat* 12

chī fàn *to eat, eating* 16

chī sù *to be vegetarian* 10

chōu (yān) *to smoke (a cigarette)* 10

chuán *ship, boat* 9

chuánzhēn *fax* 15

chúfáng *kitchen* 16

Chūnjié *the Spring Festival, Chinese New Year* 5

chūntiān *spring* 20

chūzū (qì)chē *taxi* 9

cí *word* 12

cì *measure word for trains* 13

cì *time, occasion* 12

cóng *from* 9

cónglái *ever* 20

cōngming *clever* 19

cún qián *to deposit money* 15

cuò *fault* 18

dà *big, old* 4

dǎ diànhuà *to telephone* 12

dǎ pái *to play cards* 14

dǎ tàijíquán *to do Tai Chi* 6

dàbùfen *majority* 16

dàgài *approximately* 13

dàibiǎotuán *delegation* 20

dàjiā *everyone* 16

dāng *to be; to work/to act as* 20

dāngrán *of course* 2

dānrén/shuāngrén fángjiān
  single/double room 12

dānwèi *work unit* 17

dànyuànrúcǐ *I hope so*
  (four-character phrase) 14

dào *to; to arrive, to go to* 5, 7

dāochā *knife and fork* 16

dàshǐguǎn *embassy* 18

dǎsuàn *to plan* 9

dàxiǎo *size* 8

dàxué *university* 21

de *possessive indicator* 2

. . . de shíhou *(the time)
  when . . .* 12

. . . deduō *much (more) . . .* 7

Déguó *Germany* 3

děi *to need, must; it takes* 13

dēng *lights* 18

děng *to wait* 13

děngděng *etc.* 14

dì *for ordinal numbers* 5

diǎn *o'clock* 5

diǎn *to count* 15

diànchē *tram* (lit. *electric
  vehicle*) 18

diànhuà *telephone* 3

diànshì *television* 9

diànyǐng *film, movie* 6

diànzǐ yóujiàn/yīmèi'ér
  e-mail 15

dìdi *younger brother* 4

dìfang *place* 9

dìng *to book* (a ticket) 6

dìqū *district* 15

dìtiě *underground/
  subway* 18

diū *to lose* 18

dōng *east* 9

dǒng *to understand* 21

Dōngnányà *South-East
  Asia* 19

dǒngshìzhǎng *managing
  director* 16

dōngtiān *winter* 14

dōngxi *thing, object* 6

dōu *all, both* 5

dòufu *beancurd, tofu* 10

dù *degree* (°C) 20

dǔchē *(to be in a) traffic
  jam* 18

dùjià *to take a holiday* 9

duì *yes, correct* 3

duì *to, for* 10

duìbuqǐ *excuse me/I'm
  sorry* 1

duìfu *to cope with* 18

duìhuànlǜ *exchange rate* 15

duìmiàn *opposite* 9

duō *many, more* 10

duō cháng? *how long?* 7

duō yuǎn? *how far?* 7

duōshao? *how much, how
  many, what's the number
  of?* 3

dùzi *tummy, stomach* 17

è *hungry* 10

Éguó-rén *Russian
  (person)* 19

èrděng *second-class
  (ticket)* 13

èrhú *a two-stringed musical
  instrument* 19

érzi *son* 4

fā *to send* (a fax, e-mail
  etc.) 15

fā chuánzhēn *to send a fax* 15
fā fēng *mad* 9
fādá *developed* 20
Fǎguó *France* 3
fàn *food, meal* 12
fàn hòu *after meals* 17
fàn qián *before meals* 17
fàndiàn *hotel* 3
fàng *to put* 15
fāngbiàn *convenient* 14
fāngfǎ *method* 19
fángjiān *room* 3
fǎngwèn *visit; to visit (formal)* 16
fāngyán *dialect* 19
fānyì *interpreter, translator* 19
fǎnzhèng *no way, in any case* 9
fāzhǎn *to develop* 21
fēicháng *extremely* 8
fēijī *plane* 3
fēn(zhōng) *minute* 5
fēnchéng *to divide/to be divided into* 17
fēng *measure word for letters* 15
fēng *wind* 20
fēngjǐng *scenery* 20
fèngzhǎo *chicken feet* 16
fēnháng *branch (of a bank)* 15
fù qián *pay (money)* 10
fù zhàng *to pay bills* 15
fūren *wife (formal), madam* 16
fúwù *service* 12

fúwùtái *reception* 12
fúwùyuán *assistant, housestaff* 6
fúyòng fāngfǎ *instruction (for taking medicine)* 17

gān bēi! *cheers!* 16
gānjìng *clean* 10
gǎnmào *to have a cold* 17
gàosu *to tell* 12
gāoxìng *happy* 18
gè *measure word* 4
gēge *elder brother* 4
gěi *for; to give* 6
gēn *and, with, to follow* 6
gèng *even more* 8
gèzhǒng gèyàng de *all kinds* 12
gōnggòng qìchē *bus* (lit. *public together steam vehicle*) 18
gōngjīn *kilogram* 7
gōngsī *company* 16
gōngyuán *park* 14
gōngzuò *to work, work* 20
guā fēng *windy* (lit. *blow wind*) 20
guǎi *to turn* 18
guān (mén) *to close (a door)* 5
guānfāng *official* 19
Guǎngdōng *Canton (Province)* 3
guāngpán *CD* 15
guì *expensive; honourable* 2
guò *to pass, spend (of time)* 8
-guo *have ever done* (verbal, suffix) 9
guójì *international* 15

guójiā *country* **18**

guòjiǎng *to exaggerate, to flatter* **19**

guóyǔ *national language* **19**

hái *still* **5**

hái kěyǐ *just so so* **8**

háishi *or (used in question forms)* **6**

háishi *would be better* **9**

hǎiyùn (to post) *by sea* **15**

háizi *child/children* **2**

hángkōng (to post) *by air* **15**

Hánguó-rén *Korean (person)* **19**

Hànzì *Chinese characters* **11, 17**

Hànzú *Han nationality* **19**

Hànzú-rén *the Han people* **19**

hǎo *good, well* **1**

hào *number* **3**

hǎochī (de) *delicious, tasty* **10**

hǎokàn *nice-looking* **15**

hàomǎ *number* (often used for telephone, telex, fax numbers and car registration plates) **3**

hǎoxiàng *to seem* **18**

hē *to drink* **10**

hé *and* **4**

hé *box* **16**

hē de *something to drink* **12**

hēi(sè) (de) *black* **7**

hěn *very* **1**

hépíng *peace* **3**

héshì *suitable* **8**

hézī qǐyè *joint venture* **21**

hézuò *co-operation, to cooperate* **16**

hóng(sè) (de) *red* **7**

hòu *later* **16**

hòulái *later* **18**

hòutiān *the day after tomorrow* **13**

hú *lake* **14**

Huá *another word for China* **19**

huá bīng *to skate* **14**

Huá-rén *overseas Chinese people* **19**

huài *broken, not working; bad* **18**

huán *to return something to* **12**

huàn *to change* **9**

huàn qián *to change money* **6**

huáng(sè) (de) *yellow* **7**

huānyíng *to welcome* **16**

huì *can, be able to* **2**

huì *meeting* **5**

huí guó *to return to one's own country* **20**

huí lái *to come back* **20**

huí qù *to go back* **16**

huò(zhě) *or (used in statements)* **16**

huǒchē *train* **5**

huódòng *activity* **14**

huǒtuǐ *ham* **12**

hùshi *nurse* **17**

hùzhào *passport* **12**

jǐ *how many?* (usually less than ten) **4**

jǐ *crowded* **7**

kuàilè *happy* **21**
kuàizi *chopsticks* **10**
kuòdà *to expand* **21**

là *hot, spicy* **10**
lā dùzi *to have diarrhoea* **17**
lái *to come* **1**
lái *I'll have* (colloquial) **10**
lán(sè) (de) *blue* **7**
lǎo *old* **14**
lǎoshī *teacher* **1**
le *grammatical marker* **4**
lèi *tired, tiring* **9**
lěng *cold* **20**
lí *distance from* **7**
lǐ *inside* **18**
lì *pill* **17**
liǎng *two (of anything)* **4**
liàng (measure word for vehicles (inc. bicycles)) **18**
liáng(kuai) *cold, cool* **16**
liànxí *to practise; exercise* **14**
líng *zero* **3**
líng (brakes) *work well* **18**
lìng yí gè *another; another one* **18**
línghuó *flexible* **15**
línyù *shower* **12**
lìshǐ *history* **19**
liúlì *fluent* **19**
liúxuéshēng *overseas student* **21**
lóu *floor; building* **7**
lóushàng *upstairs* **14**
lóuxià *downstairs* **14**
lù *road, street* **3**
lǜ(sè) (de) *green* **7**
lǚguǎn *hotel* **12**

Lúndūn *London* **3**
lǚxíng *to travel; travel* **14**
lǚxíngtuán *tourist group* **14**
lǚyóu *to travel* **21**

ma (question particle) **1**
máfan *(to) trouble* **12**
mǎi *to buy* **6**
mài *to sell* **7**
mǎlù *road* **9**
māma *mum, mother* **4**
màn *slow* **8**
mǎnyì *satisfied* **21**
màn zǒu *take care* (as in goodbye; lit. *walk slowly*) **16**
màoxiǎn *adventurous; to take the risk* **9**
máoyī *woollen pullover* **7**
mápó dòufu *spicy beancurd/ tofu* **10**
mǎshàng *at once* **18**
méi *no, not, (have not)* **2**
měi *every* **8**
měi *beautiful* **20**
méi guānxi *it's OK, it doesn't matter* **2**
Měiguó *USA* **3**
méi shénme *it's nothing, don't mention it* **9**
měi tiān *every day* **8**
méi wèntí *no problem* **6**
mèimei *younger sister* **4**
měiyuán *US dollar* **12**
mén *door* **5**
míngbai *to understand* **13**
míngnián *next year* **5**
míngpiàn *namecard* **3**
míngtiān *tomorrow* **1**

shūfu *comfortable* 9
shuǐ *water* 12
shuì *to sleep* 13
shuǐguǒ *fruit* 16
shuō *to speak, to say* 2
shūshu *uncle* (on father's side or someone of his father's generation) 16
sì jì *four seasons* 20
sòng lái *to send over* (to the speaker) 12
sòng qù *to send over* (away from the speaker) 12
suàn-cuò le *calculated wrongly* 10
Sūgélán *Scotland* 3
... suì ... *years old, age* 4
suíbiàn *casually* 10
suǒ (measure word for schools, houses, etc.) 21
suǒyǐ *so, therefore* 13
suǒyǒude *all* 16

tā *she, he, it* 1
tāde *his, her, its* 2
tài ... le! *too ...!* 7
tàitai *Mrs, wife* 1
tāmen *they, them* 21
tán *to talk, to chat* 14
tán liàn'ài *to be in love, go steady* (lit. *talk love*) 14
tán(yi)tán *to talk (a bit) about* 21
tāng *soup* 10
táng *sugar* 12
tānzi *stall* 10
tè *extremely* (colloquial) 20
tèkuài *special express* (*train*) 13

téng *pain; painful* 17
tèsè *feature, characteristic* 21
tiān *day* 9
tián *to fill* (in a form) 12
tián (de) *sweet* 7
tiānqi *weather* 10
tiánshí *dessert* 16
tiào dísīkē *to go to a disco* 14
tiào wǔ *to dance* 14
tiáojiàn *condition* 12
tīng *to listen to, (attend concert)* 6
tīng (measure word for cans (of drink)) 10
tǐng *quite, fairly* 14
tīngshuō *I heard, I am told* 9
tóngshì (men) *colleague(s)* 21
tóngxué (men) *fellow student(s)* 21
tōngzhī *to inform* 18
tóu téng *headache* 17
tóuděng (piào) *first-class (ticket)* 13
tóupán *starter* 16
tuìxiū *to retire* 9

wàiguó *foreign country* 16
wàiguó-rén *foreigner* 16
wàizī qǐyè *foreign enterprise* 21
wǎn *bowl* 10
wàn *ten thousand* 21
wǎn'ān *good night* 12
wán(r) *(Chinese medicine) ball* 17
wǎnfàn *dinner, supper* 12
wǎng/wàng *in the direction of* 9

wǎnshang *evening* 5
wèi (measure word for person (polite)) 2
wèi *for* (formal) 16
wèi . . . gān bēi! *to* . . . (used in a toast) 16
Wēi'ěrshì *Wales* 3
wèishēng *hygiene, hygienic* 10
wèishénme? *why?* 12
wēixiǎn *dangerous* 9
wèizi *seat* 14
wēn *warm* 17
wén *language, writing* 19
wèn *to ask* 1
wénhuà *culture* 21
wèntí *question, problem* 6
wénxué *literature* 19
wǒ *I, me* 2
wǒde *my* 2
wǒmen *we, us* 2

xī *west* 9
xià chē *to get off* (a vehicle) 9
xià qí *to play chess* 14
xià xuě *to snow* (lit. *descend snow*) 20
xià yǔ *to rain* (lit. *descend rain*) 8, 20
xià(yí)ge *next* 9
xiān *first* 6
xiàndàihuà (de) *modern* 16
xiāng *fragrant* 16
xiǎng *would like to; to think* 6
xiǎng *to miss, long for* 20
xiàng *to (look) like* 4
Xiānggǎng *Hong Kong* 9

xiāngjiāo *bananas* 7
xiǎngyào *would like* 12
xiànjīn *cash* 10
xiànmu *to envy* 9
xiānsheng *Mr; husband; gentleman* 1
xiànzài *now* 5
xiǎo *little, young, small* 1
xiǎojie *Miss, young lady* 2
xiǎoshí *hour* 12
xiāoxi *news, information* 18
xiàtiān *summer* 14
xiàwǔ *afternoon* 5
xiě *to write* 19
xièxie (nǐ) *to thank; thank you* 1
Xīfāng *the west, western* 6
xíguàn *habit, customs* 16
xǐhuan *to like* 3
xīn *new* 8
xìn *letter* 15
xìnfēng *envelope* 15
xíng *OK* 9
xìng *surname* 2
xīngqī *week* 5
xìngqu *interest* 19
xìntǒng *postbox, mailbox* 15
xīnxian *fresh* 7
xìnyòng kǎ *credit card* 10
xiōngdì *brothers* 4
xiū *to repair* 12
xiūxi *to rest* 6
xīwàng *to hope; hope* 16
Xīyào *western medicine* 17
Xīyī *western medical (doctor)* 17
xǐzǎojiān *bathroom* 12
xuǎnzé *to choose* 12

yóulǎn *sightseeing* 13
yóupiào *stamp* 15
yǒuyì *friendship* 16
yóuyǒng *to swim* 14
yú *fish* 10
yǔ *rain* 20
yǔ(yán) *language* 19
yuǎn *far* 7
yuànyì *would like to, to be willing to* 15
yuányīn *reason* 12
yùbào *forecast* 20
yùdìng *to book* (a table, a room) 10
yuè *month* 5
yuè . . . yuè . . . *the more . . . the more . . .* 13
yuè lái yuè . . . *more and more . . .* 21
Yuènán *Vietnam* 3
yǔfǎ *grammar* 19
yúkuài *happy, pleasant* 20
yúlè *entertainment* 14
yùndòng *sports, to take exercise* 14
yùndònghuì *sports meeting, games* 14
yǔyīn *pronunciation* 19

zài *to be at/in* 1
zài (indicating continuing action) 6
zàijiàn *goodbye* 1
zájì *acrobatics* 6
zánmen *we/us* (including listener) 7
zǎo *early* 14
zǎocān/zǎofàn *breakfast* 12

zǎo jiù *for a long time, ages ago, for ages* 8
zǎoshang *morning* 5
zěnme? *how?* 9
zěnmeyàng? *how is it? how about it?* 8
zhā *to pierce, to put in a needle, to do acupuncture* 17
zhá *brakes* 18
zhàn *(bus) stop, station* 7
zhàn xiàn *(line) engaged* 15
zhāng (measure word for flat objects) 8
zhàntái *platform* 5
zhǎo *to look for* 12
zhǎo (qián) *to give change* 13
zhàoxiàngjī *camera* 18
zhè/zhèi *this* 2
zhèixiē/nèixiē *these/those* 15
zhème (gui) *so (expensive)* 7
zhēn *real, really* 2
zhēn dǎoméi! *how unfortunate! bad luck!* 18
zhēnde *really* 4
zhèngcān *main course* 16
zhènghǎo *just right* (amount) 15
zhěngtiān *all day* 14
zhèngzài *at this moment* 12
zhēnjiǔ *acupuncture* 17
zhěnsuǒ *clinic* (open to the general public) 17
zhèr *here, this place* 7
zhéxué *philosophy* 19
zhèyàng *like this, in this way* 17

English–Chinese vocabulary

afternoon   xiàwǔ
afterwards   ránhòu
alcohol   jiǔ
all + noun   suǒyǒude + noun
all, both   dōu
already   yǐjīng
also   yě
always   zǒngshì
America   Měiguó
apple   píngguǒ
arrangement; to arrange   ānpái
to ask   wèn
assistant, housestaff   fúwùyuán
autumn   qiūtiān

bag   bāo
bank   yínháng
banquet   yànhuì
bathroom   xǐzǎojiān
to be   shì
to be at/in   zài
beautiful   měi, piàoliang
because   yīnwei
beer   píjiǔ
before   yǐqián
bicycle   zìxíngchē
big   dà
birthday   shēngrì
black   hēi(sè) (de)
blue   lán(sè) (de)
to board (a vehicle)   shàng (chē)
boiled water   kāishuǐ
book   shū
to book (a ticket)   dìng (piào)
both   dōu
bottle   píngzi

breakfast   zǎocān/zǎofàn
broken, not working; bad   huài
bus   gōnggòng qìchē
business   shēngyi
but   kěshì
to buy   mǎi
to call, to be called   jiào

camera   zhàoxiàngjī
can, be able to   néng
can, know how to   huì
car   qìchē
cash   xiànjīn
CD   guāngpán
certainly, definitely   yídìng
to change   huàn
to change money   huàn qián
cheap   piányi
cheers!   gān bēi!
cheque, check   zhīpiào
child/children   háizi
China   Zhōngguó
Chinese (language)   Zhōngwén
Chinese characters   Hànzì
chocolate(s)   qiǎokèlì
to choose   xuǎnzé
chopsticks   kuàizi
city   chéngshì
clean   gānjìng
clear   qīngchu
clever   cōngming
to close (a door)   guān (mén)
coach (vehicle)   chángtú qìchē
coffee   kāfēi
cold   lěng
cold, cool   liáng(kuai)

colleague tóngshì
to come lái
to come back huí lái
comfortable shūfu
company gōngsī
concert yīnyuèhuì
convenient fāngbiàn
to cook zuò (fàn)
cough; to cough késou
country guójiā
credit card xìnyòng kǎ
crowded jǐ
cup(ful) bēi

dad, father bàba
dangerous wēixiǎn
daughter nǚ'ér
day tiān
to decide juédìng
delicious, tasty hǎochī (de)
difficult nán
dish cài
to do zuò
doctor yīshēng, dàifu
don't bié
door mén
double room shuāngrén fángjiān
downstairs lóuxià
to drink hē
to drive kāi

early zǎo
east dōng
easy róngyì
to eat chī
economy jīngjì
elder brother gēge
elder sister jiějie
e-mail diànzǐ yóujiàn/yīmèi'ér
embassy dàshǐguǎn
English (language) Yīngwén

to enter jìn
euro ōuyuán
every měi
everyone dàjiā
everything yíqiè
excuse me duìbuqǐ
expensive; honourable guì
extremely fēicháng, tè

far yuǎn
fast kuài
fat pàng
fault cuò
fax chuánzhēn
to feel, to think juéde
few; less shǎo
to fill (in a form) tián (biǎo)
film, movie diànyǐng
first xiān
fish yú
floor/storey lóu
food, meal fàn
football zúqiú
for; to give gěi
foreign country wàiguó
foreign enterprise wàizī qǐyè
form biǎo
free; freedom zìyóu
friend péngyou
friendly yǒuhǎo
friendship yǒuyì
from cóng
fruit shuǐguǒ
to get off the bus xià chē
to go back huí qù
to go to qù, dào

good; well hǎo
goodbye zàijiàn
green lǜ(sè) (de)
guest kèren

half bàn
hand shǒu
happy gāoxìng/kuàilè
to have yǒu
to have a cold gǎnmào
to have diarrhoea lā dùzi
he/she/it tā
headache tóu téng
health, body shēntǐ
health; healthy jiànkāng
to help bāng
here, this place zhèr
to hire, to rent zū
his, her, its tāde
holiday, vacation jià(qī)
home jiā
to hope; hope xīwàng
hospital yīyuàn
hot rè
hot, spicy là
hotel fàndiàn, bīnguǎn, lǚguǎn
hour xiǎoshí
how far? duō yuǎn?
how is it? how about
   it? zěnmeyàng?
how much? how
   many? duōshao?
how? zěnme?
hundred bǎi
hungry è
husband xiānsheng, àiren

I, me wǒ
idea zhǔyì
identity card shēnfènzhèng
if rúguǒ, yàoshi
illness bìng
to inform tōngzhī
inside lǐ
interest xìngqu
interesting yǒu yìsi

international guójì
interpreter, translator; to interpret,
   translate fānyì
to introduce; introduction jièshào
to invite; please qǐng

joint venture hézī qǐyè

key yàoshi
kilogram gōngjīn
knife and fork dāochā
to know (a fact) zhīdao
to know (people) rènshi

language yǔyán
last zuìhòu
later, after yǐhòu
to leave; to walk zǒu
left zuǒ
to let, allow ràng
letter xìn
letter box xìnxiāng
light(s) dēng
to (look) like xiàng
to like xǐhuan
to listen to tīng
a little yìdiǎn(r)
little, young, small xiǎo
to live (in/at a place) zhù (zài)
long cháng
to look at, watch kàn
to look for zhǎo
to lose diū
to love; love ài

male nán
many; more duō
to marry jié hūn
meaning yìsi
meat ròu
medicine yào

to meet   jiàn miàn
meeting   huì
menu   càidān
minute   fēn(zhōng)
Miss, young lady   xiǎojie
to miss   xiǎng
mobile (phone)   shǒujī
money   qián
month   yuè
morning   shàngwǔ
morning (early)   zǎoshang
most   zuì
mountain   shān
mountain bike   shāndìchē
Mr; husband;
   gentleman   xiānsheng
Mrs; wife   tàitai
mum, mother   māma
music   yīnyuè

near   jìn
to need, must; it takes   děi
new   xīn
news, information   xiāoxi
next   xià(yí)ge
nice looking   hǎokàn
no, not, (have not)   méi
noisy   chǎo
north   běi
not   bù
not bad, pretty good   búcuò
now   xiànzài
number   hào
number (telephone, telex,
   fax)   hàomǎ
nurse   hùshi

o'clock   diǎn(zhōng)
of course   dāngrán
often   chángcháng
old   lǎo

Olympic Games   Àolínpǐkè
   Yùndònghuì
on   shàng
only   zhǐ
opportunity   jīhuì
opposite   duìmiàn
other   biéde

pain; painful   téng
park   gōngyuán
passport   hùzhào
to pay (money)   fù qián
peace   hépíng
person   rén
pharmacy   yàofáng
place   dìfang
to plan   dǎsuàn
plane   fēijī
platform   zhàntái
pleasant, happy   yúkuài
police officer   jǐngchá
polite   kèqi
possible; possibly   kěnéng
to post   jì
post office   yóujú
postcard   míngxìnpiàn
pound (money)   (Yīng)bàng
to practise; exercise   liànxí
prescription   yàofāng
pretty good   búcuò
purse/wallet   qiánbāo
to put   fàng

question, problem   wèntí
quiet   ānjìng

rain   yǔ
to rain   xià yǔ
real; really   zhēn
really   zhēnde
reason   yuányīn

receipt shōujù
recent; recently zuìjìn
to recognize, to know
  (people) rènshi
red hóng(sè) (de)
to rest xiūxi
to return something (to) huán
  (gěi)
right (the opposite of left) yòu
road, street lù
room fángjiān

safe ānquán
same yíyàng
sandwich sānmíngzhì
satisfied mǎnyì
seat wèizi
to see kàn-jiàn
to see a doctor kàn bìng, kàn
  yīshēng
to seem hǎoxiàng
to sell mài
service fúwù
she, he, it tā
ship, boat chuán
a short while, after a
  moment yìhuǐ(r)
sightseeing yóulǎn
simple jiǎndān
to sing (a song) chàng (gē)
single room dānrén fángjiān
to sit zuò
size dàxiǎo
to sleep shuì
slow màn
to smoke (a cigarette) chōu (yān)
to snow xià xuě
so, therefore suǒyǐ
some yìxiē, yǒude
sometimes yǒu shíhou
son érzi

soup tāng
south nán
to speak, to say shuō
sports; to take exercise yùndòng
spring chūntiān
stamp yóupiào
to start kāishǐ
station, (bus) stop (chē) zhàn
still hái
to stroll sàn bù
student xuésheng
to study, to learn xué(xí)
success; successful chénggōng
sugar táng
summer xiàtiān
sunny (day) qíngtiān
surname xìng
sweet tián (de)
to swim yóuyǒng

to take a holiday dù jià
to take the bus zuò chē
to take, to fetch ná
to talk, chat tán
taxi chūzū (qì)chē
tea chá
teacher lǎoshī
telephone diànhuà
to telephone dǎ diànhuà
television diànshì
to tell gàosu
to thank; thank you xièxie (nǐ)
that nà/nèi
there nàr/nàli
these/those zhèixiē/nèixiē
they, them tāmen
thin shòu
thing, matter, issue shìqing
thing, object dōngxi
to think, believe rènwéi
to think, to assume yǐwéi

this zhè/zhèi
this year jīnnián
thousand qiān
ticket piào
time shíjiān
time, occasion cì
tired, tiring lèi
to; to arrive, to go to dào
today jīntiān
together yìqǐ
toilet cèsuǒ
tomorrow míngtiān
too . . . ! tài . . . le!
train huǒchē
transport, traffic jiāotōng
to travel; travel lǚxíng, lǚyóu
to try shìshi
to turn guǎi
TV diànshì
two (of anything) liǎng

underground, subway dìtiě
to understand dǒng, míngbai
university dàxué
upstairs lóushàng
to use yòng
US dollar měiyuán
usually yìbān

vegetables qīng cài
vehicle (bus, bike, car) chē
very hěn
video (tape) lùxiàngdài
visa qiānzhèng
visit; to visit (formal) fǎngwèn

to wait děng
to walk, on foot zǒu lù
to want (to), need, will yào
to want to, would like to; xiǎng

warm nuǎn(huo)
water shuǐ
we, us wǒmen
weather tiānqi
week xīngqī
weekend zhōumò
to welcome; welcome huānyíng
west xī
what kind? shénme yàng de?
what? shénme?
when, what time? shénme shíhou?
where? nǎr?/nǎli?
which number? jǐ hào?
which? nǎ/něi?
white bái(sè) (de)
who? shéi/shuí?
whose? shéide?/shuíde?
why? wèishénme?
wife tàitai, àiren
wife (formal); *madam* fūren
wind fēng
wine pútáojiǔ
winter dōngtiān
to work; work gōngzuò
to write xiě

year nián
. . . year (of age) . . . suì
yellow huáng(sè) (de)
yes, correct duì
you (singular) nǐ
you (polite form) nín
you (plural) nǐmen
young niánqīng
younger brother dìdi
younger sister mèimei
your (singular) nǐde
your (plural) nǐmende

Appendix: character texts

---

1 Hello! how are you? 第一课 你好！你好吗？

Dialogue 1

格林太太：	你好，小王！
格林先生：	小王，你好！
小王：	格林先生，格林太太，你们好！
格林太太：	你太太好吗？
小王：	她很好，谢谢。

Dialogue 2

格林先生：	小王，谢谢你。
格林太太：	谢谢你，小王。
小王：	不用谢。
格林先生：	再见。
小王：	再见。
格林太太：	再见。

Dialogue 3

李先生：	请进。
格林先生：	(enters the room)
李先生：	格林先生，你好！
格林先生：	你好，李先生。
李先生：	请坐。
格林先生：	谢谢。
李先生：	格林太太好吗？
格林先生：	她很好。谢谢。

Dialogue 4

Frank:	请问，张老师在吗？
李老师：	对不起，她不在。
Frank:	她今天来吗？
李老师：	不来。她明天来。
Frank:	谢谢你。
李老师：	不用谢。明天见。
Frank:	明天见。

2 What's your name? 第二课 你叫什么？

Dialogue 1

Jane:	您贵姓？
陈：	我姓陈。您呢？
Jane:	我姓 Lord。这是您的孩子吗？
陈：	不是。我没有孩子。这是李太太的孩子。
Jane:	(to the child) 你叫什么名字？
孩子：	我叫盼盼。

Dialogue 2

White:	郑先生，你好！
常：	我姓常，不姓郑。 我叫常正。
White:	对不起，常先生。
常：	没关系。White 先生，你有没有中文名字？
White:	有。我叫白彼德。
常：	白先生，你会不会说英文？
White:	当然会。常先生，你也会说英文吗？
常：	会一点儿。

Dialogue 3

白：	那是谁？你认识不认识她？
吴：	认识。她是郭小姐。
白：	她真漂亮。
	⋯⋯
白：	你好！我叫白比德。你呢？
郭：	你好，我叫郭玉婕。
	⋯⋯
郭：	这是我的男朋友。他叫刘文光。
	这是白先生。
刘：	白先生，你好！
白：	哦，你好！

3 Where are you from? 第三课 你是哪国人？

Dialogue 1

林：	您是哪国人？
白：	我是英国人。这是我的名片。
林：	谢谢。哦，白先生，你住在伦敦？
白：	对。你是中国人吧？
林：	是，我是广东人。

Dialogue 2

营业员*：	这是您的飞机票。
白：	谢谢。我住在什么饭店？
营业员：	你住在和平饭店。
白：	和平是什么意思？
营业员：	和平是 peace 的意思。
白：	很好。我喜欢和平。
*营业员	**yíngyèyuán** *assistant*

Dialogue 3

林:	你住在哪儿?
白:	我住在和平饭店。
林:	几号房间?
白:	五零八号房间。你住在哪儿?
林:	我住在平安路七号。
白:	平安路在哪儿?
林:	平安路在西城区。
白:	和平饭店也在西城区,是不是?
林:	不在。在东城区。
白:	你的电话号码是多少?
林:	六五五二 九三二四。你的呢?
白:	我的是六六七三 八八三零。

4 Do you have brothers and sisters? 第四课 你有兄弟、姐妹吗?

Dialogue 1

丁:	您叫什么名字?
刘:	我叫刘富贵。
丁:	刘先生结婚了吗?
刘:	结婚了。
丁:	有没有孩子?
刘:	有两个,一个儿子,一个女儿。
丁:	他们几岁?
刘:	儿子两岁,女儿五岁。

Dialogue 2

丁:	您有兄弟、姐妹吗?
刘:	有两个弟弟、一个妹妹。没有哥哥和姐姐。
丁:	您弟弟、妹妹多大?

刘：	大弟弟二十六，小弟弟二十四。
丁：	妹妹呢？
刘：	妹妹二十八。
丁：	很好，谢谢您。
刘：	不客气。
丁：	再见！
刘：	再见！

Dialogue 3

吴：	你爸爸、妈妈多大年纪？
陆：	爸爸五十三，妈妈四十九。
吴：	不像、不像。这是你妹妹吧。她真漂亮。
陆：	她今年二十二。
吴：	真的？她结婚了吗？
陆：	没有。可是有男朋友了。
吴：	哦。

5 What time is it now? 第五课 几点了？

Dialogue 1

顾客*：	请问，你们几点开门？
营业员：	上午八点到下午五点半。
顾客：	中午关门吗？
营业员：	不关。
顾客：	周末开不开？
营业员：	星期六开，星期天不开。
*顾客	**gùkè** *customer*

Dialogue 2

小许：	现在几点了？
老万：	两点一刻了。
小许：	噢，会已经开始了。

老万：	什么会？你不是明天开会吗？
小许：	今天星期几？
老万：	星期三。
小许：	噢，我还以为是星期四呢。

Dialogue 3

Jane：	您去哪儿？
中国人：	我去利物浦。
Jane：	几点的火车？
中国人：	我不知道。票上没有时间。
Jane：	我帮你看看。(Looks at the notice board) 啊，三点一刻，在第六站台。
中国人：	现在三点差五分，还有二十分钟。
Jane：	祝你一路顺风。
中国人：	谢谢你。再见。

Dialogue 4

Ann：	明年春节是几月几号？
朋友：	二月十二号。
Ann：	真可惜。我的生日是二月十一号。
朋友：	没关系。英国十一号的晚上就是中国十二号的早上。

---

6 What do you want to do today? 第六课 你今天想做什么？

Dialogue 1

小吴：	今天休息。你想做什么？
Frank：	我想去买东西。可是我要先换钱。
小吴：	好。我们先坐车去中国银行换钱，然后去商店买东西。

Frank:	好。下午我想去北海公园。
小吴：	没问题。晚上呢？
Frank:	晚上我们去看杂技好不好？
小吴：	太好了。我请服务员给我们订票。

Dialogue 2

小吴：	今天晚上你想看电影还是看京剧？
Frank:	我不喜欢京剧。
小吴：	那么我们看电影吧。电影比京剧有意思。
Frank:	有没有音乐会？
小吴：	你想听中国音乐还是听西方音乐？
Frank:	在中国当然听中国音乐。

Dialogue 3

Frank:	早上好！
Passer-by:	早上好！
Frank:	他在做什么？
Passer-by:	他在打太极拳。
Frank:	那个人也在打太极拳吗？
Passer-by:	不。他在做气功。
Frank:	气功跟太极拳一样吗？
Passer-by:	不一样。
Frank:	气功比太极拳难吗？
Passer-by:	不一定。我说气功比太极拳容易。

7 How much is it? 第七课 多少钱？

Dialogue 1

顾客：	请问，在哪儿买毛衣？
营业员：	在二楼。
	········

营业员：	您买什么？
顾客：	我想买一件毛衣。
营业员：	要哪件？您喜欢什么颜色的？
顾客：	那件红色的给我看看行吗？
营业员：	这件很好。
顾客：	哦，太大了。那件黄色的我试试可以吗？
营业员：	这件也不错。
顾客：	哦，太小了。
营业员：	这件蓝色的很适合你。
顾客：	太好了。多少钱？
营业员：	五百块。
顾客：	嗯，太贵了。对不起，谢谢你。
营业员：	....

Dialogue 2

小芳：	我们去自由市场看看吧。
Ann：	好。自由市场离这儿多远？
小芳：	很近。坐车两、三站就到了。
Ann：	车太挤了。咱们走路去吧。
小芳：	可是走路太远了。
Ann：	走路要多长时间？
小芳：	走路要二、三十分钟才能到。
Ann：	好吧。那么咱们坐车去吧。

Dialogue 3

顾客：	苹果怎么卖？
摊贩：	四块一斤。
顾客：	真贵！他们的苹果三块八一斤。
摊贩：	可是我的苹果比他们的大一点儿。
顾客：	葡萄多少钱一斤？
摊贩：	四块两毛五一斤。
顾客：	这么贵！他们的四块一斤。
摊贩：	可是我的葡萄比他们的甜多了。
顾客：	草莓一斤多少钱？

摊贩:	八块二。
顾客:	太贵了！
摊贩:	可是我的草莓比他们的新鲜得多！
顾客:	你的东西最贵。
摊贩:	可是我的东西最好！

8 What's it like? 第八课 怎么样？

Dialogue 1

素兰:	这是我新买的毛衣。你看怎么样？
Colin:	不错，不错。
素兰:	大小合适吗？
Colin:	嗯，有点儿大。
素兰:	颜色好看吗？
Colin:	嗯，不难看。
素兰:	你摸模 .... 你觉得质量怎么样？
Colin:	嗯，还可以。多少钱？
素兰:	不贵，只要一百五十块。
Colin:	什么？！ 一百五十块我可以买三张足球票！

Dialogue 2

罗太太:	假期过得好吗？
李先生:	非常好，就是东西不便宜。
罗太太:	我早就知道了。
李先生:	我以前觉得英国的东西贵，现在才知道法国的东西更贵。
罗太太:	意大利的东西也很贵是不是？
李先生:	意大利的东西也不比法国的便宜。你的假期过得怎么样？
罗太太:	不怎么样。
李先生:	怎么了？
罗太太:	每天都下雨。

Dialogue 3

宝婕：	你的中文说得真好。
Martin:	哪里，哪里。我的中文没有你的英文好。
宝婕：	不。你的中文比我的英文好得多。
Martin:	以后我帮你学英文，你帮我学中文，怎么样？
宝婕：	好主意。可是我学得不快。
Martin:	没关系，我学得也很慢。

9 How do I get to . . . ? 第九课 去......怎么走？

Dialogue 1

乔：	听说你快要去度假了。
冯：	对，我有三个星期的假，从六月二十七号到七月十八号。
乔：	你打算去哪儿？
冯：	香港和澳门。这两个地方我都没去过。
乔：	你怎么去？
冯：	我先坐飞机到香港，在那儿住五天。再从香港坐船到澳门。
乔：	我真羡慕你。
冯：	你什么时候度假？
乔：	我？噢，十二月。
冯：	多长时间？
乔：	不知道。
冯：	怎么会不知道？
乔：	今年十二月我就要退休了。
冯：	我真羡慕你。

Dialogue 2

Ann:	请问，去天坛怎么走？
Passer-by:	天坛在西南边。坐车四站就到了。
Ann:	坐几路车？

Passer-by:	你先从这儿往东走。再坐往南开的车，十五路、二十三路都行。车站在银行对面儿。
Ann:	用换车吗？
Passer-by:	不用。下车以后往前走一点儿。天坛就在马路西边儿。
Ann:	谢谢您。
Passer-by:	没什么。

Dialogue 3

James:	你去过天津吗？
黄：	没去过。
James:	下个周末咱们一起去吧。
黄：	好啊。你打算怎么去？坐汽车还是坐火车？
James:	咱们骑车去，怎么样？
黄：	什么？你发疯了！骑车去天津要两、三天，又累又危险。
James:	我不怕累，也喜欢冒险！
黄：	反正我不跟你一起去。我在家看电视，又舒服又安全。

---

10 What would you like to eat? 第十课 您想吃什么？

Dialogue 1

服务员：	你们预订了吗？
Brown:	预订了。我叫 John Brown.
服务员：	我看一看。……Mr Brown, 七点半，两个人。
Brown:	对，对。
服务员：	好，请跟我来。
	……
服务员：	这是菜单。你们先喝点儿什么？
余乔：	我要一杯桔子汁。

Brown:	你们有什么葡萄酒？
服务员:	我们有长城白葡萄酒和中国红葡萄酒。
Brown:	来一杯白葡萄酒吧。
	…… ……
服务员:	酒来了。你们要什么菜？
余乔:	我不吃肉。
Brown:	你吃不吃鱼？
余乔:	不吃。我只要青菜和豆腐。
Brown:	什么？你现在吃素了？
余乔:	是啊。我已经很胖了。
服务员:	你们喜欢吃辣的吗？
余乔:	喜欢。可是别太辣了。
服务员:	来一个麻婆豆腐吧。
Brown:	好啊。先来两个酸辣汤。
余乔:	今天已经很热了，我们应该少吃辣的。
服务员:	没关系。吃完饭以后，你们多吃点儿冰淇淋。我们的冰淇淋非常好吃。

Dialogue 2

Brown:	抽支烟吧。
余乔:	我不抽烟了。
Brown:	为什么？
余乔:	我爱人不让我抽了。她说抽烟对我的身体不好，对她的身体也不好。
Brown:	我也不想抽了。可是我有一个朋友，戒烟以前不胖，戒烟以后就胖了。我怕胖。
余乔:	我也怕胖，可是今天的菜太好吃了。
Brown:	你吃饱了吗？
余乔:	吃饱了。
Brown:	我们结账吧。服务员，请结账。
服务员:	你们吃好了吗？
余乔:	吃好了，谢谢。
Brown:	你们收不收信用卡和支票？
服务员:	对不起，我们只收现金。

Dialogue 3

Ann:	我饿了，我们随便吃点儿吧。
方：	那儿有个小摊子，他们的炒面好吃极了。
Ann:	(*At the food stall*) (*whispering*) 我看这儿不太干净。
方：	没关系，他们会给我们卫生筷子。
	. . . . .
方：	请来两碗儿炒面、两听可口可乐。
服务员：	请先付钱。两碗儿炒面十二块，两听可口可乐十四块，一共二十六块。
方：	什么？你算错了吧。上次炒面五块一碗儿。
服务员：	没算错。上次是上次，现在一碗儿六块了。

12 At the hotel 第十二课 选择旅馆

Hotel 这个词的中文可以是宾馆、饭店、旅馆和旅店。饭店和宾馆一般很大，旅馆和旅店一般不大。"馆"和"店"都是 house 的意思。"宾"的意思是 guest，"旅"的意思是 travel. "饭"是 food 的意思。

在中国很多旅馆和旅店以前不让外国人住。为什么？有各种各样的原因。以前很多大饭店、大宾馆也不让中国人住，现在让了。大饭店、宾馆的条件比旅馆、旅店的条件好多了。当然也贵多了。

Dialogue 1

服务员：	您好！
Frank:	你好！我想要一间单人房间。
服务员：	您预订了吗？
Frank:	没有。
服务员：	您要住几天？
Frank:	三、四天。我明天告诉你我什么时候走，可以吗？
服务员：	可以。

Frank:	一天多少钱？
服务员：	单人房间每天五十美元。
Frank:	包早餐吗？
服务员：	当然包。
Frank:	有洗澡间吗？
服务员：	有。不过只有淋浴和厕所。
Frank:	好吧。
服务员：	请先填一下儿这张表。......请给我您的护照。您走的时候还给您。
Frank:	这是我的护照。
服务员：	您的房间是二零一，在二楼。这是钥匙。
Frank:	谢谢。
服务员：	如果您有问题，请给服务台打电话。
Frank:	不会有问题吧。

Dialogue 2

服务员：	您好。服务台。
Frank:	我是住二零一房间的 Frank. 我的房间太吵了。能不能换一间安静一点儿的？
服务员：	对不起，没有别的单人房间了。只有双人房间。
Frank:	双人房间一晚上多少钱？
服务员：	比单人房间贵二十美元。
Frank:	太贵了。
服务员：	如果明天我们有别的单人房间，一定给您换。
Frank:	好吧。哦，还有，我的淋浴怎么没有热水？
服务员：	对不起，现在正在修。五个小时以后就有了。
Frank:	五个小时以后？不行。我要找你们的经理。

Dialogue 3

服务员：	您好。服务台。
Frank:	我是二零一房间的 Frank. 能不能麻烦你们给我送来一点儿吃的？我饿了。
服务员：	对不起，餐厅现在关门了。我们只有三明治和饮料。

Frank:	可以。你们有什么样的三明治？
服务员：	我们有奶酪的、火腿的、鸡肉的和牛肉的。
Frank:	我要一个奶酪的、一个牛肉的和一杯咖啡。
服务员：	好的。咖啡要加奶、加糖吗？
Frank:	要加奶，不加糖。
服务员：	行。我们一会儿就送去。
Frank:	还有。明天早上我要起得很早。你们能不能打电话叫醒我？
服务员：	可以。几点？
Frank:	七点半。
服务员：	没问题。
Frank:	谢谢你。晚安。
服务员：	晚安。

13 Trains, tickets and taxis 第十三课 火车、票和出租车

Dialogue 1

Frank:	我想买一张去上海的火车票。
售票员*：	哪天的？
Frank:	后天的。
售票员：	要哪次车的？
Frank:	我不明白你的意思。
售票员：	去上海的火车有十三次、二十一次和一六一次。
Frank:	它们有什么不一样？
售票员：	十三次和二十一次是特快，一百六十一次是直快。
Frank:	什么是特快和直快？
售票员：	特快就是非常快的意思。十三次特快比一六一次直快快四、五个小时。
Frank:	是不是特快的票也比直快的票贵？
售票员：	那当然了。
*售票员	**shòupiàoyuán** *ticketseller, assistant*

Dialogue 2

Ann:	请问，还有十八号二十一次的票吗？
售票员：	有。您要哪种票？
Ann:	我要三张硬卧。
售票员：	对不起。硬卧只有一张了。我们还有软卧和硬座。
Ann:	软卧比硬卧贵多少？
售票员：	一百八十块。
Ann:	那么十八号一六一次还有硬卧吗？
售票员：	有。
Ann:	太好了！我买三张十八号一六一次的硬卧票。
售票员：	一六一次比二十一次慢四个小时。
Ann:	没关系。我们可以在火车上多睡四个小时。

Dialogue 3

司机：	您去哪儿？
乘客：	我想先去雍和宫，再去天坛。
司机：	请上车吧。
乘客：	你能不能先告诉我去这两个地方大概得多少钱？
司机：	去雍和宫四十五块，再去天坛也是四十五块。
乘客：	是人民币还是美元？
司机：	人民币。
乘客：	好吧。
	(Getting off at Tiāntán Park)
乘客：	谢谢你。这是一百块。别找（钱）了。
司机：	对不起。一共一百九十块。
乘客：	怎么是一百九十块？
司机：	你去雍和宫的时候，我等了你两个小时。等一个小时五十块。所以一共一百九十块。
乘客：	你怎么没先告诉我？
司机：	你没问呀。

14 Free time and entertainment 第十四课 娱乐活动

去公园

很多中国人起得很早。他们认为早睡早起对身体好。早上他们做什么？不少人去公园。

在公园里，他们打太极拳、作气功、唱歌、跳舞，等等。有的老人在公园里散步、下棋、打牌、唱京剧。

很多公园都有湖。在北方夏天可以在湖里游泳，冬天可以在湖上滑冰。

Dialogue 1

Edward:	你喜欢什么运动？
小付：	我最喜欢网球和游泳。
Edward:	我也喜欢网球，可是更喜欢足球。
小付：	你喜欢踢足球还是看足球？
Edward:	都喜欢。
小付：	我只喜欢看，不喜欢踢。

Dialogue 2

明力：	听说今年秋天你要去中国旅行。
Ann:	对。可是我还没决定怎么去。
明力：	怎么去？当然坐飞机去。坐火车又慢又不舒服。
Ann:	我不是那个意思。我还没决定跟旅行团去还是自己去。
明力：	跟旅行团去很方便，可是又贵又不自由。
Ann:	自己去又便宜又自由，可是真不方便。
明力：	怎么不方便？
Ann:	我要自己去办签证、订飞机票，找旅馆、等等。
明力：	可是自己去可以有更多的机会练习中文。
Ann:	对，我一定要学好中文，二零零八年去北京看奥林匹克运动会。

Dialogue 3

小赵：	老钱，好久不见。
老钱：	小赵，是你呀！
小赵：	您现在在做什么？
老钱：	跟以前一样。每天打打牌、下下棋、打打太极拳，挺有意思。
小赵：	你比以前年轻多了。
老钱：	哪里、哪里。老多了。小赵，你最近在做什么？
小赵：	我正在谈恋爱。整天买东西、看电影、跳迪斯科真没意思。
老钱：	你比以前瘦多了。
小赵：	谈恋爱又累又不自由。
老钱：	你的女朋友呢？
小赵：	她还没来呢。我在等她。

Dialogue 4

Edward:	你坐哪儿？
小付：	五排四号。
Edward:	你的位子真好。
小付：	你在哪儿？
Edward:	我在楼上十排三十号。
小付：	你觉得今天的表演怎么样？
Edward:	他们唱得挺好。你觉得呢？
小付：	我觉得他们唱得还不错。可是演得不怎么样。
Edward:	听说后面的表演很棒。
小付：	但愿如此。

15 At a post office and changing money
第十五课 在邮局和换钱

邮局

中国的邮局跟英国的邮局差不多。在邮局你可以寄信、寄钱、寄包裹，也可以买邮票、信封和明信片，还可以在邮局存钱、取钱和付账。在中国的邮局你还可以打长途电话和国际电话。

邮局的开门时间常常不一样，有的上午八点开门，有的八点半开门。有的下午五点半关门，有的晚上七点关门。星期六、星期天都开门。

顺便说一下，中国的信筒是绿色的，英国的信筒是红色的。

Dialogue 1

Ann:	请问，这封信寄到英国多少钱？
营业员：	请放在秤上。……超重了。三块九。
Ann:	几天能到？
营业员：	不一定。一般五、六天。这是您的邮票。
Ann:	这张邮票真好看，我能买一套吗？
营业员：	当然可以。一套六块七。
Ann:	我还想寄一个包裹。
营业员：	是什么东西？
Ann:	都是书和光盘。
营业员：	也请放在秤上。……两公斤。您寄航空还是海运？
Ann:	航空。

Dialogue 2

Colin:	小姐，请问，可以在这儿发（一）个传真吗？
营业员：	可以。发到哪儿？
Colin:	德国。
营业员：	一共几页？
Colin:	两页。
营业员：	好的。请给我传真号码。
Colin:	这是传真号码。
营业员：	请等一等。……发完了。这是收据。
Colin:	多少钱？
营业员：	四十块。请到那边付钱。
Colin:	谢谢你。顺便问一下，可以在这儿上网和发电子邮件吗？
营业员：	当然可以。

Dialogue 3

总机：	您好。南方大学。
谢：	请转四二七分机。
总机：	对不起，四二七占线。您愿意等一等还是一会儿再打来？
谢：	我这是国际电话。您能不能叫四二七的王葆平给我打个电话？
总机：	您的号码是多少？
谢：	英国伦敦是四四二零七。我的电话是二一六七七九二。
总机：	您贵姓？
谢：	我叫谢群毅。
总机：	没问题。
谢：	谢谢您。

换钱

在中国换钱一般只能在大银行的分行换，兑换率都差不多。有的大饭店和大商店也有换钱的地方。银行的开门时间跟普通的商店不一样，比商店开门时间晚一点，关门时间早一点。可是在大饭店里的换钱的地方开门时间比较灵活，可能会开到很晚。

将来，取款机多了，取钱更方便了，就不用去银行换钱了。

Dialogue 4

顾客：	请问，今天美元和人民币的对换率是多少？
营业员：	一比八点九。
顾客：	一美元换八块九，对吗？
营业员：	对。
顾客：	我想换两百美元的人民币。
营业员：	请先填这张兑换单。
顾客：	... ... 填好了。这是两百美元。
营业员：	请等一等。... ... 这是一千七百八十块。请点一点。
顾客：	正好。谢谢你。
营业员：	不客气。

16 Being a guest 第十六课 作客

吃中国饭

中国人常常为客人做很多菜。他们希望客人多喝酒、多吃菜。

中国人和西方人吃饭的习惯不一样。大部分中国人一般先吃饭，后喝汤。在西方，人们一般先喝汤，后吃饭。中国人常常先喝酒，吃凉菜，然后吃热饭、热菜，最后吃水果。西方人先吃头盘，然后吃正餐，最后吃甜食或水果。中国人吃饭用碗和筷子；西方人吃饭用盘子和刀叉。

中国人在家里吃饭和在饭馆吃饭差不多，大家一起吃所有的菜。西方人在饭馆自己吃自己的菜。在家吃饭的时候，不同的菜先放在的盘里，然后才吃。

Dialogue 1

袁先生：	老白，欢迎，欢迎。
白先生：	老袁，你好。我知道你爱喝酒。 这是给你的酒。
袁先生：	法国葡萄酒！你太客气了。
白先生：	这盒巧克力是给你们女儿的。
袁先生：	珍珍，快谢谢白叔叔。
珍珍：	谢谢白叔叔。
白先生：	不用谢。……真香啊！袁太太， 做什么好吃的呢？
袁太太：	没什么好吃的。都是家常便饭。
白先生：	你们的厨房挺现代化的。
袁太太：	可惜太小了。
袁先生：	老白，客厅里坐吧。
白先生：	好，好。你们的客厅真漂亮。
袁先生：	哪里，哪里。老白，你想喝点儿什么？
白先生：	喝点儿茶吧。

Dialogue 2

袁先生：	老白，咱们先喝一杯。
白先生：	好啊。
袁先生：	你喝啤酒、葡萄酒还是来点儿白酒？
白先生：	白酒我喝不了。喝点儿葡萄酒吧。
袁先生：	白的还是红的？
白先生：	红的吧。
袁先生：	这种酒不甜。我知道外国人一般不喜欢喝甜的酒。
白先生：	是，我不喜欢喝甜的酒。
袁先生：	咱们先干一杯！祝你工作顺利、生活愉快！
白先生：	祝你们全家幸福，万事如意！
袁先生：	干杯！
白先生：	干杯！
袁太太	别客气，多吃点儿。
白先生：	好，好，我自己来。
	......
白先生：	菜都非常好吃。
袁先生：	再多吃一点儿。
白先生：	我已经吃饱了。
袁太太：	你吃得太少了。
白先生：	我真的吃不下了。
袁先生：	你太客气了。
白先生：	我没客气。

Dialogue 3

白先生：	我可以用一下你们的厕所吗？
袁先生：	左手第二间就是。
	......
白先生：	喔，已经九点多了。我该回去了。
袁先生：	还早呢。再坐一会儿吧。
白先生：	不坐了。明天早上我还有事情。
袁先生：	好吧。那就不留你了。
白先生：	给你们添麻烦了。
袁先生：	没什么。欢迎你再来。

338

白先生：	一定，一定。
袁先生：	我送送你。
白先生：	不用了。请回去吧。
袁先生：	慢走。
袁太太：	路上小心。
白先生：	没问题。再见！
袁先生 & 袁太太：	再见！

Dialogue 4

董事长：	白先生，您筷子用得真好。
白先生：	我常常吃中国饭。
夫人：	您自己做饭吗？
白先生：	我做得不好。我常去中国城的饭馆儿吃饭。
董事长：	来，先喝一杯。这是茅台酒。您喝过吗？
白先生：	喝过两次。
董事长：	为我们两个公司的成功合作干杯！
白先生：	为董事长和董事长夫人的健康干杯！
夫人：	这是燕窝汤，非常有营养。
白先生：	我听说过，可是没喝过。
董事长：	这是凤爪，不知道你吃过吗？
白先生：	看见过，还没吃过。
夫人：	正好，请尝尝吧。
	······
夫人：	多吃点儿菜。
董事长：	再喝一杯。
白先生：	我吃不下了，也喝不下了。
董事长：	再喝最后一杯。为中英两国人民的友谊干杯！
白先生：	干杯！希望你们有机会去英国访问。

---

17 Seeing a doctor 第十七课 看医生

中国的医疗

在中国，很多单位有自己的医务所。小的医务所只有一个医生，大的可以有几个医生和护士。如果你有病，你可以去单位的医务所，也可以直接去医院。

中国的医院一般分成不同的科。有的医院是专科医院，只看一、两种病。大的医院一般又有中医，又有西医。你可以看中医，也可以看西医。

Dialogue 1

医生：	你哪儿不舒服？
白先生：	我肚子不舒服。
医生：	拉肚子吗？
白先生：	有一点儿。
医生：	你昨天吃什么了？
白先生：	我参加了一个宴会，吃了凤爪，喝了燕窝汤。
医生：	那些都是好东西，对你身体好。
白先生：	我可能吃得太多了。
医生：	你喝了很多酒，是不是？
白先生：	不多。只喝了八杯。
医生：	我明白了。我给你一些药。你愿意试试中药吗？
白先生：	我没吃过中药。听说中药很苦，是吗？
医生：	有的苦，有的不苦。我给你的药不苦。
白先生：	那我试试吧。
医生：	这是药方。请到药房去拿药。
白先生：	医生，谢谢您。
医生：	不用谢。

Dialogue 2

药济师*：	这是您的药。
白先生：	怎么吃呀？
药济师：	瓶子上有服用方法。
白先生：	对不起，我还不认识汉字。
药济师：	哦，对不起。我告诉你。一天吃三次，一次吃二十粒。
白先生：	什么？一天吃六十粒？！
药济师：	对。
白先生：	我的天啊！
药济师：	吃药的时候不要喝咖啡、茶和酒。应该喝温开水。
白先生：	为什么？
药济师：	吃药都应该这样。
白先生：	我的药饭前吃还是饭后吃？

药济师：	都可以。
白先生：	谢谢您。
药济师：	不谢。
*药济师	**yàojìshī** *pharmacist*

Dialogue 3

参观者*：	你们诊所病人多吗？
医生：	不少。
参观者：	你们都看什么病？
医生：	各种各样的病。你看，这个病人常常头疼。她看过西医，吃过西药，可是还不好。我们给她扎了针灸，现在她好多了。
参观者：	真的？我也有时候头疼。她扎了几次了？
医生：	四次了。
参观者：	针灸是不是很疼？
医生：	针灸是不舒服，可是常常很有效。
参观者：	真的吗？
医生：	你有什么病？我可以给你扎。
参观者：	不用、不用。我没病。我的身体很好。谢谢您。
*参观者	**cānguānzhě** *visitor*

18 Coping with problems 第十八课 对付问题

中国的交通

在中国，开车和骑自行车都走路的右边。这跟在美国和欧洲大陆一样，跟在英国不一样。

中国是世界上自行车最多的国家。在大城市有很多自行车道。现在在中国租汽车还很难，可是租自行车比较方便。骑自行车又便宜又有意思。

在中国有地铁的城市很少。不少城市有电车。

因为中国人太多，所以路上总是很挤，常常堵车。公共汽车也非常挤。当然你可以坐出租车。出租车不挤，可是不便宜。

要是你从一个城市去另一个城市，你可以坐飞机、火车，也可以坐长途汽车。长途汽车有时候不太舒服。

Dialogue 1

Ann:	我想租两辆自行车。
店主*:	有身份证吗？
Ann:	有。这是我的护照。
店主:	好。您租哪种车？
Ann:	我要一辆小的。我的朋友要一辆大的。
店主:	你们租几天？
Ann:	一天。
店主:	那两辆山地车不错。你们试试吧。
Ann:	这辆车的闸好象不太灵。
店主:	是吗？我给你紧一紧。
Ann:	这些车怎么都没有灯？
店主:	在城里用不着灯。
Ann:	好吧。我租这两辆。多少钱？
店主:	这辆大的一天十八块。那辆小的一天十五块。一共三十三块。
Ann:	给您四十块。
店主:	找您七块。
*店主	**diànzhǔ** *shopkeeper*

Dialogue 2

Ann:	师傅，我的车带坏了，您能帮我修修吗？
师傅:	没问题。
Ann:	得多长时间？
师傅:	一会儿就行。
Ann:	师傅，抽支烟吧。
师傅:	好、好。谢谢、谢谢。
Ann:	师傅，去香山还有多远？
师傅:	往北骑二十分钟，再往西拐就到了。······修好了。

Ann:	真快。谢谢您。这辆车的闸不太灵，您能看看吗？
师傅:	可以。我给你紧紧。……行了。
Ann:	谢谢您。一共多少钱？
师傅:	补车带两块五。紧闸就不收你钱了。
Ann:	谢谢师傅。您再抽支烟吧。

Dialogue 3

安音:	你好象有点儿不高兴。
Ben:	没什么。
安音:	你的手怎么了？
Ben:	哦，我摔了一跤。
安音:	怎么回事？
Ben:	真倒霉！我跟别人撞车了。
安音:	是谁的错？
Ben:	我说是他的错，他说是我的错。
安音:	车撞坏了吗？
Ben:	撞坏了。
安音:	你们找警察了吗？
Ben:	找了。警察说我们都有错。
安音:	后来呢？
Ben:	后来，我们都去修自己的车了。

Dialogue 4

警察:	您有什么事？
Ben:	我的包丢了。
警察:	包里面有什么？
Ben:	有我的护照和钱包。钱包里有我的信用卡、四百多人民币和两百美元。哦，还有一个小照相机。
警察:	您丢了护照，应该通知你们国家的大使馆。
Ben:	我给大使馆打电话了。
警察:	您现在住在哪儿？
Ben:	玉龙饭店三零一房间。
警察:	请您先回去。我们一有消息就马上通知您。

19　Learning Chinese　第十九课　学中文

中文还是汉语?

中文一般指汉语。中文的"中"是中国的中。文是 writing 或者 language 的意思。汉语的"汉"是汉族的汉。"语"是语言的语，也是 language 的意思。汉语就是汉族人的语言。中国的很多少数民族都有自己的语言。

汉语有很多种方言。上海话是一种方言。上海人说上海话。广东话也是一种方言。广东人和香港人说广东话。

我们学习的中文是普通话。普通话不是方言，是官方语言。台湾人叫它国语，东南亚的华人叫它华语。国语和华语就是普通话。普通话不是北京话。北京话和普通话差不多。很多北京人说的普通话有北京口音。

Dialogue 1

华岩:	你的中文真棒，说得真流利。
兰音:	哪里、哪里，说得不好。
华岩:	你的语音、声调都非常好。
兰音:	不行，不行，还差得很远。
华岩:	你学了几年了?
兰音:	三年了。
华岩:	什么? 只有三年? ! 你太聪明了。
兰音:	你过奖了。
华岩:	我学了六年英语了，可是说得还很差。
兰音:	你真谦虚。
华岩:	你一定要告诉我你的学习方法。
兰音:	很简单。我先生是中国人。

Dialogue 2

老师:	你们好。我姓唐，是你们的老师。你们可以叫我唐老师。我还不认识你们。先请大家介绍一下儿自己。

为民：	我是俄国人。我叫白为民。白是李白的白。我 很喜欢中国文学。将来我想当翻译。
安芳：	我姓崔，叫崔安芳。我是韩国人。我对中国音 乐很有兴趣。我现在在学习二胡和琵琶。
文哲：	我是美国人。我的中文名字叫史文哲。史是历 史的史，文是文学的文，哲是哲学的哲。我也喜欢 中国文学。我更喜欢中国哲学。我要研究孔子、老 子和庄子。
兰音：	我是英国人。我对中国的少数民族很有兴趣。 我将来想研究他们的历史和语言。
老师：	你叫什么名字？
兰音：	哦，对不起。我叫兰音，我还不知道将来做什 么，可能当记者。
山本：	我叫山本，是日本人。我现在在研究中国经济。
老师：	谢谢大家的介绍。

Dialogue 3

老师：	你们觉得中文难不难？
山本：	汉字不难，语音很难。
兰音：	因为你是日本人，会写汉字，所以你觉得汉字 不难。我觉得汉字太难了。
兰音：	汉字不容易，可是语法更难。我总是不知道什 么时候用'了'，什么时候不用'了'。
为民：	汉语语法不太难，声调真不容易。我常常说不 好第二声和第四声。
安芳：	我觉得第三声最难。
老师：	中文不容易，可是只要我们多听、多说、多 读、多写，我们就一定可以学好。

20 Travel and weather 第二十课 旅行和天气

气候和天气

中国很大，东、西、南、北的气候常常很不一样。一般来说，南方
的夏天比北方的热，北方的冬天比南方的冷。

在中国，大部分地方有四个季节：春、夏、秋、冬。春天从三月到五月。六月、七月、八月是夏天。秋天是九、十和十一月。十二月到二月是冬天。一般七、八月最热；一、二月最冷。

中国人比较喜欢春天和秋天，因为春天和秋天不冷也不热。

Dialogue 1

Colin:	这几天天津特冷，可是风景真美。昨天下雪了。
素兰:	雪大吗？
Colin:	不小。天气预报说，明天还要下雪。
素兰:	昆明从来不下雪。我真想去天津看雪。
Colin:	你那儿天气怎么样？
素兰:	不暖和。今天的气温是十五度。
Colin:	什么？十五度？跟天津的春天一样暖和。
素兰:	可是我觉得冷。今天上午下了小雨。
Colin:	我最喜欢小雨。可是天津冬天很少下雨。
素兰:	你来昆明看雨，我去天津看雪，怎么样？
Colin:	真是个好主意！我来安排吧。
素兰:	等一等，那么我们在哪儿见面呢？

Dialogue 2

老师:	假期你们打算去哪儿？
山本:	我喜欢大城市。我想去上海，然后去广州。上海和广州的经济最发达。
兰音:	我不喜欢大城市。我要去云南和贵州。那儿有很多少数民族。
文哲:	云南和贵州都在中国的南方，夏天一定很热。我去山西的五台山。那儿一定很凉快。
为民:	这个假期我有工作。我去天津给一个代表团当翻译。
老师:	安芳，你呢？
安芳:	我真羡慕你们。可是我要回韩国。我太想我爸爸、妈妈了。开学的时候我再回来。

Dialogue 3

老师：	你们怎么去？
为民：	天津不远。我坐火车去。两、三个小时就到了。
兰音：	云南离北京很远。我可以坐火车，也可以坐飞机。 我还没有决定。
老师：	飞机比火车快多了，可是也贵多了。
文哲：	五台山不远也不近。我想先坐火车，再坐长途汽车。
老师：	山本，你要去两个地方。你怎么去？
山本：	我想先坐飞机到上海，再坐火车去广州。
安芳：	我不喜欢坐飞机，可是我只能坐飞机回国。
老师：	好。祝大家假期愉快。

21 Experiences, feelings and reflections
第二十一课　谈感想

去中国学习、旅游和工作

每年有很多外国人去中国学习。他们学习中国的语言、文学、文化、历史、宗教，等等。在中国的几百多所大学里，有几万个外国留学生。

去中国旅游的外国人越来越多。他们很多人对中国的文化和历史感兴趣。很多人去过中国很多次。

这几年去中国工作的外国人也越来越多。在中国的外资企业和合资企业也越来越多。很多公司都想在中国扩大生意。

Dialogue 1

老师：	同学们，你们假期过得好吗？
学生们：	很好。/不太好。/非常好。/还可以。
老师：	请每个人都谈一谈，好吗？
文哲：	我去了五台山。那里一切都好，就是饭不好。
老师：	饭怎么不好？

文哲:	他们不吃肉。可是我最爱吃肉，所以我常常觉得饿。
为民:	你应该跟我一起去天津。我们的代表团每天都有宴会。
老师:	兰音，少数民族的饭你吃得惯吗？
兰音:	开始的时候吃不惯，后来就吃得惯了。那些少数民族的人真友好。
老师:	那儿是不是很热？
兰音:	我去的地方是山区，所以不太热。那儿的风景美极了。
老师:	山本，你对上海和广州有什么印象？
山本:	这两个城市的经济都发展得很快。可惜我听不懂上海话和广东话。
老师:	这两种方言都不容易懂。安芳，你爸爸、妈妈都好吗？
安芳:	他们都很好，谢谢您。 我爸爸、妈妈说下个假期他们要来中国。我们一起在中国旅游。
大家:	那太好了！

Dialogue 2

记者:	福特先生，祝您生日快乐！
福特:	谢谢，谢谢。
记者:	您在中国几年了？
福特:	差不多十二年了。
记者:	您一直在大学工作吗？
福特:	对。我非常喜欢当老师。
记者:	在中国您对什么最满意？
福特:	当然是我的工作。我们学校的教学越来越好。
记者:	那么您对什么最不满意？
福特:	我对很多事情不满意。可是很难说对什么最不满意。
记者:	您打算怎么庆祝您的生日？
福特:	早上我太太给我做了中国的长寿面。晚上同事们来我家包饺子。
记者:	您的生日过得真有中国特色。
福特:	我现在已经是半个中国人了。